Bloom's Modern Critical Views

Bloom's Modern Critical Views

THE ROMANTIC POETS

Edited and with an introduction by
Harold Bloom
Sterling Professor of the Humanities
Yale University

BLOOM'S
LITERARY CRITICISM
An Infobase Learning Company

Bloom's Literary Criticism
An imprint of Infobase Learning
132 West 31st Street
New York NY 10001

Library of Congress Cataloging-in-Publication Data
The romantic poets / edited and with an introduction by Harold Bloom.
    p. cm.—(Bloom's modern critical views)
Includes bibliographical references and index.
ISBN 978-1-60413-871-9 (hardcover)
1. English poetry—19th century—History and criticism.   2. English poetry—18th century—History and criticism.   3. Romanticism—Great Britain.
I. Bloom, Harold.
PR590.R594 2011
821'.809—dc22
                                    2011014749

Bloom's Literary Criticism books are available at special discounts when purchased in bulk quantities for businesses, associations, institutions, or sales promotions. Please call our Special Sales Department in New York at (212) 967-8800 or (800) 322-8755.

You can find Bloom's Literary Criticism on the World Wide Web at
http://www.chelseahouse.com

Contributing editor: Pamela Loos
Cover designed by Alicia Post
Composition by IBT Global, Troy NY
Cover printed by Yurchak Printing, Landisville PA
Book printed and bound by Yurchak Printing, Landisville PA
Date printed: September 2011
Printed in the United States of America

This book is printed on acid-free paper.

All links and Web addresses were checked and verified to be correct at the time of publication. Because of the dynamic nature of the Web, some addresses and links may have changed since publication and may no longer be valid.

Contents

Editor's Note

My introduction assesses the six indispensible figures making up the romantic tradition in England. Jerome Christensen opens the volume with a discussion of tragic delight primarily in Wordsworth, followed by Leslie Brisman's analysis of Shelleyan intersections with Christianity.

Helen Vendler astutely explores Keats's attempts to reconcile his philosophical emphasis on the social versus aesthetic concerns of poetry, after which Paul de Man returns us to Wordsworthian concepts of time and history.

Jonathan Wordsworth then turns his attention to Shelley's "Mont Blanc," tracing the author's ability to invest the material world with spiritual significance. Jean Hall applies a broader focus to the development of Byron's career.

John L. Mahoney takes up elements of the tragic imagination in Coleridge's late work, followed by David Bromwich's consideration of the ramifications of the term *romanticism*. John Beer concludes the volume with an overview of romantic visions of apocalypse and millennial transition.

HAROLD BLOOM

Introduction

William Blake

After *Jerusalem*, Blake wrote very little poetry and devoted himself to his work as painter and engraver. The most considerable poem left in manuscript from his later years is *The Everlasting Gospel*, a series of notebook fragments on the theme of the necessity for the forgiveness of sins. There are powerful passages among these fragments, but they do not add anything to *Jerusalem* as imaginative thought, and Blake did not bother to arrange them in any definite form. The rhetorical directness of some of the fragments has made them popular, but their very freedom from the inventiveness of Blake's mythmaking has the effect of rendering them poetically uninteresting.

This is not true of Blake's last engraved poem, "The Ghost of Abel," a dramatic scene composed in 1822 as a reply to Byron's drama *Cain*. Byron's Cain fights free of natural religion and its fears only to succumb to a murderous dialectic by which every spiritual emancipation of a gifted individual is paid for through alienation from his brethren, the consequence being that a dissenter from the orthodoxy of negations in moral values is compelled to become an unwary Satanist. Blake's very subtle point is that the covenant of Christ, as he interprets it, takes man beyond the "cloven fiction" of moral good and moral evil, the "hateful siege of contraries" experienced by Milton's Satan on Mount Niphates, and into the clarification of seeing that only a part of what is called moral good is actually good to the imagination of the real life of man. Vengeance and every similar mode of hindering another can have no part in an imaginative morality, and for Blake there is no other morality worthy of the name. "The Ghost of Abel," which makes surprisingly effective use of Blake's long line, the fourteener, as a medium for dramatic dialogue, is

1

the true coda to Blake's poetry, rather than *The Everlasting Gospel*, for it makes explicit the moral basis of the laconic *Marriage of Heaven and Hell*.

At about the time he wrote *The Everlasting Gospel*, Blake reengraved a little emblem book, *The Gates of Paradise*, which he had first engraved as early as 1793, adding a number of rhymed couplets and an epilogue in two quatrains to the engravings and their inscriptions. The Gates of Paradise are "Mutual Forgiveness of each Vice," and the story told in epilogue is something rarer, an address "To the Accuser who is the God of This World," and one of Blake's most perfect short poems:

> Truly, My Satan, thou art but a Dunce,
> And dost not know the Garment from the Man.
> Every Harlot was a Virgin once,
> Nor can'st thou ever change Kate into Nan.

> Tho' thou are Worship'd by the Names Divine
> Of Jesus & Jehovah, thou art still
> The Son of Morn in weary Night's decline,
> The lost Traveller's Dream under the Hill.

The tone of this is unique in Blake, and I have not found the equivalent in any other poet. There is enormous irony here, mitigated by a gentle and mocking pity for the great antagonist, the Satan adored as Jesus and Jehovah by the religious of this world. Blake is past argument here; he has gone beyond prophetic anger and apocalyptic impatience. The Accuser is everywhere and at all times apparently triumphant, yet he is a delusion and so but a dunce. He cannot distinguish the phenomenal garment from the Real Man, the Imagination, and his spouse Rahab is only a delusion also.

States change; individuals endure. The god of the churches is still that light bearer, son of the morning, who fell, and he is now in his weary night's decline as history moves to a judging climax. The vision of a restored man, Blake's vision, is the clear sight of a mental traveller in the open world of poetry. The Accuser is the dream of a lost traveler in the phenomenal world, but Blake has found his way home and need not dream.

William Wordsworth

After Shakespeare, Chaucer, and Milton, Wordsworth is the strongest poet in the English language. Shakespeare and Chaucer created men and women, which is the highest poetic achievement. Wordsworth, like Milton, is a poet of the sublime, of the transcendental striving that is a vital part of the human endowment. Sir John Falstaff and Hamlet, the Wife of Bath and the Pardoner—these are beyond Milton and Wordsworth. Milton's Satan is an extraordinary creation, but he belongs to a different order of persuasiveness than Shakespeare's Iago represents. Wordsworth's Margaret, in *The Ruined Cottage*, is a figure of heroic pathos, but again this is in a different realm from the terrifying pathos of King Lear and Cordelia. This of course is to catalog the modes of greatness and is intended to appreciate Wordsworth, since no other poet writing in English, after nearly two centuries, approaches Wordsworth's power and originality. *Originality* is the key term in apprehending Wordsworth; he made a larger break with literary tradition than anyone after him, be it Whitman, Dickinson, or Eliot. After Wordsworth, poetry became Wordsworthian, which is still its condition. Modern and postmodernism alike are still in Wordsworth's shadow.

Before Wordsworth, poems had subjects; after Wordsworth, poems are subjective, even when they struggle not to be. The change, so commonplace that we now have difficulty in observing it, is the largest I know of in literature since Shakespeare's pragmatic invention of the human—that is to say, of the ever-growing inner self. No one before Wordsworth would have written a poem at all comparable to *The Prelude*, an epic whose principal concern is the growth of the poet's own mind. "Mind," for Wordsworth, was a very complex metaphor for consciousness, not just in the cognitive sense but also in the mode of affect. Wordsworth's best critics always have emphasized his uncanny fusion of the sublime—"Something evermore about to be"—and of the educational mission of teaching us how to *feel*, more subtly and more acutely. The most profound function of Wordsworth's poetry is *consolation*, not through otherworldly hopes and speculations but through the human heart and its universal struggle with the burden of mortality. No poet since Wordsworth can rival him in his power of evoking our deepest fears, longings, and anxieties of expectations. Wordsworth's cognitive originality, profound as it is, nevertheless is dwarfed by his emotional range and intensity.

We are at a bad moment, at least in the English-speaking world, in the study and appreciation of the greatest literature, whether it be Shakespeare or Wordsworth. An extraordinary number of those who now teach Wordsworth, and write about him, manifest their political and cultural exuberance in denouncing the poet of *The Prelude*, "Tintern Abbey," and *The Ruined Cottage* because of his "betrayal" of the French Revolution. This peculiar fashion of academic abuse will pass away in a decade or so, while Wordsworth's greatest poetry will abide. To be one of the four most essential poets of the English language is to be inescapable. Wordsworth will bury his historicist, Marxist, and pseudofeminist undertakers. Even those who never have read Wordsworth are now overdetermined by him; you cannot write a poem in English without treading on his ground. Doubtless all of us would prefer that Words-worth had retained the generosity and social vision of his youth in his later years, but political objections are absurdly irrelevant to the perpetual great-ness of *The Prelude*, "Tintern Abbey," and *The Ruined Cottage*. If we reach the twenty-second century, then Wordsworth will be there, undiminished and imaginatively powerful, a blessed consolation in our distress.

Samuel Taylor Coleridge

Coleridge had the dark fortune of being eclipsed by his best friend, William Wordsworth. What we think of as modern poetry is Wordsworthianism, the evanescence of any poetic subject except for the poet's own subjectivity. Two years younger than Wordsworth, Coleridge actually invented what was to be the Wordsworthian mode in such early poems as "The Eolian Harp" (1795) and "Frost at Midnight" (1798), the immediate precursors of Wordsworth's "Tintern Abbey" (written later in 1798). But Coleridge had an almost Kafkan sense of guilt and of self-abnegation. He became Words-worth's follower, enhancing their joint volume, *Lyrical Ballads* (1798) with his magnificent *The Rime of the Ancient Mariner*. Since the two parts of *Christabel* were composed in 1798 and 1800, "Kubla Khan" around 1798, and "Dejection: An Ode" in 1802, Coleridge's crucial poetic achievement is pretty much the work of four years and essentially ended when he was 30. When one considers how unique and original Coleridge's poetic endow-ment was, it is a great sorrow that only a few fragments attest to his gift after 1802.

Perhaps Coleridge's greatest achievement, like Emerson's after him, was in his notebooks, which afford an extraordinary image of his complex and restless mind. Yet, for the common reader, Coleridge is no longer the Sage of Highgate but the author of a few absolute poems, "Kubla Khan," and *The Rime of the Ancient Mariner*, in particular. Coleridge had projected an epic on the fall of Jerusalem to the Romans (C.E. 70), and rather wonderfully "Kubla Khan" somehow issued from that outrageous ambition. No reader could know this from chanting the gorgeous fragment, which should be memorized and indeed recited aloud. But this foreground helps explain the sense of "holy dread" in "Kubla Khan" and its general atmosphere of potential profanation.

The hidden theme of "Kubla Khan" appears to be Coleridge's fear of his own genius, his own daemonic powers. The poem's genre is what William Collins, following John Milton, established in his "Ode on the Incarnation of the Poetical Character." There a new Apollo, a "rich-haired youth of morn," is manifested in the guise of the post-Miltonic, preromantic Bard of Sensibil-ity, a direct ancestor of William Blake as well as of Coleridge. "Kubla Khan" concludes with a vision of a youth with flashing eyes and floating hair, who has found his way back to an unfallen existence, where he has drunk "the milk of Paradise." This youth is the poet that Coleridge both longed and feared to become, the celebrant of a new imaginative power, one who would repair the fall not only of Jerusalem but of Man.

The Rime of the Ancient Mariner, so frequently interpreted as a Christian parable of the Fall of Man, instead is a phantasmagoria of the unlived life, one so compulsive that the poem never will know (nor can we) why gratuitous crimes and gratuitous releases should take place. Whereas the Christian Fall results from an act of disobedience, the Ancient Mariner simply *acts*, without willing and yet with terrible consequences. As I read this great ballad, it is a poem of the imagination's revenge on those who live in a world without imagination. Coleridge rightly said that it had no true moral and indeed should have had no moral at all. Instead, it offers a visionary cosmos as compelling as that in Kafka's stories and parables. Coleridge, like Kafka, makes his work uninterpretable, but in turn the matter for interpretation becomes just that movement away from interpretability. Kafka gives us a New Kabbalah, and so does Coleridge. The cosmos of *The Rime of the Ancient Mariner* is not sacramental but Gnostic; the divinity is estranged or hidden, and we find ourselves in the emptiness the ancient Gnostics called the Kenoma. There we wander, there we weep, unless we suffer the ultimate, compulsive fate of the Ancient Mariner, who ends as a haunter of wedding feasts, always retelling his own story, in a kind of parody of ecological wisdom.

We can surmise that the two extreme figures of Coleridge's bipolar vision are the youth of "Kubla Khan" and the Ancient Mariner. Perhaps they are caught in a perpetual cycle together, in which at last the newly incarnated poetic character must age into a fundamentalist of what Coleridge called the primary imagination. That is "primary" only in being initial; otherwise it is repetition, unlike the secondary or higher imagination that has drunk the milk of Paradise, with consequences immediately ecstatic but finally catastrophic.

George Gordon, Lord Byron

George Gordon, Lord Byron, is literature's most notorious instance of a writer's life becoming his work, indeed taking the place of it. The illustrious Goethe is something of a rival instance, and later examples include Oscar Wilde, Ernest Hemingway, and Norman Mailer. To endeavor to speak of the work in the writer in regard to Byron is therefore a considerable challenge, which I will take up here, though on a modest scale.

Byron was a cinema idol two centuries before there was a cinema, and a rock star centuries before rhythm and blues metamorphosed into rock-and-roll. Valentino and Elvis lag in the Byronic wake, as any other popular luminary would have to run well behind the noble Lord Byron: great poet, gallant martyr to Greek independence from the Turks, reformist British politician, and an authentic anthology of every sexual possibility: incestuous heterosexuality, sodomizing of male and female, Satanic sadomasochism, pederasty, and whatever else nature makes available (with perhaps a restraint or two).

Externally, Byron's work strongly affected his life with the publication of *Childe Harold's Pilgrimage*, cantos 1 and 2, in 1812, when the twenty-four-year-old poet "awoke one morning and found myself famous." But that is hardly a matter of the work in a writer, except that Byron's persona or mask as romantic adventurer never left him after that. It was not a question of following the big wars, like the Byronic Hemingway, nor even of achieving authentic disgust with the limits of sexual experience. Instead, there was the impossible quest somehow to reconcile personal idealism and the demands of celebrity, probably the ultimate instance of celebrity ever, in the long cavalcade from Cleopatra in the ancient world down (very much down) to the present.

Everything crucial about Byron is an enigma, simultaneously ambiguous and ambivalent. The best of him emerged in his long, complex friendship with Shelley, a kind of a brother in poetic greatness, aristocratic ambivalence, and revolutionary temperament but hardly a double or twin. Byron, according to the flamboyant Trelawny, wished to save Shelley's skull from the funeral pyre, but Trelawny would not consent, saying he feared Byron was capable of using it as a drinking cup. And yet Byron said to his London friends that they were all wrong about Shelley, who made everyone else seem a beast in comparison.

Shelley, a superb critic, uniquely saw and said that Byron's *Don Juan* was the great poem of the romantic age, surpassing even Goethe and Wordsworth. It depends on perspective, to some degree, but time seems to have agreed with Shelley. Certainly, the effect of *Don Juan* on Byron himself was extraordinary. At last, the work became the life.

William Hazlitt found throughout Byron's poetry the story of "a mind preying upon itself." That can be phrased, more generously, as the record of a mind influencing itself. Byron exuberantly said of *Don Juan*: "It may be profligate but is it not *life*, is it not *the thing*?"

Indeed it is the celebrated thing-in-itself, the reality for which all of us search. Its protagonist, the amiable but passive Juan, decidedly is *not* Byron. Rather, the great voice narrating the poem is more than Lord Byron's, the voice *is* Byron himself, in all his diversity and self-contradictions, an identity larger than that of the noble lord. George Wilson Knight brilliantly remarks that, in *Don Juan*, Byron and the ocean became one, as if to resolve the poet's simultaneous faith both in nature and in eternity. I think of Hart Carne invoking the Caribbean as "this great wink of Eternity" in *Voyager II* and reflect at the closeness of sexual dynamics in Byron and in Hart Crane.

Northrup Frye remarks that Byron, unlike his public, was not enthralled by the Byronic hero. Since that hero reappeared, in the next generation, in Charlotte Brontë's Rochester and Emily Brontë's Heathcliff and lived on in Hemingway's bullfighters, big-game hunters, and heroically literate soldiers, Byron had no way of stopping what he had begun. He might have blanched at many of our current female Byrons, who have a charming way of turning into vampires.

Byron's chief debt to *Don Juan* was that it turned him inexorably to revolutionary action, perhaps because he needed to demonstrate that he was *not* Don Juan. The first two cantos of *Don Juan* were published in July 1819. A year later, Byron joined the Carbonari in their revolution against Austrian rule. The Carbonari were defeated, but in 1823 Byron and Trelawny were exiled to Greece, where "the Trumpet Voice of Liberty" died a hero's death at Missolonghi on April 19, 1824. After that, his life and work fused forever. It is good to remember however the essential Byron, who scribbled this fragment on the back of his manuscript of *Don Juan*, canto 1:

> I would to heaven that I were so much clay,
> As I am blood, bone, marrow, passion, feeling—
> Because at least the past were passed away—
> And for the future—(but I write this reeling,
> Having got drunk exceedingly today,
> So that I seem to stand upon the ceiling)
> I say—the future is a serious matter—

Percy Bysshe Shelley

Shelley was a lyric and Pindaric poet who desired to write revolutionary epic and lyrical drama. At heart a skeptic and not a Platonic visionary, he nevertheless broke through to a Gnostic vision very much his own, curiously parallel to the work of William Blake, whom he never read.

A.D. Nuttall, in his *Alternative Trinities*, studies Christopher Marlowe, John Milton, and Blake as three intricate instances of poetic heresies that approach Gnosticism. The Gnostic religion, to most scholars, is a second century of the common era Christian heresy. I myself agree with Henry Corbin, who argued that Gnosticism (or esotericism) was an eclectic world religion and the truest form therefore of Islam, Christianity, and Judaism.

Perhaps Shelley's *gnosis*, his poetic way of knowing, was not altogether a Gnosticism, but his visionary drama *Prometheus Unbound* opposes Jupiter as a kind of Gnostic *archon* or Demiurge to Prometheus as a Gnostic savior, almost indeed a stranger or alien god.

Shelley's magnificent "Ode to the West Wind," composed between
the third and fourth acts of *Prometheus Unbound*, demands to be read on
several levels of interpretation: political, personal, heretical-religious, and
agonistic in relation to Shelley's poetic precursors, John Milton and William Wordsworth, in particular. Politically, Shelley was of the permanent
left: almost the Leon Trotsky of his day. Yet Shelley's personal stance
strangely blended hope and despair. Like Job, the poet falls on the thorns
of life, and he prays to the wind to lift him as a leaf, a wave, a cloud, as anything but a human being. From this nadir, Shelley makes a great recovery
when he urges the West Wind to make him its lyre and to be "through my
lips . . . the trumpet of a prophecy." A revolutionary spirit, the west wind is
also the harbinger of a Gnostic revelation, correcting the Creation-Fall by
going beyond nature.

I suspect that Shelley's deepest struggle in the poem is with Wordsworth, the prophet of nature, whose "sober coloring" is answered by the "deep
autumnal tone" of "Ode to the West Wind." Shelley's impatient and apocalyptic temperament will not wait on nature's revelation of herself.

Shelley set himself against Milton in *Prometheus Unbound* and against
Wordsworth in the "Hymn to Intellectual Beauty," "Mont Blanc," and the
"Ode to the West Wind." In his final poem, the great death march of the
fragmentary *The Triumph of Life*, Shelley turned to Dante, whose *Inferno* and
Purgatorio provided the context for a vision of judgment. Shelley hymns the
triumph of life over individual human integrity, while showing how the natural sun blots out the light of the stars, or poetic imagination, while the sun
itself vanishes in the glare of the cold Chariot of Life. Something like a new
Gnostic heresy is darkly suggested by Shelley's last vision, a sublime fragment
but profoundly despairing of any hope in ordinary human life.

John Keats

John Keats is unique among all major poets after Shakespeare in that his
consciousness is so profoundly normative; that is, it is so natural, sane, sympathetic, balanced, and equable as to give us an example of what human life
can be at its most wise and compassionate. A normative person is very rare,
whether in life or in literature, and this rareness enhances Keats's value for
us as a poet and as a human being.

Keats died at twenty-five and left us a truncated canon. His two major
long poems—*Hyperion* and *The Fall of Hyperion*—are fragments, but they
manifest a greatness that transcends his art in the great odes, the sonnets and
major lyrics, and in *Lamia* and *The Eve of St. Agnes*.

Here I desire only to note a few of the particular excellences of the
great odes, and of the astonishing ballad, "La Belle Dame Sans Merci." The
most famous of the odes is "On a Grecian Urn," which has haunted poetic

tradition down to its reappearance in Wallace Stevens's "The Poems of Our Climate," where Keats's powerful estrangement: "Thou, silent form, doth tease us out of thought / as doth eternity: Cold pastoral" is echoed as: "cold, a cold porcelain." It is strikingly bitter that Keats becomes more and more distant from what he contemplates on the urn as the poem proceeds. This is akin to the transition from the last line of stanza 7 to the opening of stanza 8 in the "Ode to a Nightingale." "Faery lands forlorn" leads to the tolling of the word *forlorn*, like a bell, as Keats is tolled back from the state of being one with the nightingale's song to the isolation of "my sole self."

I have a personal preference for the "Ode to Psyche" and the "Ode on Melancholy" but would have to grant that the superb "To Autumn" is probably the most eminent of the Great Odes of Keats. But, in these poems, we choose among sublimities:

> Sometimes whoever seeks abroad may find
> Thee sitting careless on a granary floor,
> Thy hair soft-lifted by the winnowing wind;

Keats's harvest girl, profoundly erotic, lingers halfway between Milton's Eve and Tennyson's Mariana. The influence of Keats has been enormous; he fostered not only Tennyson and the pre-Raphaelites but rather more subtly helped to form Emily Dickinson's oxymoronic rhetoric. Keats has remained a presence in subsequent American poetry from Trumbull Stickney, Wallace Stevens, and Hart Crane on to the remarkable Henri Cole, one of the most accomplished of our contemporary poets. In England, Keats fathered Wilfred Owen, the great poet of World War I, while in Ireland his effect lingered always on William Butler Yeats.

In his closing days, Keats began a crucial transition from his agon with Milton and with Wordsworth to a larger, loving contest with Shakespeare. The sonnet "On the Sea" suggests *King Lear*'s: "When last the winds of Heaven were unbound," while Keats's final fragment could be inserted in many Shakespearean contexts and be altogether at home, in its power of apprehension and its eloquence:

> This living hand, now warm and capable
> Of earnest grasping, would, if it were cold
> And in the icy silence of the tomb,
> So haunt thy days and chill thy dreaming nights
> That thou wouldst wish thine own heart dry of blood
> So in my veins red life might stream again,
> And thou be conscience-calm'd—see here it is—
> I hold it towards you.

JEROME CHRISTENSEN

"Thoughts That Do Often Lie Too Deep for Tears": Toward a Romantic Concept of Lyrical Drama

Near the end of his influential essay on the Immortality Ode, Lionel Trilling surmises that "thoughts that lie too deep for tears are ideally the thoughts which are brought to mind by tragedy" and summarily comments that "It would be an extravagant but not an absurd reading of the Ode that found it to be Wordsworth's farewell to the characteristic mode of his poetry . . . and a dedication to the mode of tragedy. But the tragic mode could not be Wordsworth's."[1] Trilling's extravagance comes at the expense of his own argument, which had begun by rejecting the conventional reading of the Ode as Wordsworth's conscious farewell to his art;[2] for even though Trilling describes the forecast of tragedy as a dedication to a new poetic subject, insofar as it is both a farewell to what is *Wordsworthian* in the poet's art and a promise never to be fulfilled, the last line of the Ode is freighted with pathos.

In the words of the poem, however, not tragedy but "the meanest flower that blows" brings to mind "thoughts that do often lie too deep for tears." Wordsworth surely knew that tragedy had not traditionally been assigned such a task. Exceedingly rich and various, eighteenth-century tragic theory proposed explanations of the kinds of pleasures tragedy ideally provides which ranged from versions of Aristotle's principles of catharsis and mimesis to variations on the Lucretian return on the self.[3] But whatever design

From *The Wordsworth Circle* 12, no. 1 (Winter 1981): 52–64. Copyright © 1981 by Marilyn Gaull.

by which tragedy was said to achieve its ends, theorists agreed that tragedy deserved its rank as the noblest form of dramatic art, capable rival of epic narrative, because it brought to the mind thoughts too *high* for tears, filled and elevated the mind with exalted conceptions. It is likely that tragedy, certainly as the eighteenth century conceived it, is meant to fall under the general proscription of "supposed Height" that Wordsworth announces in the Preface to *Lyrical Ballads*; his programmatic removal to "safe ground" is explicable in part as a retreat from tragic means and aims.[4]

Tragic theory was not, however, the same as tragic practice. As it was staged in the later eighteenth century, tragedy was most esteemed for its sensationally sentimental capacity to bring "thoughts" just right for tears. One account, from a review of the Edinburgh opening of John Home's *Douglas: A Tragedy* (the great weepy hope of Scottish tragic theatre), may suffice as example of the general standard of taste: "The applause was enthusiastic, but a better criterion of its merits was the tears of the audience, which the tender part of the drama drew forth unsparingly."[5] This criterion of merit, the capacity to draw forth what Keats called "barren Tragedy-tears,"[6] was distasteful to Wordsworth, who repudiated that standard in one of his few explicit comments on tragedy: "We [Wordsworth and Klopstock] talked of tragedy," he notes; "he seemed to rate too highly the power of exciting tears. I said that nothing was more easy than to deluge an audience. That it was done every day by the meanest writers." Wordsworth's objection to the tidal powers of contemporary tragedy is of a piece with his contemptuous dismissal of "sickly and stupid German Tragedies" and other forms of violent and disgusting sensation in the Preface to *Lyrical Ballads*.[7]

Wordsworth does not work toward tragedy, he works *through* it—especially in the Immortality Ode, where the difficulties attendant on the project of carrying "relationship and love" intimately involve the problem of genealogy.[8] The epigraph, which divides between the proposition that "The Child is Father of the Man" and the conditional "wish" for days to be "Bound each to each by natural piety," designs the Ode, as an oedipal drama that is never brought to catastrophe or resolution.[9] Indeed, the fulfillment of the wish for a binding natural piety depends on the overcoming of the potential for tragedy in the relations of child and father.

If the topic is genealogy and the tendency is deeper, the synthetic metaphor is descent—an uncongenial metaphor for the sublimity of tragedy but apt for the "complex and revolutionary" pathos that Wordsworth defines in the 1815 "Essay Supplementary to the Preface" and which in turn describes the mental passage in the Ode: "There is also a meditative, as well as a human, pathos; and enthusiastic, as well as an ordinary, sorrow; a sadness that has its seat in the depths of reason, to which the mind cannot sink gently of itself—but to which it must descend by treading the steps of thought" (*Prose*, III, 83). The Immortality Ode is the splendid example of this "profound passion," which eludes both the awful reverence of an inhuman sublime and the ordinary tears of an all too human pathos. Natural piety is staged in the poem, and particularly in stanzas VII–IX, as an art of sinking in a step by step descent from father to son to man—a genealogy of thoughts.[10]

Unlike the Virgilian descent, the Wordsworthian begins with a flower that is not plucked but read, which tells a tale put in the form of two questions: "Whither is fled the visionary gleam? / Where is it now the glory and the dream?" (55–56). The three sections of stanzas V, VI–VII, and VII–IX propose answers to those questions; but I shall confine my analysis to the last, where the answer is, in effect, a correction of the nature of the questions.

Before the child can father, it must be a child with its own paternity. The paternity of the child who, in one guise or another, is the subject of stanzas V–IX is "God" (65) or "Immortality" (119), and the complex affiliations between father and child are most intensely reflected on in stanza VIII. The six-year-old child is initially lauded for yet keeping a "heritage" that makes him an "Eye among the blind" (112). That eye is not put to the service of the blind, however, but directed backward to the gracious source of light and sight. And although called "Seer blest" (115), the mighty eye is not merely a visionary camera; it reads: "thou Eye among the Blind, / That deaf and silent, read'st the eternal deep" (112–13). To be stationed at the edge of the eternal deep is, by sublime paradox, the "being's height" (123). A correlative of the "Soul's immensity," which the child's "exterior semblance doth belie" (110, 109), the eternal deep is *in* the child but *of* the father—an extension in the child of the eternity of the godhead, which appears to the child like one of those ghostly scripts so common in Wordsworth: read not out of spontaneous reverence but because the child is "Haunted for ever by the eternal mind" (114). His heritage a haunting, the child's only privilege at his being's height is to read the will of an eternal father, a legacy that is the condition of and on his privilege. The difference between what is his and what is the father's constitutes the text read by the child positioned on the margin between who he is and where he came from. Or at least one supposes. It is constitutive of the meditative distance between ourselves and the seer that we cannot look over his shoulder to see what he reads but must read *him* reading and infer the conditions of his privilege from an exterior semblance that belies.

Constrained by the despotism of the spiritual eye and shouldering the truths that rest on him, all that unfixes the child is the unrest of his reading. Hence the answer to the poet's rhetorical question (asked of a child not here and who could not hear), "Why with such earnest pains dost thou provoke / The years to bring the inevitable yoke, / Thus blindly with thy blessedness at strife?" (124–26), seems clear: the child summons the years that he may exchange marginal uneasiness for earnest pains, forget a haunting blessedness beneath the hard fact of an earthly yoke. But the poet's imposing rhetoric forestalls easy answers. If the child has provoked the future, the poet provokes the past as, with forgetfulness at strife, he depicts the child's plight in language that limns the oedipal nexus of tragedy: the child's "freedom" is entailed by the epithet "heaven-born" (123); he is blessed by an "Immortality" that "Broods" over him like a "Master over a Slave" (119–20). The poet tropes uneasiness as strong ambivalence and implies a choice: the child could surrender to the mastery of Immortality, or he could, in the fashion of Oedipus, turn to confront the father, either to murder or transcend. But the child neither succumbs to the father nor succeeds to the sublime; instead he turns away from his patrimony, summons the years, and flees from being's height to begin his grave descent. Now there is nothing odd about the child's flight and the repression of his ambivalence, but peculiar are the poet's endorsement of slavery and his supercilious representation of the choice of the child, so-called eye among the blind, as a *blind* striving. What is especially odd is that the thought of this repressive turn, flight, and descent is followed by "O joy!" (130).

The poet's joy is odd because it marks his nearest approach to a thought too great for tears, to that delight which Edmund Burke identified as tragic affect, but which seems an indecorous response to an evasion of tragic conflict. The poet explains his joy (and in explaining again transgresses sublime decorum) as his reaction to the discovery that "nature yet remembers / What was so fugitive" (132–33). Now "fugitive" is usually referred to the transient glory of the soul, surprisingly persistent in the memory of mortal nature. But "fugitive" is equally descriptive of and more proximate to the buried child who has blindly fled his father. And if, as Thomas Weiskel has observed in *The Romantic Sublime* (1976) of Burke's theory of the sublime, "Delight is what you feel on escaping from the bewildering emotions and consequences surrounding a [real or imagined] murder" (p. 89), it would seem that Wordsworth's dramatic joy must be something different, for it is provoked not by escape from a murder real or imagined but by evasion of a conflict that *might* have led to the *thought* of a murder. Like tragic delight, the poet's joy prepares a renewal of power, but the poet's power appears only as the capacity to recollect what has been repressed—not a cathartic release from consequences but an acceptance of the return of all consequences all over again—without tears.

We can address the significance of this moment by comparing the recollection of this fugitive with the tragic scene of wonder and awe in the *Iliad* cited by Burke and elaborated by Weiskel as an example of the oedipal complexity of the sublime moment. Burke quotes four lines (590–93) from Pope's translation of the scene in Book 24 of the *Iliad*, when Priam suddenly appears before Achilles to plead for the body of Hector. Weiskel quotes the context:

> Unseen by these, the King his entry made;
> And prostrate now before *Achilles* laid,
> Sudden, (a venerable Sight!) appears;
> Embrac'd his Knees, and bath'd his Hands in Tears;
> Those direful Hands his Kisses press'd, embru'd
> Ev'n with the best, the dearest of his Blood!
>
> As when a Wretch, (who conscious of his Crime
> Pursu'd for Murder, flies his native Clime)
> Just gains some Frontier, breathless, pale!
> All gaze, all wonder: Thus *Achilles* gaz'd
> Thus stood th' Attendants stupid with Surprize;
> All mute, yet seem'd to question with their Eyes:
> Each look'd on other, none the Silence broke,
> Till thus at last the Kingly Suppliant spoke,
>
> Ah think, thou favour'd of the Pow'rs Divine!
> Think of thy Father's Age, and pity mine!
> In me, that Father's rev'rend Image trace,
> Those silver Hairs, that venerable Face:
> His trembling Limbs, his helpless Person, see!
> In all my Equal, but in Misery! (584–603)

Weiskel notes that "for the moment anger is suspended—sublimated—into wonder. Priam has cleverly assumed the role of the father in Achilles' mind, thereby engaging in his own interest powerful prohibitions against anger and parricide." He goes on to generalize that, "Wonder, the 'sense of awe' Burke will find in the sublime moment, is the affective correlative of a positive 'identification' with the Father, an identification which both presupposes the renunciation of parricidal aggression and facilitates an escape from the imagined consequences of a murder (pp. 90–91). I would like to stress the momentary quality of this sublime awe, suspension, and identification, as does Pope, who in his commentary on the passage (24.634–39) remarks on (what Weiskel parenthetically acknowledges) Priam's acute perception of the striking effect the paternal image has and who calls attention to the way the king "sets him [Achilles' father] before his [Achilles'] Imagination by this Repetition, and softens him into Compassion. (Twickenham ed., VIII,

562 n.). This compassion, Wordsworth's "human pathos," issues in what Wordsworth has led us to suspect:

> These Words soft Pity in the Chief inspire,
> Touch'd with the dear Remembrance of his Sire.
> Then with his Hand (as prostrate still he lay)
> The Old Man's Cheek he gently turn'd away.
> Now each by turns indulg'd the Gush of Woe;
> And now the mingled Tides together flow. . . . (634–39)

Like the meanest tragedian, Priam deluges his audience with tears; like the amateur he is, he gets caught up in the flood that annihilates not only the awful integrity and positive identification of the sublime moment but all distinctions whatever: between Hector and Achilles' father, between Priam and Achilles, between the two principals and the attendants, who join in "One universal, solemn Show'r . . ." (645).

The Homeric scene is a remarkable collection of familiar Wordsworthian *topoi*, assembled as if by negatives; and it is a suggestive illustration of the relationship between sublimity and beauty adumbrated by Wordsworth in his fragmentary essay on their respective provinces and powers. Like Burke, Wordsworth affirms that the sublime and the beautiful can "coexist" in the same object, even though they cannot act on the perceiver simultaneously: "the sublime always precedes the beautiful in making us conscious of its presence . . ." (*Prose*, III, 82). The sublime precedes the beautiful as the stunning effect of Priam's sudden manifestation precedes his eloquent utterance, during which he contrives a subtle weave of repetition that produces the soft languor which Burke in *A Philosophical Enquiry into the Origin of Our Ideas of the Sublime and Beautiful* describes as an effect of the beautiful (ed. Boulton, [1968], pp. 50–51). Tears, which Burke does not mention, follow. What, it may be asked, could Wordsworth have found offensive in such a turning of sublimity into human pathos? Observe the consequence of tears. The action resumes in *The Iliad* with the heroes "Satiate at length" (647), but Pope, who has already read to the end of the poem, cancels this new beginning in his note to line 634: "We are now come almost to the end of the Poem, and consequently to the end of the Anger of Achilles . . ." (Pope, *Iliad*, 563, n.). Once foreseen, the consequences cannot be aborted; human pathos has mortal consequences for mimetic narrative: the tears occur near the end of the poem; they mark the end of the anger of Achilles; consequently, like a deluge they sweep away Achilles, who *is* his anger, and drown the remainder of the Homeric epic in what Coleridge would call Wordsworthian pathos. Wordsworth's own evasion of the tragic prevents the tears that would dissolve those distinctions—the reading of which is life. Taking joy in the recollection of a repressed fugitive is to bring nothing to an end; instead it is to accept the legible pathos of repression after repression: a continual deepening that yields its "complex and revolutionary" returns to the eye that steadily cons the mental deep, continually evading a recognition of what it reads.

The joyous recollection prepares another scene which evokes oedipal complications:

> Not for these I raise
>   The song of thanks and praise;
> But for those obstinate questionings
> Of sense and outward things
> Fallings from us, vanishings;
> Blank Misgivings of a Creature
> Moving about in worlds not realised,
> High instincts before which our mortal Nature
> Did tremble like a guilty Thing surprised. . . . (140–148)

This passage revised the earlier scene in stanza VIII: "high instincts" conform to the soul's project at its "being's height," and mortal nature corresponds to the fugitive. By depicting a dualism this side of eternity, however, the revision advances the Ode one more step in its meditative descent. "Descent" not only because one scene follows another farther down the page and seems to come from deeper in the poetic memory, but because if in his provoking of the years the fugitive enacts a repressive turn away from his immortal legacy, the obstinate questioning is descendant from that repression: it too turns away from the eternal deep and from contest with the immortal father. If that turn is not, like its predecessor, with its blessedness at strife but, on the contrary, about its father's blessed business, it is because the precedent of the mortal nature offers a target to turn toward and against, a surrogate for the immortal master who is privileged by repression in order that days might be bound each to each in a pathetic descent which will not produce awe or tears but will "call forth and bestow power of which knowledge is the effect . . ." (Essay, Supplementary to the Preface [1815], *Prose*, III, 82). The descent of reading to strife, then, devolves into questioning that in turn represses its descent by interrogating the mortal nature, which starts back "as if a guilty Thing surprised."

Why guilty? If anything the persistence of the memory of the obstinate soul reasserts the failure of the mortal nature to murder or even threaten the master light. I would suggest that the emergence of this guilty figure marks a crucial threshold in the downward passage of the stanza. As the repressed power of the flight from the father is transferred to the pious soul, so, the source of these lines suggests, does the child cross over into father. The line of guilt has been persuasively glossed as an echo of Horatio's remark on the reaction of the ghost of Hamlet's father to the crowing of the cock: "And then it started like a guilty thing / Upon a fearful summons" (I, i, 148–49)—an echo which implies for the Ode the translation of haunted child into haunting father and identifies the guilt not as a consequence of a crime committed by a son against the father but for a crime *about to be* committed against the son.[11] The child is father of the man. Here that father halts on the threshold between the poet and his being's height, haunting the future of the man who will have to assume the heritage of his mortal nature. The poet's stern lack of sympathy for the fugitive in stanza VIII is explained by the intervention of this ghost which bars him from participation in what he recollects by fathering his distance from the source of light. Nonetheless, that repression is the condition of the poet's capacity *to* recollect, to observe a vital distance, and to acquire the power that descends to him as his thoughts deepen.

With a choice of fathers the poet may reject the mortal for the immortal, choose "the master-light of all our seeing" (156). Yet the continuity to which the poet adheres qualifies the identification to which he aspires. The repudiation of the mortal nature permits the poet to silence phenomenal noise and to repeat the scene at the margin of the eternal deep, now revised so that the particular child in whom was lodged all privilege and all possibility, becomes "Children" (167), who, with no eyes for the deep, do not suffer the act of reading but sport innocently on the shore. But revision is not vision. Although the poet affirms a return, what he *sees* is not the gift of a sublime transcendence but the consequence of restless thought. Linked into the stages of the poem by the "Hence" (162), the seashore scene is an exterior semblance of vision, which the poet has the ability to see only because he has the mortal power to read.

The inconclusiveness of that wishful thought characterizes the tension of the Ode: the poet stages his past in tragic figures (as Freud tells us he must, if they are to be staged at all)[12] within a meditation that evades a tragic dynamic which would transcend then deluge human suffering. Despite its repression, the intimation of immortality does persist and can be read beneath the belying of exterior semblance. But, because of its repression, that intimation can only be read as part of a mortal descent into which the fugitive fits like a dark glass. The poet is the father's child as he is the child's father. Although immortality be the master light of all our seeing, all we see comes to us transcribed in the ineradicable characters of our mortality. In recollecting the paternity from which no tragic act has severed him, the poet recalls a genealogy of repression, of which his recalcitrant reading is the legacy—a bestowal of power, if not of an effective knowledge. The distance the poet travels from stanza VIII to the end is a descent from a recollected reading of an eternal deep by a privileged child of light down the steps of thought toward the deepening of all semblances, fugitives between the first light and final deluge. Repetition has been bound to an orderly descent that works through the same question without the compensation of easy or final answers that could harmonize or reconcile. In natural piety the poet concludes; he acknowledges his legacy as the gift of a semblance that will always belie and often brings thoughts too deep for tears.

I should not suppress that it is the "human heart" (201) that Wordsworth gratefully identifies as the bestower of his sober receptiveness. Yet it is in line with the spirit of the text, in which all identifications are specious, to suspect Wordsworth's profession here. Certainly it would be impossible for the poet to thank meditative pathos, for it is the quality of that declension of mind not to be able to refer to itself—that is, to be incapable of positing an elevation from which consciousness, *spectator ab extra*, could congratulate the mind on the method of its acting. Self-consciousness, the stagey gesture that approves the hypostasis of head and heart so dear to Romantic psychology, belongs to the tragic theatricality of human pathos. Indeed, I would ally myself, albeit somewhat gingerly, with those who have, as a policy of taste or principle, withheld their applause from Romantic exploits of self-consciousness. Self-consciousness, as it has been conventionalized by Romantic poets and critics, is not a wound of the soul but a weakness for the limelight. The knowing *ecstasis* of self-consciousness transports the mind out of itself in order to place it dead center on the stage of history so that "I" can tearily watch myself suffer. This weakness is not foreign to Wordsworth, of course: it has been the subject of brilliant commentary, received its full measure of praise and blame. But it is my argument that the Immortality Ode ought to be politely withdrawn from the visionary company. Wordsworth does not face human suffering. He does not face it because it cannot be seen by the poet at large in the world any more than it can be seen by spectators gaping at stagelit actors. On the defective vision of a theater audience Charles Lamb is all but authoritative:

> Some dim thing or other the spectators see; they see an actor presenting a passion, of grief, or anger for instance, and they recognize it as a copy of the usual external effects of such passions; or at least as being true to *that symbol of the emotion which passes current at the theater* for it, for it is often no more than that: but of the grounds of the passion, its correspondence to a great or heroic nature, which is the only worthy object of tragedy,—that common auditors know anything of this, or can have any such notions dinned into them by

the mere strength of an actor's lungs—that apprehensions foreign
to them should be thus infused into them by storm, I can neither
believe, nor understand how it can be possible.[13]

Lamb is all *but* authoritative because Wordsworth does not equate the theatrical with Drury Lane, nor exempt the worthiest objects of tragedy from
the class of "dim things" that obstruct the descent to the grounds of human
passion. Nothing "human" is alien to a tragic scenario that progresses from
conflict to climactic transcendence and closes with a curtain of tears. The
poet's return to a flower brings him back to exactly what is *not* the face
of human suffering because in whatever mask that face might appear, the
witness of the human would be suborned to tragic testimony for theatrical
convenience. It is both pathetic and an occasion for further meditation that
the poet must depersonify to deepen, if not fully unmask, the human; he
must remark on semblances that belie in order to be true to life.

What is life? Life for the critic is a line to be read: "Thoughts that do
often lie too deep for tears." That critical reading lines up behind, descends
from, the poet's "own" reading of the line of descent which makes legible the
"meanest flower that blows." And, to string out the word one more sentence,
that descent is a line of readings. What is reading? Surely a difficult question. But an answer can be suggested by noting that reading, or at least the
Wordsworthian reading of the Ode, has an uncertain structure which can be
tracked, if not fully determined, by marking its deviance from a more categorical norm.

Such a norm is proposed by Kenneth Burke in the "Dialectic of Tragedy" section of *A Grammar of Motives* (1945). There Burke cites the Greek
proverb "*ta pathemata mathemata*," the sufferer is the learned, and argues that
to complete the proverb "at the risk of redundancy" would requite reference
to an initial action. The true tragic grammar is realized, Burke says, by the
sequence "*poiemata, pathemata, mathemata*, suggesting that the act *poiemata*
organizes the opposition (brings to the fore whatever factors resist or modify
the act), that the agent thus 'suffers' this opposition, and as he learns to take
the oppositional motives into account, widening his terminology accordingly,
he has arrived at a higher order of understanding" (rpt. 1969, pp. 39–40). The
dialectic could hardly be more symmetrical: Burke opposes the tragic Greek
proverb in order to make it proverbialize Greek tragedy; the realization of a
tragic grammar requires the assembling of the proverbial act into a higher
order of understanding. The providential calculus of dialectic brings the classical to a climax in our knowledge. Whether Burkean, Coleridgean, Frank-
fortian, or Bloomian, dialectic translates poetry into criticism and transfigures
us dialecticians into the higher, even the highest, critics—the last comers to a

cultural stageplay whose finale is cued to our long awaited arrival. From this perspective the *exemplum* of Priam's scene in Homer's epic can be generalized and dialectic conceived of as the intersection of drama and narrative. This is true whether we consider the Burkean schema of first action, then suffering, and, finally, knowledge, or whether we think of dialectic in terms of the oedipus complex, which posits family drama as family romance, the structure of tragedy as the story of one's life.

The story of Wordsworth cannot be so neatly rationalized, however. Indeed, if the power of understanding inheres in the topographical paradox that to stand under is to *be* higher, Wordsworth's wholly unparadoxical strength as a poet is that, as Coleridge continually reminds us, he understands nothing. Again and again Wordsworth rejects the dialectical lure, to which all Coleridgeans are susceptible, the bait which tempts the epigone to complete Greek proverbs, to assemble tragedy from classical ruins according to the mathematics of a supposedly higher grammar. There is nothing of the classical about Wordsworth. If the fugitive allusion to Pope's "Homer" in the Immortality Ode is convincing, then it should follow that Wordsworth's repudiation of the tragic scene casts out not only the Homeric ethos but its neo-classical redaction as well. But even should that argument want killing force, only lack of space prevents a cataloging of Wordsworth's less oblique dismissals not only of classical precedents and neo-classical grammars but of the very notions of precedent and grammar which "classical" implies. And it is only the grammarians' funereal impulse that tries to strap Wordsworth to ratios of revision. Rather than assemble proverbs into grammars, Wordsworth might be said to *de*proverbialize tragedy according to the rarely grammatical dissemblance of repression: he does not impose the formula "to act, suffer, and know"; he adheres to the repetitive process "to act, to suffer, to act, to suffer"—an interminable series in which each cause is the effect of its effect, under its own influence. Or, as Wordsworth intimates: like father, like son, like father. Each term, moment, or character is constituted by its repression of its affiliations with the other; each is an exterior semblance latent with its supposed antithesis. The sequence plots no resolution; instead it configures thought as an indefinite dissembling in which each character is doubly distinguished: as its disguise of itself and as the obstinate questioner of its neighbor. The sequence "act, suffer, act, suffer" represents reading as a differential movement through a tissue of latencies. One always reads along the same lines, always, however, sinking deeper. The line of reading, to paraphrase D. H. Lawrence, is no free fall. It is a narrow, tight descent, where the mind meditates hemmed in by compulsions. That's nothing to cry about. The Romantic complicity of dissembling characters—the never quite understood differential of an action that is already suffering and a suffering already acting evades the human pathos of tragic knowledge and adumbrates what I would describe as the generic equivalent of meditative pathos: lyrical drama.

The concept of a lyrical drama is not Robert Langbaum's invention; nor is it my own; nor is its application to the Immortality Ode more than a slight anachronism; it is, of course, the subtitle that Shelley attached to *Prometheus Unbound*, a term, however, curiously isolated in Romantic literary history, uncommonly overlooked in critical commentary—a hybrid which, though it could not have come from nowhere and has not dropped out of sight, appears to have no natural father and no child.[14] Unlike the ideal of the myth, which, as Earl Wasserman describes it in *Shelley* (1971), is composed of "eternal mental possessions" which ask "to be interwoven into a beautiful whole 'containing within itself the principle of its own integrity'" (p. 272), the lyrical drama is an unpropertied child of contradictions, a composite which is itself the act and suffering of its potential disintegration. Lyrical insofar as it is the aspiration of ego, a song transcribed for one voice, and composed of imagery "drawn from the operations of the human mind";[15] dramatic in that what is the mind is a *scene*, not simply an agent—the lyrical drama is passionate and implicit, not theatrical. As a drama of thought which can neither be staged nor closeted, the lyrical drama does not so much take place in the depths of the mind as continually displace the mind in an indefinite deepening, which is unmotivated and unlimited by the teleological and topographical prejudice of a destined profound. To risk a tentative definition: lyrical drama is the pathetic representation of the mind in the meditative passage of characters.

Among the consequences that follow from such a definition, several are especially salient. First, to begin the criticism of lyrical drama presupposes an abandonment of the familiar epistemological theme in Romantic criticism. Instead of a problem of knowledge or understanding, the lyrical drama presupposes a problem of reference. One does not ask, that is, which is prior or ulterior, subject or object? Or, can the self ever know an other through a poetry of experience? One does not project a bookkeeping of the dialectical profit taken by a knowing subjectivity. Instead one asks, to what do the characters in meditative passage refer? Is that reference constant? To what are we to refer for the production and reproduction of these characters? Are those operations rule governed, mechanical, or, perhaps, indeterminate? Is the pathos of meditation reducible to the coercion (or, perhaps, the license) of reference? To propose a genre as a problem of reference rather than a project of knowing is another way of opting for the tension of reading instead of the quiet pride of understanding.

A second point, closely associated with the first, is that although the concept of a lyrical drama brackets the questions regarding the transactions of subject and object—indeed, all questions of knowledge—the consequence is neither a simple idealism nor a horrific solipsism. For this is a drama *of* the mind, not *in* the mind. Not an hypothetical ideal or an hallucination of diseased self-regard, the drama of the mind is a formal contrivance; it follows a script and is represented in characters which are orthographical *dramatis personae* fully fledged by an inky plume. Like the words of Prometheus' curse these characters can be recalled, dissembled, and read, yet never fully known for what they are, never finally erased. If the characters of lyrical drama will not pose as beautiful idealisms, they cannot be antithetically consigned to the inert state of mere things either. They are, to employ once again Wordsworth's resonant term, exterior semblances—seemings whose materiality appears as the curious effect of a kind of rich redundancy (What, after all, would an *interior* semblance be? Is not semblance logically always the false front on authentic innerness?)—a redundancy that characterizes the materiality of the signifier by attributing to it a depth, however insubstantial, and a potential for dramatic conflict, however irresolvable. Once again, one cannot know what cannot reasonably be assigned to the ideal or the material; one can but read the differentials or, better, the intimations. One reads, I wish, with the same sort of meditative pathos with which Wordsworth intimately regards the meanest flower, thereby binding flower, poet, and reader each to each in hermeneutical piety.

Finally, however, I want to make it clear that I advance no claim for the lyrical drama as a positive genre. Although the name does appear in the sub-title to *Prometheus Unbound*, lyrical drama does not identify a genre which we have always dimly known and that has been lying around somewhere waiting to be recognized by an ingenious critic. And if it were, it would probably not be noticed by a Romanticist, who, though as ingenious as most, has not historically exercised that capacity in either the invention or study of genres. The word itself comes strange to the pen. Among the instances of what might be called Romantic genre study exemplary is that of M. H. Abrams, which began with the structure and style of the greater Romantic lyric, applicable to most Romantic poetry, and ended (thus far, at least) in a mythus of the spirit of the age. In essential rapport with such a plot are most studies of the sublime, which initially posit a generic locus, only to find the critical wagon hitched to a fierce dynamic of dislocation and aggrandizement. The sublime is a "genre" which devours the very notion of kinds. It would probably suit neither the Romanticists I have brusquely categorized nor specialists in genre theory to have either natural supernaturalism or the sublime be denominated a genre. In fact, the Romantic period has always been a predicament for genre theorists and historians. Most influential has been the organization of the Romantic lyric from a Victorian retrospect from which it can be assigned to the plastic class of dramatic lyric and accredited as a tendency toward the dramatic monologue (see Langbaum, pp. 38–75). That organization has recently been contested, however, according to definite principles of form which sharply distinguish the Romantic lyric from both the eighteenth-century dramatic lyric and the Victorian dramatic monologue, and which reinscribe for genre theory the brackets around the Romantic era.[16] Hybrid norm, the genre is an invention—not of mine but of a rhetoric of crossings. Each the act of the other's suffering, the suffering of the other's act, lyric and drama will always mix, never merge. In what I take to be a particularly Romantic sense of genre, lyrical drama designates a crossing or a threshold— a *limen* which marks out neither a progress nor a regress but a transgress: the transgression of child and man, action and suffering, lyric and drama. I would like to designate a genre whose one actively redundant rule (including this one) is that its every rule will be broken, its formal design breached, its purest pleasures the dissemblance of pain.

I shall conclude by nudging this designation one more step toward the promised conceptualization. In his superb essay "Positive Negation," Angus Fletcher describes personification as "the figurative emergent of the liminal scene."[17] Although Fletcher elaborates that phrase with subtle attention to the liminality of Coleridge's verse, there is little doubt that the uncanniness of personification that Fletcher's phrase captures would whet the appetite of Coleridge the critical censor. The critic quite properly regarded the dissembling characters of personification as vagrant, agnostic misfits which his theology could not tolerate and his dialectics neither capture nor kill. The uncanny emergence of personification, its liminal passage, transgresses "the sacred distinction between things and persons" which in the *Biographia Literaria* Coleridge affirms as the first tenet to which a true philosophical criticism must subscribe (Shawcross ed., I, 137). What goes for philosophical criticism applies to philosophical poetry as well; and in his criticism of the potentially great philosophical poet, Wordsworth, Coleridge prepares us to suppose that the same transgression that characterizes a particular figure also applies to a particular kind of Wordsworthian poem—a kind delimited in the *Biographia* primarily by Coleridge's ostensibly excessive objections to poems like "The Thorn" and the Immortality Ode, which otherwise have no conspicuous affinities.[18] That kind of poem, I would suggest, is lyrical drama: a mixed genre of transgression, which is the liminal scene where personifications, like fathers and sons, emerge—a scene affectively like Stonehenge, where the "circle of reddening stones" utter the groans of human sacrifice; like a graveyard alive with epitaphic inscriptions; like a plot of turf forming into characters of fatal legibility. But unlike all because the liminal scene of the lyrical drama diagrams no charmed circle, hides no daemonic spot. It represents a poetic genre which transgresses the orders of master and slave, priest and victim, nature and supernature, the quick and the dead, by provoking all dualisms with the variable flight of fugitive form.

NOTES

1. This essay is an extended version of a paper delivered at the 1980 meeting of the Wordsworth-Coleridge Association. Lionel Trilling, "The Immortality Ode," *The Liberal Imagination: Essays on Literature and Society* (1950), p. 152.

2. Trilling, p. 129. My interest in Trilling is that he gives me a line on the Ode. For a full scale assault on the principles of Trilling's criticism based on a full reading of the Ode, see Helen Vendler, "Lionel Trilling and the Immortality Ode," *Salmagundi*, 42 (Spring, 1978), 68–86.

3. See W. P. Albrecht, *The Sublime Pleasures of Tragedy* (1975), pp. 1–2, and James H. Averill, *Wordsworth and the Poetry of Human Suffering* (1980), p. 122, for summary accounts of eighteenth-century tragic theory.

4. Preface to *Lyrical Ballads* (1802) in *The Prose Works of William Wordsworth*, eds. W. J. B. Owen and J. W. Smyser, 3 vols. (1974), I, 143.

5. *Scots Magazine* XVII (1756). Quoted in E. C. Mossner, *The Life of David Hume* (1970), pp. 359–60. For discussions of the tearfulness that tragedy was expected to provoke see James T. Lynch, *Box, Pit, and Gallery: Stage and Society in Johnson's London* (1953), pp. 283–85, Leo Hughes, *The Drama's Patrons: A Study of the Eighteenth-Century London Audience* (1971), pp. 112, 134–36.

6. In a letter, November 22, 1817, to Benjamin Bailey, *The Letters of John Keats, 1814–1821*, ed. Hyder E. Rollins, 2 vols. (1958), I, 186.

7. "Conversation with Klopstock," *Prose Works*, I, 95. The editors suggest the connection (n98).

8. For a version of this working through, see Averill's discussion narrative of "The Ruined Cottage" (*Wordsworth and the Poetry of Human Suffering*, p. 122).

9. All quotations from "Ode: Intimations of Immortality from Recollections of Early Childhood" are from *The Poetical Works of William Wordsworth*, eds. Ernest de Selincourt and Helen Darbishire, 5 vols. (1947), Vol. 4.

10. On "thought" in the Ode, see Francis Ferguson, *Wordsworth: Language as Counter-Spirit* (1977), pp. 123–25. On the relation of tears and narrative in Wordsworth, see Neil Hertz, "Wordsworth and the Tears of Adam," in *Wordsworth: A Collection of Critical Essays*, ed. M. H. Abrams (1972), pp. 107–22.

11. I take the gloss from *Major British Poets of the Romantic Period*, ed. William Heath (1973), p. 259, n2 (corrected).

12. For an analysis of the complications of Freud's theatricalism, especially as it is represented in the essay "Psychopathic Characters on the Stage," see Phillipe Lacoue-Labarthe, "*Theatrum Analyticum*," trans. Robert Vollrath and Samuel Weber, *GLYPH 2* (1977), 122–43.

13. Charles Lamb, "On the Tragedies of Shakespeare, Considered with Reference to their Fitness for Stage Representation," *The Works of Charles and Mary Lamb*, ed. E. V. Lucas (1903; rpt., 1968), I, 102.

14. Robert Langbaum's use of the term in *The Poetry of Experience* (1957) is no exception. Langbaum neither attributes the term to Shelley nor discusses *Prometheus Unbound*. For Langbaum, lyrical drama is another version of the dramatic lyric; both are subsumed within the category "poetry of experience." See pp. 57–65.

15. Shelley, Preface to *Prometheus Unbound, Shelley's Poetry and Prose*, eds. Donald H. Reiman and Sharon Powers (1977), p. 133.

16. See Ralph W. Rader, "The Dramatic Monologue and Related Lyric Forms," *Critical Inquiry*, Vol. 3, No. 1 (Autumn, 1976), 145–46.

17. Angus Fletcher, "'Positive Negation': Threshold, Sequence, and Personification in Coleridge," *New Perspectives on Coleridge and Wordsworth, Selected Papers of the English Institute*, ed. Geoffrey Hartman (1972), p. 158.

18. For a reading of "The Thorn" which endeavors to follow through on Coleridge's objections and analyzes the poem as a lyrical drama, see my "Wordsworth's Misery, Coleridge's Woe: Reading 'The Thorn,'" *PLL*, Vol. 16, No. 3 (Summer, 1980), 268–86.

LESLIE BRISMAN

Mysterious Tongue: Shelley and the Language of Christianity

The wilderness has a Mysterious tongue
Which teaches awful doubt, or faith so mild,
So solemn, so serene, that man may be
But for such faith with nature reconciled.

("Mont Blanc")

Professor Thomas Weiskel used to quote with approval the urbane apho-
rism that Christianity is our most successful metaphor.[1] A metaphor, like
the modern Greek word for *truck* to which it is related, is a vehicle of convey-
ance; a metaphor transports meaning—sometimes packaged or packageable
as the tenor, the signified, sometimes a looser cargo. Whether loaded or
empty and making a dry run, a metaphor is a vehicle for making or crossing
a certain figurative distance, like the distance between biological life and
imaginative life, or earthly life and eternal life. Sometime after the death of
Thomas Weiskel, his father, a practicing Congregational minister, showed
me a photograph of his son's posthumous daughter, about whose head there
appeared to hover, in a configuration of lights and shades, what the Reverend Mr. Weiskel saw as the spiritual form of his dead son not yet "meta-
phorized" or carried hence. For the Reverend Mr. Weiskel, Christianity
was the most successful metaphor, *the* faith by which one could understand
how a man might "pass away" and still be a spiritual presence. For his son,

From *Texas Studies in Literature and Language* 23, no. 3 (Fall 1981): 389–417. Copyright ©
1981 by the University of Texas Press.

27

however, Christianity was the most successful *metaphor*, a figure or set of figures of speech by which passages of poetry (rather than the narrow passes in the valley of the shadow of life) were to be negotiated.

Translation to an afterlife or translation, through commentary, of what Wordsworth called the "after-images" of memory and literature: it may be that there is no crossing the distance between these two senses of translation, the distance between those who value Christian beliefs as beliefs and those who value Christian metaphors as metaphors. Yet in some way that distance is always being crossed not only between orthodox father figures and the heretical sons but between God the Father and *His* metaphor-making Son. Jesus undertook to teach that the water of life is not literal water, that the blindness that matters is not literal blindness. Circumcision, both in Deuteronomy and the New Testament, can mean circumcision of the heart, a troublesome figure of speech, or circumcision of the flesh, a troublesome literalism; and to this day the interpretation of circumcision as metaphoric separates Christians from Jews. On the other hand, atonement is a metaphor for Jews—a symbolic action in the Levitical code—and something closer to literalism for Christians. More troublesome is the question whether "eternal life" is a figure of speech for a state of mind on this earth, or in some sense a literalism in relation to which the earthly awareness of being saved is the vehicle or shadowy figure. Blake, who repeatedly punctuated one of his most beautiful passages with the refrain, "mark well my words; they are of your eternal salvation," meant something else by "eternal salvation" than the more conventionally pious Coleridge might have meant. For Blake, one can be saved from this world or saved in this world by setting aright the relations between one's passions, intellect, imagination, and integrative instincts. There is no divinity but that which resides in the human breast, and a man may be translated to God in Blake's sense by translating for himself, by making his own, the divine Word of William Blake. Radical as this may seem, there is also something very Protestant about it. As the eighteenth-century divine John Asgill put it, understanding Jesus' metaphors is salvation: "God will not deliver out Eternal life to man faster than he makes him understand it; for the knowledge of Eternal Life is the essence of it. *This is eternal life*: to know God and Jesus Christ."[2] The tree of knowledge is the tree of life.

The position that eternal life begins in this life at the moment of acceptance of Christ remains in the end a different thing from the position that eternal life is coextensive with (i.e., a figure for) a state of consciousness in this life. For a space, however, the Christian and the poetic visionary share the metaphor of eternal life, and this happy coexistence may be taken as a synecdoche for the Romantic poets' sharing of certain essential Christian metaphors or Christian doctrines understood as metaphors. The surprising thing is that

Blake and Shelley, hostile to traditional Christianity, should have been even more immersed in Christian metaphor than were the more overtly Christian poets Wordsworth and Coleridge. Like Yeats, who said in *A Vision* that his spirits brought him metaphors for poetry, the Romantic poets commandeered the Christian metaphors, those giant tractor-trailers of the mind, and found in them "grand store-house[s] of enthusiastic and meditative imagination."

This last phrase, Wordsworth's in the 1815 Preface, sums up two qualities or habits of mind that the Romantics took over from Protestant religion: meditation and enthusiasm. Poetic meditation, with its privileged apostrophes, and daemonic enthusiasm, with its visitations of Imagination, are contraband goods "transported" from prayerful meditation and spiritual zeal. Where they thought they were going with these goods is a question we may be inclined to answer a little too readily with a phrase like "natural supernaturalism." It is true that in general the poets were going from heaven to earth, from a source of power to which the priests and practitioners of organized religion once had privileged access, to a secularized or humanized godlike power. But for Keats, the poetic journey is characteristically a round trip, away from and back to this earth, even if the bare earth or the mind that perceives it emerges more sublime for the redoubled distances of metaphor. And what shall we say of Wordsworth's "direction" when he says "trailing clouds of glory do we come / From God who is our home." Is the Intimations Ode headed from God to a dispirited earth and the meanest flowers? Is "God" Wordsworth's abbreviation for the comforts of an older faith, or Wordsworth's ultimate tenor, *the* signified, toward which the laden language of poetry wishes to go? If the soul's home is with infinitude, as he says in *The Prelude*, if we are most at home when the language of the sublime has carried us furthest from our sole selves, then God may be the end—the final signified—rather than a rejected signifier for the sublime spirit.

One generalization about the "direction" of Romantic religious metaphor will, I think, hold. It has been remarked of Byron that he was certainly a Calvinist even if he was not a Christian, and in general the Romantics were radical Protestants (of varying degrees and kinds of radicalism) even if they were not Christians. By this statement I mean not only that they all had their equivalents for "inner light," not only that they all thought they could read God's book for themselves (be that scripture or the book of nature), but that they saw themselves recovering the spirit of primitive, prechurchly Christianity, the spirit of Jesus the maker of metaphors. For example, one of the most "High Church" figures of mystification for Shelley is the Shape all Light who offers Rousseau, in a mysterious communion ritual, a "new Vision never seen before." Blake would have called her Mystery, the Whore of Babylon, and indeed her walking on water (like that of Christ the maker of miracle) and her mystifications about origins (she purports to answer the question "shew whence I came, and where I am, and why") can suggest that far from inner light her illumination has about it all the darkness of *The Four Zoas'* nine nights. The scene of rebirth that follows, like Rousseau's earlier account of his reorigination (*The Triumph of Life*, ll. 325–42), forms a radical critique of Christian rebirth as a figure for the ultimate "difference." So impossible is it to tell rebirth from repetition or refiguration that we are led back from the mystifications of Pauline Christianity and of poetry in general to the making of metaphors of a more protestant, deconstructionist Jesus. St. Paul, whose writings are the earliest Christian documents in the Bible, specifies to the Corinthians that *rebirth* means literal rebirth into a life elsewhere. Paul does use rebirth as a religious metaphor, calling those who believe men "risen with Christ" (Col. 3:1)—already raised with Christ, *as it were*. But he cautions against limiting the meaning of resurrection to this metaphoric sense, this "as it were." "If in this life only we have hope in Christ," he says in 1 Corinthians 15:19, "we are of all men most miserable." I suspect that he writes this to the Corinthians because some among the Christians there held just the view Paul rejects, and that Shelley in his own way sanctioned—the view that Christ and his power of resurrecting us is for this life only, that resurrection is a metaphor for the sense of renewal one feels in accepting the sovereignty of love. If what Paul rejects was already known in Corinth, then it is back to Corinth, back to "primitive" Christianity, back to Jesus himself (as he was understood in Corinth) that Blake, Shelley, and Wordsworth take us.

In this essay I turn to Shelley, the Romantic poet most vociferously hostile to Christian dogma, to illustrate some of the striking ways in which Christian metaphors were appropriated for poetry and the human spirit at large. I single out three types of natural supernaturalism—three Christian concepts reinterpreted by the Romantic poets: faith, hope, and love.[3] With a crucial reinterpretation of faith as "self-esteem" rather than the esteem of a power outside the self, these three concepts make up Shelley's own list in "Hymn to Intellectual Beauty." Shelley agreed with Paul (1 Cor. 13:13) that the greatest of these is love, and he regarded the gospel of love as the true teaching of Jesus to which the protestant spirit of the poet (protesting against the abuses of interpretation and power on the part of church, state, and selfhood) must return.[4] It is under the rubric of love that Shelley elucidates his central religious and philosophic ideas, and I include here Shelley's revision of the traditional concept of atonement. More than themes or messages, Shelley's ideas on love influence the plot and tone of all his poems. Here, and in Shelley's handling of the other virtues, we can see how complexly thematics are related to poetics, despite the poet's repeated disclaimer of didactic poetry.

Love

In *A Defence of Poetry*, Shelley at once identifies the core of his radical prot-estantism and his theory of imagination:

> The great secret of morals is love, or a going out of our own nature and an identification of ourselves with the beautiful which exists in thoughts, action, or person, not our own. A man, to be greatly good, must imagine intensely and comprehensively; he must put himself in the place of another and of many others; the pain and pleasure of his species must become his own. The great instrument of moral good is the imagination; and poetry administers to the effect by acting upon the cause.

In thus revealing highest truths, Shelley also reveals himself, his most deeply held convictions. One might say that the rhetoric of revelation is responsible for the beautiful opening phrase, "the great secret of morals," but that is to pass on to an abstraction a responsibility that Shelley makes his own. Love is the *secret* of morals because "poetry lifts the veil from the hidden beauty of the world," presenting commonplaces like love "as if they were not familiar." The secret is that morality is not transmitted as moral science but as poetry, as principles and exempla encoded in myths that hold the imagination. In the next sentence, Shelley writes a little prose poem by substituting Everyman for Christ: "A man, to be greatly good, must imagine intensely and comprehensively; he must put himself in the place of another and of many others; the pain and pleasure of his species must become his own." For Mark, the secret of Jesus was his divinity—something repeatedly made manifest yet repeatedly felt to be secret, wholly other, and the subject of an enjoined silence. For Shelley, the secret that God is love is repeatedly to be "leaked" in poetry. In one place Shelley does obscurely encode the secret of love in the more limited sense of a literary secret. Count Cenci joyfully announces that his two sons died on the twenty-seventh of December—the feast day of John, who proclaimed "God is love" (1 John 4:8). To suppose that Cenci himself shares this irony is not necessary; the greater irony of the play is that the church and the traditional concept of a loving, omnipotent God are stumbling blocks in the path of love. More generally, works like *The Cenci* contribute to the kingdom to come by strengthening the faculty of sympathy: "Poetry strengthens that faculty which is the organ of the moral nature of man in the same manner as exercise strengthens a limb."

In the *Defence*, Shelley distinguishes cultivation of the general capac-ity for sympathy from promulgation of specific notions of morality. "A poet therefore would do ill to embody his own conceptions of right and wrong, which are usually those of his place and time, in his poetical creations which participate in neither."[5] Though poems like *Queen Mab* and *The Revolt of Islam* are general enough in their condemnation of the tyrannies of church and state, the greater success of *The Cenci* may be linked with Shelley's willingness to ground the general doctrine of love in the specific moral issues of the play. In the Preface, Shelley repeats his notion that poetry does not preach specifics:

> The highest moral purpose aimed at in the highest species of the drama, is the teaching the human heart, through its sympathies and antipathies, the knowledge of itself; in proportion to the possession of which knowledge, every human being is wise, just, sincere, tolerant, and kind. If dogmas can do more, it is well: but a drama is no fit place for the enforcement of them.

What Shelley goes on to write is couched so as not to present itself as a specific dogma, though it comments in no uncertain terms on the rape and parricide of the play:

> Undoubtedly, no person can be truly dishonoured by the act of another; and the fit return to make to the most enormous injuries is kindness and forbearance, and a resolution to convert the injurer from his dark passions by peace and love.

These are the Shelleyan principles of morality that Beatrice herself fails to share. What distinguishes Shelley's viewpoint from the "restless and anatomizing casuistry with which men seek the justification of Beatrice" is the sympathy he wishes to arouse for her independent of our judgment of *her* judgment. One may be tempted to condemn Beatrice for not turning the other cheek, for not making "fit return" in kindness and forbearance; yet to condemn her violates the very principles of forgiveness that she herself failed to call into practice.[6]

Unlike Coleridge, who preferred the Gospel of John and objected to Matthew, Shelley seems to have preferred Matthew and more especially Luke. In these he found what he regarded as the essential gospel, "the forgiveness of injuries which true Christians profess."[7] Its most radical statement occurs in what we call, after Matthew, the Sermon on the Mount: "Resist not evil: but whosoever shall smite thee on thy right cheek, turn to him the other also."[8] It is instructive to compare Shelley's understanding of this verse with that of Coleridge, whom Shelley took as a poetic father but never a Christian one. Here is Coleridge:

It may well bear a question ... whether some of the moral precepts do not acquire a false, nay a dangerous import, by this detachment from the occasion, circumstance, & their relation to the particular persons to whom they were addressed. Ex. gr. Matt. V. 39–42 would have a beauty, a propriety, a *wisdom*,—supposing them addressed to the 12 Apostles, or to the 70 Disciples ... which it has required many apologetic limitations, nay, arbitrary pretences, to maintain for them considered as moral Commands of universal application.

   ex. gr.—that the provocations instanced were mere trifling wrongs—no serious injuries! that is—resist not evil! means do not resist what is only an imaginary evil = Do not put yourself in a passion for trifles![9]

Coleridge's temporizing with Jesus' radical morality may strike individual Christians as untrue to the spirit of the original, even though Coleridge's interpretation has necessarily become an institutional orthodoxy of sorts—a moderate way of coping with a radical demand. What Coleridge regards as "a false, nay a dangerous import," Shelley takes as the basis of the reformation of the human heart—a reformation that must precede political reform. For Shelley, "revenge, retaliation, atonement are pernicious mistakes," regardless how trifling or overwhelming the provocation for or the mode of revenge. If one does not turn the other cheek, if one retaliates physically, legally, or through the endorsement of an imagined ultimate punishment for evildoers, one violates the gospel of love. Shelley's most radical insight about traditional Christianity is that the theology of atonement is based on revenge and retaliation: man's disobedience struck God as a slap in the face, and rather than turn the other cheek, God himself exacted retribution in approving of the Son's suffering for mankind. In writing *The Revolt of Islam*, *The Cenci*, and *Prometheus Unbound*, Shelley restored what he understood as the import of primitive Christianity by exposing myths of revenge for what they are.

   In the Preface to *Prometheus Unbound*, Shelley explicitly argues for the superiority of his Prometheus over Milton's Satan; he believes also in the superiority of his Prometheus over Christianity's Christ: Prometheus suffers for his own sins of rhetoric against Jupiter and saves himself from his own earlier manner of construing the nature of things. In the Christian scheme, Jesus (himself free of the taint of original sin) dies to bear on his back the sins of mankind; in *Prometheus Unbound*, Jupiter's child Demogorgon bears on his back the sins of his fathers—or rather, he comes to bear Jupiter (who personifies the sins) to "dwell together / Henceforth in darkness" (III, i, 55–56).

Shelley can present the eternal condemnation of Jupiter as a myth morally superior to God's eternal condemnation of Satan because Jupiter more clearly than Satan condemns himself: Shelley has no personified eternal judge who sits enthroned and declares himself free from sin. (Demogorgon is not an enthroned power but a power for dethronement, while Milton's myth of the transference of power labored under the necessity of retaining two enthroned powers, Father and Son.) More important, Shelley's Jupiter becomes less a character than a state of the soul, and Shelley—like Blake—distinguishes individuals from states and redeems individuals while he condemns the states. Prometheus individualizes himself while Jupiter becomes a name for a rejected snakeskin, shed in the apocalyptic recognition of the poem.

Looking at these differences between the action of Shelley's central myth and that of Christianity, one might be tempted to say simply that Shelley rejects the concept of atonement and the system of retributive justice on which it is based. But it would be more accurate to say that Shelley metaphorizes the supernatural concept of atonement and substitutes an individual death of the old self for the literal or scapegoat death exacted by a legalistic God the Father. Like Blake, Shelley responds to the Christian concept of atonement with a question: "Would you love one who never died for you?" We die for each other daily in little nameless acts of kindness and love, in the little or not so little acts of self-curtailment necessary for conversation, for love, for civilization. For the sake of poetry, which must not curtail its own myth-making even if it curtails its theologizing instinct, we need to represent one man dying or suffering for others; but in this new theology, this new theory of representation, the figures the poet singles out are synecdoches for human suffering and forgiveness of sins. Christians might argue that Jesus Christ is a synecdoche too, since he partakes through the incarnation of the human nature he redeems; but from the perspective of Shelleyan natural supernaturalism, the orthodox Son of Man remains an inadequate metonymy, a figure contiguous with, associated with human nature and original sin, but not part of it. Shelley's Prometheus, on the other hand, stands aside from the curse he once uttered on Jupiter, but he redeems us *in* redeeming himself. The nuptials of Prometheus and Asia might suggest the marriage of Christ and his Church, but as the spirit of the earth with playfully wanton imagination suggests, Asia and Prometheus partake of the sensual as well as the intellectual life they represent.

One aspect of the revisionary concept of atonement and its attendant theory of representation must be related less to Shelley's particular turn on Christian myth than to the necessary business of poetry. Christianity has one story to privilege; poets, in this regard, are promiscuous. We often speak of characters in literary works as "Christ figures" without working out the theological or mimetic theory—without deciding what it means to have someone who is not Christ take his place. But despite an orthodox tradition of imitating Christ, we necessarily naturalize supernatural dogma in considering any figure except Christ himself as the antitype or emblematic surrogate for humanity. We need to acknowledge the multiplicity of Christ figures in Shelley's poetry and the multiplicity of ways in which the divine nature of man is represented. I shall single out one example and let that serve, synecdochically, for the repeated opportunity Shelley's characters and readers have for discovering that the kingdom of God is not among you—the way Christ was among the disciples—but within you, within each individual's potentiality.

In *The Revolt of Islam*, Laon tries to prevent a bloody battle between the revolutionary and the tyrannic forces. He sees a soldier pointing on his foe the mortal spear, and he rushes before its point in an attempt to arrest the outbreak of violence in its first motions:

> The spear transfixed my arm that was uplifted
> In swift expostulation, and the blood
> Gushed round its point: I smiled, and—"Oh! thou gifted
> With eloquence which shall not be withstood,
> Flow thus!"—I cried in joy, "thou vital flood,
> Until my heart be dry, ere thus the cause
> For which thou wert aught worthy, be subdued—
> Ah, ye are pale,—ye weep; your passions pause,—
> 'Tis well! ye feel the truth of love's benignant laws."
>   (V, ix)

Reading thus far we may be a little uncertain just why our hero smiles. Is he relishing the opportunity to be, Christ-like, transfixed by that spear? Is it a smile of love or of power? *The Revolt of Islam* is not quite the poem *Prometheus Unbound* is, and reading Laon's speech, one may not feel the birth of love's benignant laws. But whether or not we are to imagine the soldiery, as a metonymy for the poem's readership, convinced by Laon's rhetoric or agape at the emblem of the suffering Laon, the soldiers are halted sufficiently by the sight of blood to attend his speech for brotherhood. Laon does not discourse on the nature of his suffering; he uses their instinctive horror at bloodshed (Shelley would seem to have been an optimist about our instincts) to argue for the way in which any man wounded in battle can become a sign of human suffering, an emblem of the inhumanity of war:

> Soldiers, our brethren and our friends are slain.
> Ye murdered them, I think, as they did sleep!
> Alas, what have ye done? the slightest pain
> Which ye might suffer, there were eyes to weep,
> But ye have quenched them—there were smiles to steep
> Your hearts in balm, but they are lost in woe;
> And those whom love did set his watch to keep
> Around your tents, truth's freedom to bestow,
> Ye stabbed as they did sleep—but they forgive ye now.

He does not say, "Forgive them, Father, they know not what they do"; he moves from "me" to "them," from the one they have just wounded to the many who have died. If the soldiers had not killed them, many civilians could have responded with compassion to the soldiers' wounds. Then—with a remarkable leap from the subjunctive to the indicative, "They forgive ye now." Since it is a plain truth that the dead harbor no grudge against the living, it is not a farfetched figure—or rather it *is* a farfetched figure, but the distance from negative goodness to positive moral principle is being negotiated—to say that forgiveness is "now," that forgiveness is, as it were—and why not make it as it *is*—an idea whose time has come. If the present, living Laon can smile at the man who smote him, the living do form a community with the dead; and it is a community of the loving, a community of those who can be said to share the high ideal of the forgiveness of sins. Laon does not argue, "I am suffering for your sins," or even, "The dead died for your sins." That is, he *does* argue "the dead died for your sins," but in the sense that they died because of your sins, as a direct consequence of your failure of love, and their deaths are linked to your failure in a causal chain that is still operative and still available for imaginative, redemptive breaking: You stop killing and there will be no more killing. Neither I nor the dead exact vengeance, and so the power to arrest the flow of evil from evil lies open before you:

> Oh wherefore should ill ever flow from ill,
> And pain still keener pain for ever breed?
> We all are brethren—even the slaves who kill
> For hire, are men; and to avenge misdeed
> On the misdoer, doth but Misery feed
> With her own broken heart! O Earth, O Heaven!
> And thou, dread Nature, which to every deed
> And all that lives or is, to be hath given,
> Even as to thee have these done ill, and are forgiven!

There are two dispensations from the great god Nature—the power who joins (or perhaps replaces) the antithetical couple of earth and heaven, now no longer meaning nature and supernature but land and sky. The first dispensation from nature is what nature metes out to all that lives or is. She gives us and our deeds being: "to be" hath given. The second dispensation from nature is the reprieve from a natural law of retribution: all are forgiven; one can take forgiveness for a given. The mystery, the mastery of Laon's speech is that he makes forgiveness of sins look as much or more a part of the order of nature as vengeance once had been. "The cut worm forgives the plough," Blake says. In Shelley's lines the present tense belongs to being itself: nature hath given all that lives the power "to be." But forgiveness of sins is an understood condition of being, a past participle: All "are forgiven," and "made free by love."

Hope

In his fine chapter on "The Christian Mythology" in Shelley, Timothy Webb turns to hope as second in importance only to the theme of love: "Apart from love, perhaps the most important virtue for Demogorgon, as for Shelley, is hope. It is mentioned twice in the final stanza, where it is closely connected with love ('Charity . . . hopeth all things')."[10] Though Webb is primarily interested in the thematic importance of Christian concepts to Shelley, his discussion of *Prometheus Unbound* helps us see how Shelley's naturalization of Christian hope, even more than his emphasis on love, influences his poetics. Shelley's insistence on reforming the Christian concept of atonement affects, preeminently, the plot of *Prometheus*. That Prometheus unsays his high language of defiance toward Jupiter and that Panthea is spared the harshest versions of the history Prometheus sees are matters of large-scale structure and theme, however intricately they are worked out in the verse.[11] The composition of Act II as a responsive echo to Act I and of Act IV as a celebration of the action of Acts I–III may also be regarded as related, in broad outline, to the doctrine of love. The Shelleyan idea of hope, however, is more inextricably bound to local effects, though no less splendid and resonant ones.

Consider the lines cited by Webb from the last verse paragraph of *Prometheus*:

> To suffer woes which Hope thinks infinite;
> To forgive wrongs darker than Death or Night;
>   To defy Power which seems Omnipotent;
> To love, and bear; to hope, till Hope creates
>   From its own wreck the thing it contemplates. . . .

In the broadest sense, these timeless infinitives leave us in hope, in a suspended state of expectation. Syntactically, they seem to give birth to the substantive *Hope* just as—or rather before—Hope itself creates the object of hope "from its own wreck." In a phrase, or perhaps one can say in the force of a single caesura, Shelley overturns the eschatological otherworldliness of Christian hope founded on the wreck of this world. Vain is all hope but love, and most vain is the hope for a world elsewhere, a world in which the presence of God's love atones for the insufficiency of human love on this earth. Hope creating from its own wreck the thing it contemplates is hope turning back on itself to create, on the basis of a shattered illusion, a "real" hope for a renewed world.

The turn in the verse at the end of *Prometheus* recapitulates a turn negotiated in Act I. The furies have no greater torment than the picture of lovelessness and ignorance climaxed by the quotation from Luke: "They know not what they do" (Act I, l. 631, citing Luke 23:34). It is itself a mark of the Shelleyan doctrine of hope that a reference to the last act of the Christ story is transferred to the first act of *Prometheus*. The words with which Jesus proclaims a final forgiveness become, in Shelley's hands, words preparatory to an initiatory forgiveness, an act of human sympathy and love that itself proclaims the kingdom to come. The crucified Jesus in Luke may be in a traditional Christian reading more than a personification of wrecked hope; but the story Luke tells does not permit the sudden turn, the sudden birth of things hoped for, that Shelley's play permits. No sooner does the fury raise to apocalyptic pitch the temptation to abandon all hope—they know not what they do—than Prometheus creates from hope's wreck the thing it contemplates: "thy words are like a cloud of winged snakes / And yet, I pity those they torture not." Prometheus is being tempted to abandon all hope, and thus more indelibly to inscribe on the portals of his mind the identifying mark of a hell of his own making. He responds by creating a heaven in hell's despite: It is the indifferent, the unfeeling, and the ironists among us—the souls too poor in spirit to be bothered by the fury's vision—whom Prometheus elects to the heaven of his special regard. While demythologizing Christian heaven, Shelley simultaneously mythologizes the quotidian: A commonplace, colloquial expression like "I feel sorry for them if they're not moved by this" is amplified into sorrow and love more "divine" than any provoked by more extreme circumstances such as those of Jesus on the cross. Perhaps more important to Shelley's theology of hope than the transference of the scene of forgiveness to an initiatory position in a story is the transference of the object of compassion from present to absent (only hoped for) recipients. Like the earlier recantation of the curse, this turn accentuates the internalization of divine mercy by reminding us how far off in visionary space is the object of mercy.

Shelley called hope "a worship to the spirit of good within,"[12] and we would do well not to emend his grammar to "a worship of the spirit of good within." As a prophet of hope, but no theist, Shelley uses but naturalizes the Christian concept of worship; he retains the high valuation of apostrophe and the high valuation of conversion, both of them forms of the turn *to* the spirit of good; he rejects only the investment of awe *in* a spirit of good external to the self. The progress of *Prometheus Unbound* may be regarded as the successive realization of more and more sophisticated interpretations of hope as a turn *to* a spirit within.

In the *Essay on the Devil and Devils*, Shelley clarifies how the investment in a mythology of hope can remain independent of the ontological error about personification. Shelley scorns the conventional "faith"—the belief that the personifications of good and evil are more than rhetorical figures. While distinguishing the moral necessity of hope from the supererogatory (or at least risky) personifications of hope, Shelley advances the ground of the atheist argument by considering God as a figure first of good in itself but then, in a slight but telling revision, as a figure for a hoped-for improvement: The religious imagination gives "to that which [is] most pleasing to us a perpetual or ultimate superiority, with all epithets of honorable addition, and [brands] that which is displeasing with epithets ludicrous or horrible, predicting its ultimate defeat."[13] ("Perpetual" means God had, has, and always will have the upper hand; "ultimate" allows God to be a specially charged absence, rather than a fictional presence.) The argument about a certain view of the origin of religion becomes an argument of poetry when the personification of hope is seen as the thing wrecked or deconstructed, out of which hope itself appears reborn: "The supposition that the good spirit is, or hereafter will be, superior, is a personification of the principle of hope and that thirst for improvement without which present evil would be intolerable." In this, as in the previous quotation from the same paragraph of the essay, an "or" turns us from existences to objects of hope and, in Shelley's view, from error to truth. "A perpetual or ultimate superiority" and "the good spirit is, or hereafter will be, superior" are no indifferent alternatives. In a sense the faculty with which the correction is made is part of Shelley's own hope—a rhetorical equivalent for the impatience he values in place of faith. The same may be said for a famous alternative in *Adonais*, where the poet is seen with ensanguined brow, "Which was like Cain's or Christ's—Oh! that it should be so!" Neither indifference nor casual irreverence, the "or" expresses the poet's impatience with the progress of love: from Cain to Christ and from Christ to us little progress has been made in the great cause of substituting forgiveness for retribution; the "partial moan" that identifies sympathy—the capacity to weep another's fate as one's own—is still "poetic" rather than universal, and the ensanguined brow a unique rather than a ubiquitous mark. The "or" between "Cain's or Christ's" is partly mimetic but also partly performative, symbolically hastening the progress to forgiveness.

"Would God that all the Lord's people were prophets!" (Num. 11:29). As they are not, and "as it is the province of the poet to attach himself to those ideas which exalt and ennoble humanity, let him be permitted to have conjectured the condition of that futurity towards which we are impelled by an unextinguishable thirst for immortality."[14] Without dogmatizing on the subject of the ontology of a future state in and of itself, Shelley appropriates for the poet the reification of the *thirst* for immortality, *the* hope that is motive for metaphor. Perhaps the definitive expression of the thirst for immortality is *Adonais*, where Shelley tropes temporizing limitations as "life" and represents "death" as the condition of fulfillment:

> Why linger, why turn back, why shrink, my Heart?
> Thy hopes are gone before; from all things here
> They have departed; thou shouldst now depart!

Like "the personification of the principle of hope" in the figure of a transcendental deity, the representation of Shelley's children, Clara and William, as hopes that have "gone before" is as risky as it is highly charged. The risk is that the stanza will appear suicidal and—perhaps worse—that Death will be taken as more than a figure for a state of union and fulfillment. The charge (and it is a moral injunction as well as a potentially explosive figure) is the charge that one linger on this brink and *immortalize, in such stationing, the condition of impatient expectation*. Perhaps the best commentary on the poetics of hope in such a passage is Shelley's own in the *Essay* on *Christianity*:

> We die, says Jesus Christ, and when we awaken from the languor of disease the glories and the happiness of Paradise are around us. All evil and pain have ceased forever. Our happiness also corresponds [with] and is adapted to, the nature of what is most excellent in our being. We see God, and we see that he is good. How delightful a picture even if it be not true! How magnificent and illustrious is the conception which this bold theory suggests to the contemplation, even if it be no more than the imagination of some sublimest and most holy poet who, impressed with the loveliness and majesty of his own nature, is impatient and discontented with the narrow limits which this imperfect life and the dark grave have assigned forever as his melancholy portion.[15]

If the poet prophesies anything, it is the survival of such impatience and discontent past the decay of the belief in a life hereafter. In miniature, this paragraph in the essay demonstrates such a survival by leading us on under the illusion that Shelley himself endorses the conception of a hereafter, only to turn such faith on its head with the exclamation "How delightful a picture even if it be not true." Man may be but for such faith (i.e., especially in the faith that it is not true) reconciled with death, and at the "top of speculation" where the *if* is situated, the injunction "here pause" finds moral and poetic authority. In *Adonais* the survival of impatience and discontent with natural limits is imaged at the limit; impatience and discontent are immortalized as the brinkmanship of "why linger?" Jesus himself, impatient and discontent with the literalism of Jewish law and envisioning a realm of love beyond it, remains an archetype for the poet. At the end of *Adonais*, nothing at all is left of Christian faith, but the survival of impatience and discontent stands forever as a monument to that which is immortal in us, as eternal evidence of things hoped for.

Without a doctrine of resurrection, a poem like *Adonais* can depend, at the point where Shelley pauses to inquire "Why linger?" on a hope modeled on Christian hope that such a moment will come to stand, synecdochically, for a larger salvific power. Beyond lies the abyss of death, and into that abyss the orthodox hope for life after death may be cast. Yet the very representation of a synecdochical moment of hope—the representation of a hope surviving the decay of orthodox beliefs—becomes a seed cast in the ground with something like a promise of resurrection. *The* Shelleyan text for understanding how the Christian trope of resurrection is assimilated into the general poetics of hope is the "Ode to the West Wind," but we may approach it by turning first to one of Shelley's models for the natural supernaturalism of this ode.

In a penultimate moment of "Tintern Abbey," Wordsworth cultivates a personal nostalgia like that of the Romantic for the Christian past:

> in thy voice I catch
> The language of my former heart, and read
> My former pleasures in the shooting lights
> Of thy wild eyes. Oh! yet a little while
> May I behold in thee what I was once,
> My dear, dear Sister! and this prayer I make,
> Knowing that Nature never did betray
> The heart that loved her.

In one sense Nature inevitably does betray the heart that loved her, for we each die our own death, passing thus the turning point between presence

("We see God, and we see that he is good. How delightful a picture") and absence ("even if it be not true"). Wordsworth's equivalent for this lingering over a moment of hope is the "little while" in which he is caught in the illusion of repetition or immortality. Actually, the prayer he makes is one magnificently answered in the poem itself, for the diminished request for immortal life—"yet a little while / May I behold"—is fulfilled in the very words that utter it. What gives these lines their pathetic urgency above and beyond all trick of the voice is the radical reduction on which they depend— the reduction of a period of youth, a personal memory, and the whole theme of redemption from death to that single trope, that glimmer of hope, "Of thy wild eyes."

That glimmer is the starting point of Shelley's Ode, where the wildness of the wind ("O wild West Wind," the poem opens) is the untrammeled spirit of freedom from death. This is neither the place for a history of the trope of wildness nor the place for an extended account of the wondrous relationship between Shelley and Wordsworth, but I want to suggest an analogy, if not a source for the turn to hope in Shelley's Ode, because that hope is similarly dependent on a radically abbreviated representation of the past. In reading his former pleasures in the shooting lights of Dorothy's wild eyes, Wordsworth cries "behold, behold" to what then he was, and this revelation of the synecdochic representation of the past becomes the basis of the extravagant claim that follows. Characteristically, Wordsworth's "May I behold" appears more sober and demur than Shelley's "Be thou, Spirit fierce, / My Spirit! Be thou me," but *behold* and *be thou* share a naturalization of apocalypse as the basis for a claim to present power and a hope for its survival. Something similar may be said for prayer: Wordsworth appears to be in the declarative mood ("this prayer I make"), describing the prayer he has made ("May I behold in thee . . ."), while Shelley half threatens the Power he more openly apostrophizes: "I would ne'er have striven / As thus with thee in prayer." In fact, however, both statements transcend the ostensible humility of prayerful attitude to become extraordinary assertions of power. "This prayer I make"—read it with four accented syllables—assumes something of the language of divine fiat, while "I would ne'er have striven / As thus with thee"—read the last four words similarly accented—turns from contrafactual hypothesis to performative language: *thus* do I strive with *thee!* Jacob, when he wrestled with the angel, received the new name of *Israel*, one whose strife is with the Lord. Like Jacob, Shelley in gaining the upper hand gains the privilege of kneeling under the hand extended over him in blessing.

But there is something wrong with this archetype, something wholly untrue to the energy with which the Israel of this poem prevails over the spirit he asks to inspire him. How much power, how much self-confidence there is in the concluding stanza! "Make me thy lyre, even as the forest is: / What if my leaves are falling like its own." If the first of these lines subjugates to the poet's will a spirit formerly outside him, the second triumphs in sublime obliviousness to the facts of nature and decay. In the words of the *Essay on Christianity*, here is the "imagination of some sublimest and most holy poet [apocalyptically] impatient and discontented with the narrow limits which this imperfect life and the dark grave have assigned forever." For the poet, unlike the Christian, there is no difference between glorying in one's own power and glorying in an inspired impatience—one that has been "put on" or breathed into the speaker. Yet Shelley's myth of inspiration is no simple turn against a Christian myth of humble reception of the spirit, and like St. Paul in 2 Corinthians 12, he can feel his vaunting as itself inspired, itself a mark of his striving not against but *with* the holy spirit. Paul says "Of such a one will I glory," and he goes on to describe his own conversion in terms that suggest he has been lifted "as a wave, a leaf, a cloud" up to paradise or that ultimate heaven where all seals are broken. "And lest I should be exalted above measure through the abundance of the revelations," Paul continues, "there was given to me a thorn in the flesh, the messenger of Satan to buffet me, lest I should be exalted above measure." Commentators on Corinthians have always puzzled over these verses, and it is altogether right that no one should know for certain whether to read the thorn in the flesh as a particular physical ailment, the whole burden of sexuality, or a spiritual problem like the harassment of the Jews. For Shelley, however, the thorns are those of life itself, and the poet falls from his vaunting to an awareness of his carnal nature in space and time. Vaunting: "Oh! lift me as a wave, a leaf, a cloud!" To keep him from being too elated: "I fall upon the thorns of life! I bleed!"

If Shelley had this specific text from 2 Corinthians in mind, we might be justified in going further and pointing to Paul's expostulation on the subject of his fleshly or worldly trouble: "And for this I besought the Lord thrice, that it might depart from me." The first three stanzas of Shelley's Ode with their three appeals for transcendence could be understood as three such supplications:

> If I were a dead leaf thou mightest bear;
> If I were a swift cloud to fly with thee;
> A wave to pant beneath thy power.

We need not commit ourselves to the presence of the Pauline model of triune supplication to understand the relevance of the answer God gives Paul: "But he said to me, 'My grace is sufficient for thee, for my strength is made perfect in weakness.'" In poetic terms the perfection of power means the fulfillment of poetic identity, and the identity of the poet with the inspiring wind of the concluding stanza is one of the most remarkable "revelations of spirit"—to borrow Keats's phrase for Wordsworth's egotistical sublime. So empowered, the poet is able to turn the whole of the natural world into metaphor, vehicle for crossing the distance between the sole self and the Spirit of the Whole: "Drive my dead thoughts over the universe / Like withered leaves to quicken a new birth." In the opening of the Ode, Shelley had invoked the west wind as a natural phenomenon, and he used mythological and experiential figures of speech to make more intense the picture of this destroyer and preserver in the world of nature:

> O Thou,
> Who chariotest to their dark wintry bed
>
> The winged seeds, where they lie cold and low,
> Each like a corpse within its grave. . . .

Here the power of the wind to drive seeds is the ostensible subject, while the Plutonian chariot, the dark wintry bed, and (most important) the simile "like a corpse within its grave" are all vehicles for conveying a tenor that is imagined to be the driving force of the natural world. By the conclusion of the poem, vehicle and tenor have switched places. In the end, that is, we are interested not in seeds that are like corpses in the grave, but in corpses that are like seeds, or rather in human resurrection and renewal that comes as surely and splendidly as that experienced in the natural world. What happens to the winged seeds (winged is a literal description of something like maple seedlings, but also a proleptic description, something the poet "planted" there in stanza 1 to get ready for the final transformation of his tenor to souls)—what happens to those winged seeds that lie cold and low in stanza 1? St. Paul says: "It is sown in corruption, it is raised in incorruption: it is sown in dishonor, it is raised in glory: it is sown in weakness, it is raised in power: it is sown a natural body, it is raised a spiritual body."

Here, in brief, is the whole enterprise of the Romantic's investment in nature. To be interested in nature as nature requires a mind of winter; it is a very sad thing. To conceive of the poet's antithetical spirit burning through nature is a rather Blakean thing, and sometimes appropriate enough. But on the whole the Romantics—including Blake—do not cremate nature; they bury it, *with the hope* that what written as weakness will be rewritten as power, and what is sown a natural body will be raised a spiritual one.

Faith

If Shelley the man held no clear faith in a spiritual world elsewhere, Shelley the poet held the faith that the desire itself, the "unextinguishable thirst for immortality," is immortal spirit. In part (the more Romantic part) this means that Shelley sided with Blake in identifying the desire for everlasting life with Imagination, the one god worthy to be called immortal.[16] In part (the more practical or political part), it means that Shelley naturalized the desire for a future state by channeling it into this-worldly hope for the future. In Timothy Webb's words, Shelley substitutes "hope for the more orthodox value of faith."[17] Even in the "Hymn to Intellectual Beauty," the poem that most explicitly substitutes for faith something other than hope, there is a movement (at least a recapitulated movement) to interpret "higher" sights as further sights, further aspirations for the natural future. The "faithful" poet can declare, "never joy illumed my brow / Unlinked with hope that thou wouldst free / This world from its dark slavery." What links joy and hope with a faith that there is something more than nature is a reluctance or inability of the poetic spirit wholly to rest in present joy. Whether struck by the beauties of landscape or entangled in the pleasures of sexual love, the "faithful" soul flies upward from immediacy, impelled by the desire to regard Intellectual Beauty as something other, above and beyond physical beauty. "Above" and "beyond" may prove to be motions of the soul rather than places or things outside it, but there remains at a minimum a faith that it is still worth talking in such terms. If we understand "faith" to involve a relationship to a Being or a trope of Being beyond us rather than (as with hope) a future before us, then we can reserve prayer (the trope of apostrophizing an ultimate "other") from Shelley's own substitutions of self-esteem. Or better: We can come to regard the poetic fiction of apostrophe not as a qualification of the sufficiency of self but as the furthest extension of what Shelley means by self-esteem. We must begin, however, with a consideration of how self-esteem acts not as an arbitrary third term but as a renaming of something essentially, though radically, a matter of faith.

If, as Blake puts it, "all deities reside in the human breast," then self-esteem means the worship of the divine in man, and man's capacity to fear himself is his capacity to internalize (at least the aspiration for) the divine. In a sense the poet's faith in Shelley's Hymn is precisely the faith that there is no other sublime. "No voice from some sublimer world" has ever supplied an answer to the problem of mutability, and no voice need supply an answer if we can negotiate the turn from the external afflictions of the self to those internal vicissitudes that undermine the self from within. Stanza 2 suggests this turn through a shift in the questions it raises:

> Ask why the sunlight not forever
> Weaves rainbows o'er yon mountain river,
> Why aught should fail and fade that once is shewn,
> Why fear and dream and death and birth
> Cast on the daylight of this earth
> Such gloom,—why man has such a scope
> For love and hate, despondency and hope?

Though the poet goes on to discuss the hope for answers, hope he represents as having been his in childhood (which may or may not be *wholly* a figure for our cultural past), the questions have in part already been answered in the very turn from questions about mutability in nature to questions about the mutability of the human heart. If our capacity to love sufficed, if our loves did not themselves change into the woes of love–hate, despondency–hope, we could live with the vagaries of experience and the fact of death. The turn from external to internal problems of mutability may appear no turn at all, just an accidental rather than an essential property of the list of woes; but self-esteem in this poem implies that the possibility of such a turn must be taken seriously, it implies not only the value of such a turn but the sufficiency of the self for its negotiation.

In one sense the turn inward at the end of stanza 2 is a prelude of things to come—of the grand turn inward when the poet recapitulates the rejection of an external sublime and moves from epiphanic ecstacy at the end of stanza 5 to the more sober emotional coloring of stanza 7. In a more important sense, however, *the* turn, the "conversion" to a viable poetic faith, has already occurred before the poem began. The perspective from which the whole poem is written, the perspective from which the poet can regard as a curiosity and immaturity, "I shrieked and clasped my hands in extacy," is that of the urbane, autumnal harmonics most fully articulated in the poem's close. The deep irony is that an address to Intellectual Beauty rather than her shadow serves not as a movement toward unmediated, epiphanic vision but quite the reverse. And since the turn to Intellectual Beauty rather than her shadow has already been quietly but definitely negotiated, the prevenience of this "conversion" can come to be understood as the very ground of self-esteem.

Though the Hymn is one of Shelley's most explicitly atheist texts, his strategy here is so protestant that we may clarify it if we think for a moment of an analogous argument on a more orthodox plane. A Catholic may pray to a saintly intermediary, while the Protestant disdains such shadows of Power and addresses The Power Himself. Similarly, in the Gospel of Luke, Jesus tells the parable of a publican and a Pharisee, where the Pharisee prays, "God, I thank thee that I am not as other men are," while the publican cries, "God be merciful to me a sinner!" (Luke 18:10–14). Shelley does nothing as Pharisee-like as thanking God that he is not—as other poets are—a worshiper of the shadow of the Power in nature. Though Shelley is further from Christianity than Wordsworth is, he is not a worshiper of a shadow of a shadow but a poet inspired to address the Power itself. He is thus closer to the publican than to the Pharisee, and brought closer still by recapitulating in stanza 5 the Phariseeism of an outward show of ecstacy:

> While yet a boy I sought for ghosts, and sped
> > Through many a listening chamber, cave and ruin,
> > And starlight wood, with fearful steps pursuing
> Hopes of high talk with the departed dead.
> I called on poisonous names with which our youth is fed;
> > I was not heard—I saw them not—
> > When musing deeply on the lot
> Of life, at that sweet time when winds are wooing
> > All vital things that wake to bring
> > News of buds and blossoming;
> > Sudden, thy shadow fell on me;
> I shrieked, and clasped my hands in extacy!

In *Prometheus Unbound*, Prometheus, looking at the crucified Jesus, says that he will not pronounce the name that has become a curse. The "poisonous names" here are Christ and its equivalents, fictions of Presence on which Christian youth is fed. Though Shelley wrote "that false name with which our youth is fed" and later blunted the barb of his original line's atheism, I think the plural "names" and the term "departed dead" spell a no less cogent attack. The plurals function less to remind us of the range of *this* youth's search for knowledge (Shelley knew Persian myths, for example, as well as Christian and classical ones) than to demystify terms like *God* by referring to Jesus as one out of many, one more of mankind's countless dead.[18] Against the background of the awareness that the supernatural is a fiction, the youth is represented experiencing an epiphany of sorts, a somewhat enthusiastic or at least adolescent awareness of a power in nature, a power that seemed to visit nature and impart to natural things a more than natural glow. Wordsworth called it a visionary gleam; Shelley, calling it a shadow, lets us know what he thinks of it even while he describes the youth caught by such a notion. Crucial for Shelley's adult recoil from that experience (and the experience was "real" in the youth of Romanticism, if not in the life of Shelley himself) is the concept of the distinguishability of natural supernaturalism from natural religion. Within the stanza quoted, Shelley rejects a supernatural faith (poisonous names) for a Wordsworthian, natural epiphany (the shadow); within the poem at large, Shelley rejects Romanticism's shadowy flirtation with natural religion and addresses himself to a wholly transcendent Imagination, a spirit wholly beyond and outside nature, though its effects are representable *by analogy* to some of the lovelier aspects of nature.

Looking back as a man addressing the Power itself, the poet can say with St. Paul, "When I was a child, I spake as a child, I understood as a child, I thought as a child; but when I became a man I put away childish things." Paul refers to the difference between childish and mature things in order to draw an analogy to the difference between earthly understanding here and what we will understand then, when we shall see face to face. In Shelley's poem, faith in the addressability of an ultimate Power seems predicated on a Pauline analogy, on the idea that "when that which is perfect is come, then that which is in part will be done away"; just as the shadow of the Power has vanished, so the limitations on our unmediated confrontation with an ultimate, addressable Power can be lifted. But it is time my discourse ceased assuming or supporting the fiction of an ultimate, addressable Power. Shelley turns to Paul's "faith, hope, and love—these three abide"—and he replaces faith in an unseen power with self-esteem, a virtue that can not only survive but thrive on the deconstruction of the fiction of an addressable divinity. In a stunning turn—and *the* faith of the poet is in the importance and efficacy of these turns—the poet shifts his concern from the question of the uncertainty of his addressee's presence to the uncertainty of the presence in the human heart of the triad of virtues:

> Love, Hope, and Self-esteem, like clouds depart
>   And come, for some uncertain moments lent.
>   Man were immortal, and omnipotent,
> Didst thou, unknown and awful as thou art,
> Keep with thy glorious train firm state within his heart.
>   Thou messenger of sympathies,
>   That wax and wane in lovers' eyes—
> Thou—that to human thought art nourishment,
>   Like darkness to a dying flame!
>   Depart not as thy shadow came,
>   Depart not—lest the grave should be,
> Like life and fear, a dark reality.

Since the first two lines constitute a statement about the human heart made without reference to an addressee, the next three lines which are addressed to Intellectual Beauty, make of that power the abstract form of love, hope, and self-esteem. Stripped of its magnificent trope, the illusion of *addressing* the power comes to mean *believing* in love, hope, and self-esteem. Or rather: There is no going naked, and the reduction of the fiction of an ultimate addressee to the triad of virtues would leave us with another analogy, a shadow of meaning, a cloudlike "presence" rather than a final manifestation. We must love these fictive coverings, just as we love the redemptive spirit of mediation that is love between persons. Love, the greatest of Shelley's as well as Paul's triad of virtues, is the means we have of transcending our own will to meaning; but Intellectual Beauty, behind rather than identical with love, remains a messenger of sympathies, not an ultimate, reified "message."

If a boy (at least a Wordsworthian boy) can experience an epiphany of the shadow of the power, an adult can know what it is to see less darkly, to see face to face—face to human face, even if the adult knows also that the sympathies between lovers are themselves no great constancy, that causing his or her face to shine upon you and be gracious unto you is nothing that can be definitively, finally caused. In addressing the Power as "thou—that to human love art nourishment, / Like darkness to a dying flame," the poet both acknowledges the power of love, of nourishing *caritas*, at the same time that he acknowledges and represents, through simile, the insubstantiality of both love and the representations of its agency. That is, just as darkness does not really feed but only serves as a backdrop for a dying flame, so the address-able Power of Intellectual Beauty is only fictionally representable as an active agent feeding human thought and listening to human prayers.

If one is thinking of the passage in 1 Corinthians, one might approach the poet's prayer "Depart not as thy shadow came" with an expectation that the prayer will be one for direct revelation: then we saw through a glass darkly, but let us see face to face. Depart not unseen, the way your shadow came. The opening lines of the Hymn establish the visual context: "The awful shadow of some unseen power / Floats though unseen amongst us." The Power itself is always unseen; the shadow of the power is physically seen or rather metaphys-ically perceived at special privileged moments of visual contact with nature heightened into "Vision." Shelley's draft version, "The lovely shadow of some awful power" made clearer still the *illusion* of what Wordsworth called "the glory" and the awfulness (awesomeness) of something beyond the natural.[19] But the Power itself could no more be perceived by the natural poet than could the face of God by the traditional Christian or Hebrew. Moses saw not God's face but God's departure, the trail of His glory. Wordsworth thought the glory had passed away from the earth; Shelley, that the shadow of the glory has passed away—or rather, that the "lovely shadow" comes and goes, just like rainbows, roses, and other natural phenomena. There is no definitive loss of the "shadow of the power," only a lamentable loss if one is concerned about *that* coming and going rather than about the transcendent power of Imagination itself.

It may have been Shelley's turn against the Wordsworthian "glory" that first prompted him to write, in the draft version of the Hymn, "thy shade alone ... / Gives truth and grace to life's tumultuous dream." If, in revising this to "thy light alone," Shelley renounced the force of accumulated habit of regarding light as a trope for illusion, he gained extraordinary clarity and strength in return. The poem as published is consistent in treating the Wordsworthian glory as a shadow—and reserving for Shelley's addressee a higher status transcendent of nature. Most remarkable is the way Shelley is able to ignore Wordsworth's own "sober coloring" in the conclusion of the Intimations Ode, to ascribe apocalyptic desire to the Wordsworthian myth of memory, and to make all his own the sober, autumnal tone.

We surmise, from the existence of a draft lacking stanza 4, that the prayer to the Spirit to "Depart not as thy shadow came!" is an expression of a revised or clarified will on the part of the poet. What Shelley was revising, summed up in the distinction between the way the shadow came and the way the Spirit herself is asked to depart—was Wordsworth. Actually, Wordsworth himself was preoccupied with the departure of what Shelley calls the shadow, though Wordsworth would have thought it identical with Shelley's Intellectual Beauty: "Wither is fled the visionary gleam? / Where is it now, the glory and the dream?" But in Shelley's revisionary memory, it is Wordsworth who emphatically represents the coming of what Shelley calls the shadow. The quintessential line from the Intimations Ode is, for Shelley, not the statement of absence but the statement of presence: "Trailing clouds of glory do we come / From God, who is our home." What makes Shelley's prayer so Romantic, so radically protestant, is that he rejects Wordsworth's heaven of infancy as too High Church, too epiphanic. If the one god of "grace and truth" is the Human Imagination Divine, then its light, however suddenly it was once imagined to have arrived, must never pass away. "Depart not as thy shadow came" means depart not suddenly, in the smoke of a deconstructive explosion of illusion.

Geoffrey Hartman, who has written about this poetic ambition in Wordsworth and Keats, calls the sensibility behind it the "evening ear" or autumnal vision, for both evening in the diurnal cycle and autumn in the annual cycle represent the gradual departure of light and the naturalized binding of hour to hour, day to day, season to season, without apocalyptic breaks for sudden revelation or failure of revelation.[20] Shelley believed that Jesus himself was a poet of the evening ear—not an incarnate God epiphanically manifested in a supernatural incarnation but a human, all too human visionary who would, if he could, have turned Jewish supernaturalism into a solemn and serene brotherly love. The "protestant" poet returns to just this more sober coloring. At the conclusion of the Hymn, the poet lingers over the passing day and finds a harmony in nature that reflects the harmonized powers of the soul no longer in search of supernatural epiphany. "The day becomes more solemn and serene / When noon is past," the last stanza begins, and it ends with a prayer that, in purging itself of supplication (the last thing he actually asks for is calm) returns prayer to its purest form: not "give me" or "hear ye" but "praised be." Praising and acknowledging, he defines himself as one whom "thy spells did bind / To fear himself, and love all human kind." This is a wholly natural bondage, though a bondage to the "supernatural" or imaginative kingdom within rather than a bondage to nature as such. Bound to respect his own antiapocalyptic imagination, bound to love all humankind, Shelley becomes (quite like Wordsworth, despite Shelley's need to misread Wordsworth as someone whose natural religion is to be overgone) a redeemed man whose days are bound each to each in natural piety.

Borrowing the term from the Abraham and Isaac story, Hartman in his book on Wordsworth calls this binding *akedah*. In Genesis, God establishes a covenant with Abraham, a covenant based on the fact that Isaac is bound but not sacrificed, unlike the only beloved Son of Christian tradition. Though prayer to a supernatural power remains a fiction, covenanting oneself to the view of things represented by Isaac, rather than what Jesus came to be understood to be, remains an authentic statement of hope and choice. In praying "Depart not as thy shadow came," Shelley rejects the suddenness of both private ecstatic vision and of Eastern, epiphanic religion. Measuring his distance from the mode of our collective spiritual youth when we were drawn to the possibility of supernatural revelation, Shelley utters a self-fulfilling prayer: To say "Depart not as thy shadow came" is not simply to utter one's hope for a matured, nonepiphanic imagination, but to bring into being, to forge yet once more for the conscience of the race, the very power of humanistic gradualism that denies or defies supernatural interference in the goings-on of nature and the goings or voyagings of metaphoric vehicles. Because of the self-fulfilling nature of his prayer, because of his assurance that there are no sudden departures of powers once incarnate in time, the poet can remove the qualifier and move gracefully, "naturally" from "Depart not as thy shadow came" to "Depart not." Insofar as the Spirit of Intellectual Beauty has come to be seen as the power of *akedah*—the power of a mind freed from apocalyptic impulse from above, yet full of faith, fully trusting itself to negotiate and value the turn inward—that power has been called into being and made present.

This is not what St. Paul meant by faith, but it is what the Romantic takes as the basis of self-esteem, his own worthiness to address himself (in the metaphoric sense) to ultimate things, and to *turn*, to address himself (in what makes wonderful poetic sense) to the personified spirit of his own divine humanity.

Notes

1. I quote Thomas Weiskel's unpublished essay on *Adonais*, but see also his *The Romantic Sublime: Studies in the Structure and Psychology of Transcendence* (Baltimore: Johns Hopkins Univ. Press, 1976), esp. pp. 4, 11. See also M. H. Abrams, *Natural Supernaturalism: Tradition and Revolution in Romantic Literature* (New York: W. W. Norton, 1971), p. 13.

2. John Asgill, *An argument proving that according to the covenant of eternal life revealed in the Scriptures, man may be translated from hence into that eternal life, without passing through death* . . . (London, 1715), p. 68. For Asgill the knowledge is identical with the life in that true knowledge of Christ inaugurates eternal life; it remains for Blake to make the more radical statement of identity, that eternal life is a state of self-knowledge of the individual psyche, not a condition beyond or replacing death. Asgill uses the word *state* to refer to the condition of death or that of eternal life: "Now a man may change his state, without change of his Person or Place" (p. 49). Blake may have had neither Asgill nor the sense of "estate" specifically in mind when he distinguished persons from states, but his usage is parallel.

3. In *Shelley: A Voice Not Understood* (Manchester, Eng.: Manchester Univ. Press, 1977), p. 174, Timothy Webb quotes Corinthians and discusses Shelley's special valuation of love.

4. *Shelley's Prose, or the Trumpet of a Prophecy*, ed. David Lee Clark (Albuquerque: Univ. of New Mexico Press, 1954), p. 283. Subsequent quotations of Shelley's prose (except for prefaces and notes to the poems) are from this edition. For the poems (except *The Revolt of Islam*), I use *Shelley's Poetry and Prose*, eds. Donald H. Reiman and Sharon B. Powers (New York: Norton, 1977).

5. *Shelley's Prose*, p. 283.

6. By condemning a fictional character, I mean refusing to sympathize. Forgiveness of sins does depend on the recognition of sins—indeed on a heightened rather than a diminished awareness of moral possibility. Shelley would by no means have slighted the difference between believing someone to have acted in error and punishing that person with our eternal disapprobation. See note 3 above.

7. *The Letters of Percy Bysshe Shelley*, ed. Frederick L. Jones (London: Oxford Univ. Press, 1964), I, 142. Bodleian Mss. Adds e 9, pp. 3–8, contain Shelley's penciled notes on the Gospel of Luke. Shelley may have interpreted the working of miracles (especially raising the dead) as a mythologization of forgiveness of sins (reprieving us of mortality understood as original sin).

8. Mary recorded that Matthew and Luke were the Gospels which Shelley read aloud. See *Mary Shelley's Journal*, ed. Frederick L. Jones (Norman: Univ, of Oklahoma Press, 1947), entries for 31 Dec. 1819 and 1, 5, 8–9 Jan. 1820.

9. Coleridge's Notebook 41, f46 (entry 64). I am very grateful to Professor Merton Christiensen of the University of Delaware for allowing me to read his transcription for the forthcoming Volume IV of the Princeton edition of the Coleridge Notebooks.

10. Webb, p. 174.

11. See Susan Hawk Brisman, "'Unsaying His High Language': The Problem of Voice in *Prometheus Unbound*," *Studies in Romanticism*, 16 (1977), 51–86.

12. *Letters*, II, 125. I take it the phrase is not part of what Shelley purports to be quoting in the previous sentence, but in any case the phrasing is probably his own.

13. *Shelley's Prose*, p. 265.

14. Shelley's note on *Hellas*, in *Shelley's Poetry and Prose*, p. 416. See Webb, p. 232. Ellsworth Barnard discusses the "thirst" for immortality as Shelley's dissatisfaction with the limits of his own reasonable attitude that "we know nothing." See *Shelley's Religion* (Minneapolis: Univ. of Minnesota Press, 1937), esp. pp. 206–15.

15. *Shelley's Prose*, p. 205.

16. Barnard (p. 257), among others, identifies Intellectual Beauty with Imagination.

17. Webb, p. 232; see also pp. 162–81.

18. For the manuscript readings, see Judith Chernaik and Timothy Burnett, "The Byron and Shelley Notebooks in the Scrope Davis Find," *Review of English Studies*, 29 (1978), 36–49.

19. For a different estimation of the manuscript readings, see Roland A. Duerksen, "Thematic Unity in the New Shelley Notebook," *Bulletin of Research in the Humanities*, 83 (1980), pp. 210–13.

20. See especially "Poem and Ideology: A Study of Keats's 'To Autumn,'" and "Evening Star and Evening Land," both in Geoffrey Hartman's *The Fate of Reading* (Chicago: Univ. of Chicago Press, 1975).

HELEN VENDLER

Keats and the Use of Poetry

Heidegger asked, "What is the poet for in a destitute time?" I want to depart today from Heidegger's premises, though not from his question: What can we say is the use of poetry? Heidegger's premises are those of nineteenth-century nostalgia, a nostalgia for the presence of God in the universe. He writes as one deprived of theological reassurance, seeing emptiness about him, and longing for presence. He suggests that the poet exists to restore presence, to testify to its possibility—or at least, like Hölderlin, to testify to felt absence.

There are premises of a particular moment—the moment of Götterdämmerung. But Heidegger's plangent lamentation offers only one response to that moment; readers will remember Nietzsche's far more athletic and exulting response to the same moment, and some will recall Wallace Stevens's remark, in "Two or Three Ideas," that:

> to see the gods dispelled in mid-air and dissolve like clouds is one of the great human experiences. It is not as if they had gone over the horizon to disappear for a time; nor as if they had been overcome by other gods of greater power and profounder knowledge. It is simply that they came to nothing. . . . It was their annihilation, not ours, and yet it left us feeling that in a measure, we too

From *What Is a Poet? Essays from the Eleventh Alabama Symposium on English and American Literature*, edited by Hank Lazer, pp. 66–83. Copyright © 1987 by the University of Alabama Press.

had been annihilated. . . . At the same time, no man ever muttered a petition in his heart for the restoration of those unreal shapes. There was in every man the increasingly human self, which instead of remaining the observer, the non-participant, the delinquent, became constantly more and more all there "was or so it seemed; and whether it was so or merely seemed so still left it for him to resolve life and the world in his own terms. (OP, 206–207)

Perhaps we can consider a response like Heidegger's as one dictated not by the facts of the case but by a certain temperament in Heidegger himself. Another temperament, other premises. And in the confidence that the use of the poet, in human terms, remains constant even through the vicissitudes of cultural change, I want to take up today the ideas on the social function of poetry expressed by John Keats.

Keats, a resolute nonbeliever and political radical, came into a post-Enlightenment world, it is true, but it was still a world which felt some of those pangs of loss later expressed by Heidegger. Keats too felt a religious nostalgia, and it entered into many of his own meditations on the function of the poet; but he did not confine himself within that framework. I take the case of Keats to be an exemplary one of a modern poet seeking to define his own worth; Keats seems to me to have thought more deeply about the use of poetry than any subsequent modern poet. And although Keats will be my example, I want to close by bringing the topic into the present day, by quoting two contemporary poets who have reflected profoundly and long on it, the Polish poet Czeslaw Milosz and the Irish poet Seamus Heaney—both of them compelled by their history to inquire into their own social function. But I will begin with Keats as a modern posttheological poet, a forerunner to others contemplating the question of the use of secular poetry.

Keats had hoped, originally, that literary creation could confer therapeutic benefits on its audience. Admirable as the desire is that art could "beguile" Dido from her grief, or "rob from aged Lear his bitter teen" ("Imitation of Spenser"), this concept of art bars it from participation in human grief. Keats later brought this idea of art to its apogee in the "Nightingale" ode, where the poet-speaker hopes that the purely musical art of bird notes will enable him to fly away from the world of the dying young, the palsied old, fading Beauty, and faithless Love. We must distinguish Keats's "escapism" (as it has sometimes been called) from an escapism that does not promise a therapeutic result, such as comforting Dido or Lear or Ruth in grief, "charming the mind from the trammels of pain" ("On Receiving a Curious Shell").

Other ends of art early proposed by Keats include the civilizing psychological one of "attuning . . . the soul to tenderness" ("To Lord Byron") and the educative one of expanding the soul, as, by vicarious experience, it strays in Spenser's halls and flies "with daring Milton through the fields of air" ("Written on the Day That Mr. Leigh Hunt Left Prison"), a view of art given its classical Keatsian expression in the sonnet on Chapman's Homer. Keats's concept of the *utile* here is far from the usual didactic one, which emphasizes social responsibility and moral action. To become tender, to expand one's sense of imaginative possibility are early recommendations consistent with Keats's later program of turning the blank intelligence into a human "soul"; the difference we notice here is the absence of that "world of pains and troubles" that will become the chief schooling agent of the heart in the letter on soul-making.

Keats, in his early poetry, enumerates four social functions of poetry: a historical one, as epic poetry recorded history of an exalted sort, written by "bards, that erst sublimely told heroic deeds"; a representational (if allegorical) one, as Shakespeare gave, in his dramatic poetry, an incarnation of the passions; a didactic one, as in Spenser's "hymn in praise of spotless Chastity" ("Ode to Apollo"); and a linguistically preservative one, which can "revive" for our day "the dying tones of minstrelsy" ("Specimen of an Induction to a Poem"). And yet, Keats perhaps sensed that these functions—historical, allegorically representational, didactic, and linguistically preservative—were not to be his own: these claims for the social functions of poetry are, in his early work, asserted merely, not enacted. A fair example of the feebleness of the early work comes in Keats's epistle to his brother George, where, after describing the living joys of the bard, Keats passes to "posterity's award," the function of the poet's work after he has died, as society makes use of his verse:

> . . . The patriot shall feel
> My stern alarum, and unsheathe his steel . . .
> The sage will mingle with each moral theme
> My happy thoughts sententious; . . .
> Lays have I left of such a clear delight
> That maids will sing them on their bridal night.
> . . . To sweet rest
> Shall the dear babe, upon its mother's breast,
> Be lulled with songs of mine.

These uses of poetry are strictly ancillary; presumably the hero would still be heroic, the sage wise, the maids bridally delighted, and the baby sleepy, even without the help of the poet. In this conception, poetry is chiefly an intensifying accompaniment in life.

Keats's earliest notions of the power of art were concerned chiefly with the theme the poem may embody. The poet's pastoral tale will distract the grieving; his patriotic and moral sentiments will inspire hero and sage; and his love poems will wake an answering echo in the breast of the young. Poems exist to charm the fair daughters of the earth with love tales, and to warm earth's sons with patriotic sententious ideas.

It is to be expected that a poet of Keats's honesty would soon perceive that the embodying of a thematic and didactic intent was not his own sole motive in composing verse. He eventually admitted that in venturing on "the stream of rhyme" he himself sailed "scarce knowing my intent," but rather exploring "the sweets of song: / The grand, the sweet, the terse, the free, the fine; . . . / Spenserian vowels that elope with ease . . . / Miltonian storms, and more, Miltonian tenderness; . . . / The sonnet . . . / The ode . . . / The epigram . . . / The epic" ("To Charles Cowden Clarke"). This avowal of the aesthetic motives of creation, this picture of the artist investigating his medium—its vocal range, its prosodic inventions, its emotional tonalities, and its formal genres—sorts uneasily with Keats's former emphasis on the social service of poetry.

While the emphasis on social service always brings in, for Keats, the relief of pain, the emphasis in descriptions of art itself, in early Keats, dwells always on the pleasure principle, so that even woe must be, in literature, "pleasing woe" ("To Lord Byron"), and poetry must make "pleasing music, and not wild uproar" ("How Many Bards") full of glorious tones and delicious endings ("On Leaving Some Friends"). In these early poems, Keats expresses the characteristic view of the youthful poet, to whom the aesthetic can be found only in the beautiful.

Keats's first attempt to reconcile his philosophical emphasis on social service and his instinctive commitment to those aesthetic interests proper to composition appears in "I stood tiptoe," where he proposes an ingenious reconciliation by suggesting that form allegorically represents content:

> In the calm grandeur of a sober line,
> We see the waving of the mountain pine;
> And when a tale is beautifully staid,
> We feel the safety of a hawthorn glade.

The myths of the gods are said, in "I stood tiptoe," to be formally allegorical renditions of man's life in nature: a poet seeing a flower bending over a pool invents the myth of Narcissus. This is a promising solution for Keats—that form, being an allegory for content, bears not a mimetic but an algebraic relation to life. But in "I stood tiptoe," this solution is conceptualized rather than formally enacted.

In his next manifesto, "Sleep and Poetry," Keats makes an advance on the thematic level, realizing that his former advocacy of a consoling thematic happiness to cure human sorrow cannot survive as a poetic program. Rather, he says, he must "pass the realm of Flora and old Pan" for a "nobler life" where he may encounter "the agonies, the strife / Of human hearts." With the thematic admission of tragic material, formal notions of power and strength can at last enter into Keats's aesthetic and fortify his former aesthetic values— beauty and mildness—with a new sculptural majesty:

> A drainless shower
> Of light is Poesy; 'tis the supreme power;
> 'Tis might half-slumbering on its own right arm.

Nonetheless, Keats is still critical of a poetry that "feeds upon the burrs, / And thorns of life," arguing rather for the therapeutic function of poetry, "that it should be a friend / To soothe the cares, and lift the thoughts of man"—an end still envisaged in the later "Ode on a Grecian Urn." The poet is simply to "to tell the most heart-easing things"; and the poetry of earth ranges only from the grasshopper's delight to the cricket's song "in warmth increasing ever."

A far sterner idea of poetry arises when Keats hopes that something will draw his "brain / Into a delphic labyrinth" ("On Receiving a Laurel Crown"). As soon as he admits thought, prophecy, and labyrinthine mystery into the realm of poetry, Keats becomes frightened at the interpretive responsibilities that lie before him, objectified for him in the example of the Elgin marbles. He cries out that he is too weak for such godlike hardship, that these "glories of the brain / Bring round the heart an undescribable feud."

But Keats obeys the Delphic imperative and writes his first tragic poem, a sonnet on the death of Leander, forcing his art to describe his worst personal specter, the image of a dying youth whom nothing can save. Keats's chief tragic adjective, "desolate," appears for the first time at this period (in his sonnet on the sea), to reappear in the "Hymn to Pan," the passage in "Endymion" on the Cave of Quietude, and the "Ode on a Grecian Urn." Henceforth, Keats can conceive of poetry as a mediating, oracular, and priestlike art, one which, by representation of the desolate in formal terms, can interpret the mysteries of existence to others.

The long romance "Endymion" marks Keats's first success in finding poetic embodiments for the principles he had so far been able merely to assert. The tale of Endymion is not socially mimetic, but rather, allegorical of human experiences; however, it is still a "pleasing tale," a pastoral, not a tragedy. Even so, Keats admits in "Endymion" two tragic principles that he will later elaborate: that in contrast to warm and moving nature, art must seem cold and carved or inscribed (a marble altar garlanded with a tress of flowers [90–91], the inscribed cloak of Glaucus); and that the action demanded of their devotees by Apollo and Pan is a sacrifice of the fruits of the earth. Art is admitted for the first time to be effortful: Pan is implored to be "the unimaginable lodge / For solitary thinkings; such as dodge / Conception to the very bourne of heaven, / Then leave the naked brain." These daring and difficult solitary thinkings and new concepts will become, says Keats, "the leaven, / That spreading in this dull and clodded earth / Gives it a touch ethereal—a new birth."

In one sense, this passage represents the end of Keats's theoretical thinking about the nature and social value of poetry. But he could not yet describe how solitary original thinkings become a leaven to resurrect society. The poem "Endymion," as it journeys between the transcendent Cynthia and the Indian maid, may be seen as a journeying to and from between the two elements of solitude and society, as Keats looks for a place where he can stand. He would like to avert his gaze from the misery of solitude, where those solitary thinkings take place, but he summons up the courage to confront the necessities of his own writing. Eventually, he arrives at two embodying symbols. The first is the cloak of Glaucus, "o'erwrought with symbols by ... ambitious magic" (III, 198), wherein everything in the world is symbolized, not directly or mimetically, but in emblems and in miniaturizations. Gazed at, however, these printed reductions swell into mimetic reality:

> The gulfing whale was like a dot in the spell.
> Yet look upon it, and 'twould size and swell
> To its huge self, and the minutest fish
> Would pass the very hardest gazer's wish,
> And show his little eye's anatomy.

Keats faces up, here, to the symbolic nature of art. Art cannot, he sees, be directly mimetic; it must always bear an allegorical or emblematic relation to reality. Also, art is not a picture (he is speaking here of his own art of writing), but a hieroglyph much smaller than its original. However, by the cooperation of the gazer (and only by that cooperation), the hieroglyph "swells into reality." Without "the very hardest gazer's wish" the little fish could not manifest himself.

In this way, as later in the "Ode on a Grecian Urn," Keats declares that art requires a social cooperation between the encoder-artist and the decoder-beholder. The prescriptions written on the scroll carried by Glaucus announce Keats's new program for poetic immortality; the poet must "explore all forms and substances / Straight homeward to their symbol-essences": he must "pursue this task of joy and grief"; and enshrine all dead lovers. In the allegory that follows, all dead lovers are resurrected by having pieces of Glaucus's scroll sprinkled on them by Endymion. Endymion goes "onward . . . upon his high employ, / Showering those powerful fragments on the dead" (III, 784).

This allegory suggests that one of the social functions of poetry is to revive the erotic past of the race so that it lives again. But in the fourth book of "Endymion," as Keats admits to the poem the human maiden Phoebe and her companion Sorrow, the poem begins to refuse its own erotic idealizations and resurrections. At the allegorical center of Book IV, the narrator of "Endymion" finds at last his second major symbol of art, the solitary and desolate Cave of Quietude, a "dark Paradise" where "silence dreariest is most articulate; . . . / Where those eyes are the brightest far that keep / Their lids shut longest in a dreamless sleep." This is the place of deepest content, even though "a grievous feud" is said to have led Endymion to the Cave of Quietude.

Keats thought that this discovery of the tragic, hieroglyphic, and solitary center of art meant that he must bid farewell to creative imagination, to "cloudy phantasms . . . / And air of vision, and the monstrous swell / Of visionary seas":

> No, never more
> shall airy voices cheat me to the shore
> Of tangled wonder, breathless and aghast.
>   (IV, 651–55)

This farewell to "airy" imagination displays the choice that Keats at first felt compelled to make in deciding on a tragic and human art. He could not yet see a relation between the airy voices of visionary shores and human truth; and he felt obliged to choose truth. "I deem," says the narrator of "Endymion," "Truth the best music." "Endymion," uneasily balancing the visionary, the symbolic, and the truthful, had nonetheless brought Keats to his view of art as necessarily related, though in symbolic terms, to human reality; as necessarily hieroglyphic; as the locus of social cooperation by which the symbol regained mimetic force; and as a social resurrective power.

Shortly afterward, in a sudden leap of insight, Keats came upon his final symbol for the social function of art, a symbol not to find its ultimate elaboration, however, until Keats was able to write the ode "To Autumn." In his sonnet "When I have fears that I may cease to be," Keats summons up a rich gestalt:

> When I have fears that I may cease to be,
> Before my pen has glean'd my teeming brain,

Before high-piled books, in charact'ry,
Hold like rich garners the full-ripen'd grain. . . .

The poet's "teeming brain" is the field gleaned by his pen; the produce of his brain, "full-ripened grain," is then stored in the hieroglyphic charactery of books, which are like rich garners. Organic nature, after its transmutation into charactery (like that of Glaucus's magic symbols) becomes edible grain. By means of this gestalt, Keats asserts that the material sublime, the teeming fields of earth, can enter the brain and be hieroglyphically processed into print. Keats's aim is now to see the whole world with godlike range and power, with the seeing of Diana, "Queen of Earth, and Heaven, and Hell" ("To Homer") or that of Minos, the judge of all things ("On Visiting the Tomb of Burns").

Still, Keats has not yet enacted very far his convictions about the social function of art. The audience has been suggested as the consumer of the gleaned wheat that the poet had processed into grain; and the audience has been mentioned as the necessary cooperator in the reading of Glaucus's symbols, and as the resurrected beneficiaries of Glaucus's distributed scroll fragments. Now, in his greatest performative invention, Keats decides to play, in his own poetry, the role of audience and interpreter of symbols, not (as he so far had tended to do) the role of artist. This seems to me Keats's most successful aesthetic decision, one that distances him from his own investments (therapeutic and pleasurable alike) in creating. By playing the audience, he approaches his own art as one of its auditors, who may well want to know of what use this art will be to him.

In the odes on "Indolence" and to "Psyche," Keats had played the role of the creating artist; but in the "Ode to a Nightingale" and the "Ode on a Grecian Urn" he is respectively the listener to music and the beholder of sculpture. Each of these odes inquires what the recipient of art stands to receive from art. Keats here represents the audience for art as a single individual, rather than as a collective social group such as his Greek worshippers on the urn. In the absence of ideational content ("Nightingale"), no social collective audience can be postulated; and a modern beholder does not belong to the society that produced the urn. Keats seems to suggest that the social audience is, in the case of art, an aggregate of individual recipients, since the aesthetic experience is primarily a personal one; but what the individual receives, society, as a multiplication of individuals, also receives, as we conclude from the enumeration of listeners to the nightingale through the ages.

In the two "aesthetic odes" proper to the senses of hearing and sight, Keats begins to enact the theories of the social function of art that he had previously only asserted. As the listener to the nightingale, Keats enters a realm of wordless and nonconceptual, non-representational song. He leaves behind the human pageant of sorrow and the griefs of consciousness; he forsakes the conceptual faculty, the perplexing and retarding brain. He offers himself up to beauty in the form of Sensation, as he becomes a blind ear, ravished by the consolations of sweet sounds articulated together by the composer-singer, the nightingale.

In the "Ode on a Grecian Urn," by contrast, Keats as audience opens his eyes to representational (if allegorical) art and readmits his brain, with all its perplexities and interrogations, to aesthetic experience. In this fiction, one function of art is still, as in the case of the "Nightingale" ode, to offer a delight of an aesthetic and sensuous sort—this time a delight to the eye rather than to the ear. But no longer does art, with consolatory intent, ravish its audience away from the human scene; instead, it draws its audience into its truthful representational and representative pictures carved in stone. The fiction of artistic creation as a spontaneous outpouring to an invisible audience—the fiction of the "Nightingale" ode—is jettisoned in favor of admitting the laborious nature of art, as sculpted artifice. And Keats, in the "Urn," establishes the fact that appreciation need not be coincident with creation; he is appreciating the urn now, even though it was sculpted centuries ago. The freshness and perpetuity of art is insisted on, as is its social service to many generations, each of whom brings its woe to the urn, each of whom finds itself solaced by the urn, a friend to man. The social function of art, Keats discovers here, is to remind its audience, by means of recognizable representative figures, of emotions and events common to all human life—here, lust, love, and sacrifice.

The Elgin marbles, recently installed in England, were Keats's example of his aesthetic ideal—an art that exerts a powerful aesthetic effect even though created long ago, even though the audience cannot ascribe historical or legendary names to the figures represented. This ode declares that art need not be historically based in order to be humanly meaningful; that art, although representationally mimetic, is not directly or historically mimetic; that art works in a symbolic or allegorical order, like that of Glaucus's cloak. It is wrong, therefore, to demand of an artist that he treat directly—autobiographically, journalistically, or historically—of events; his means are radically other than reportage. In fact, unless he pursues things to their "symbol-essences" he will not be able to communicate with ages later than his own.

Finally, in the ode "To Autumn," Keats finds his most comprehensive and adequate symbol for the social value of art. He does this by playing, in this ode, two roles at once. Once again, as in "Indolence" and "Psyche," he will play the role of the artist, the dreamer indolent in reverie on the bedded grass or the gardener Fancy engaged in touching the fruits of the earth into life. But he will also play the role of audience, of the one who seeks abroad to behold the creative goddess and sings hymns to her activity and her music.

In "Autumn," in his final understanding of the social function of art, Keats chooses nature and culture as the two poles of his symbolic system. He sees the work of the artist as the transformation of nature into culture, the transmutation of the teeming fields into garnered grain (the gleaning of the natural into books, as his earlier sonnet had described it). Since civilization itself arose from man's dominion over nature, the processing of nature by agriculture became the symbol in Greece of the most sacred mysteries. The vegetation goddess Demeter, with her sheaf of corn and her poppies, was honored in the Eleusinian rituals. And the two symbolic harvests, bread and wine, food and drink, remain transmuted even to this day in the Christian Eucharist.

Keats's "Autumn" ode takes as its allegory for art the making of nature into nurture. The artist, with reaping hook, gleaning basket, and cider press, denudes nature, we may say, but creates food. We cannot, so to speak, drink apples or eat wheat; we can only consume processed nature, apple juice and grain. Since the artist is his own teeming field, art, in this allegory, is a process of self-immolation. As life is processed into art by the gleaning pen or threshing flail, the artist's own life substance disappears, and where wheat was, only a stubble plain can be seen; but over the plain there rises a song. Song is produced by the steady rhythm of nature transmuted by self-sacrifice into culture. Art does not mimetically resemble nature, any more than cider mimetically resembles apples. But without apples there would be no cider; without life there would be no hieroglyphs of life. In this way Keats insists again on the radically nonmimetic nature of art but yet argues for its intelligible relation to life in its representative symbolic order.

Keats is the audience for the artist-goddess's sacrifice of herself into food, as she passes from careless girl through ample maternity and into her own death vigil, when all the corn has been threshed, and all the apples pressed, she disappears; nature has become culture. As her beneficiary, Keats is full of an overflowing gratitude—for her generous omnipresence ("whoever seeks abroad / May find thee") and for her elegiac harmonies ("thou hast thy music too"). Her rhythms permeate the whole world until all visual, tactile, and kinetic presence is transubstantiated into Apollonian music for the ear.

We can now put Keats's view over against Heidegger's. Heidegger looks at the world and sees an absence; Keats looks at the world and sees, through the apparition of postharvest absence, a vision of past natural plenty—apples, nuts, grapevines, gourds, honey, and grain. For Keats, the task of the poet is to remember and re-create the immeasurable plenitude of the world and process it, by the pen, into something which draws from the sensual world but does not resemble it mimetically. The artist must find a charactery, or symbolic order, by which to turn presence into intellectual grain and cider, food and drink. The reaper's hook, the threshing flail, and the cider press are images of the mind at work, processing nature. The work of the mind in aesthetic production is not interrogative or proposition-making (as Keats had thought in the "Urn"), but rather "stationing"—composing symbolic items in a symbolic arrangement until that order bears an algebraic or indicative relation to the order of reality. Only in this way is a vision of reality made intelligible to other minds.

It is not by being a sage or a physician (two roles that appealed to Keats) that the artist produces his result in other minds; it is by his creation of symbolic equivalences arranged in a meaningful gestalt. Once the mind of the audience sees this vision of reality, this shadow of a magnitude, it shares its intelligibility, can "consume" it. The haphazard and unreadable texture of life becomes the interpreted and the stationed. We, as audience, may indeed find ourselves enlightened, solaced, or cured by art; but it cannot be the artist's chief *aim* to enlighten or solace or cure us; he must rather aim to transmute the natural into the hieroglyphic aesthetic, making his music part of a choral harmony contributed to by all his fellow artists. If his art is not music, it has not yet done its work of transubstantiation but is still inert direct mimesis.

By putting the "airy voices" of his choir of creatures, and the "barred clouds," at the end of his ode, Keats places the imaginative (the quality he thought he might have to forfeit in his quest for reality and truth) in a harmonious relation to the natural. He thus displays the aesthetic principle of music as paramount over even the algebraic or symbolic principle of allegorical representation. Music resembles apples even less than cider does; and yet it is the music of autumn, which arises cotemporally with its transmutations and because of them, on which Keats insists as he closes his ode.

I believe that every poet of substance passes through a course of realization very like those of Keats. Judging from their juvenilia, artists all begin with an exquisite, almost painful, response to the beautiful, and an equal revulsion toward the ugly. In their youth, they often equate the tragic and the deformed with the ugly and attempt therefore to create an idyllic counterspace. This space is usually not a social one; at most it is occupied only by a narcissistically conceived other, the beloved. As soon as the social scene intrudes into the young artist's poetry—either in the form of history (mythological or actual) or in the form of current political or domestic struggle—the poem is forced into the world of human tragedy. This exemplary process leads to a new aesthetic, in which the dissonant, the mutable, and the ugly must find a place. Usually, a poet writes *about* such disagreeable subjects before he can write *within* them. Later, if the poet can do the requisite work of internalization and symbolizing, there comes the discovery of a virtual order, powerfully organized, through which the complex vision of tragic reality can express

itself. The move into the symbolic order always angers those for whom the
artist's duty is a historically mimetic one, and for whom the clarity of pro-
paganda is preferable to the ambivalence of human response to the human
world. "Art," Yeats said, "is but a vision of reality." In using the concessive
"but" and the symbolic word "vision," Yeats argues for the algebraic or allegorical relation between art and reality. One who cannot recognize that algebraic relation, and bring it, by his own gaze, back into "swelling reality," is
incompetent to read art.

Those poets who encounter particularly acute political stress, like Czeslaw Milosz and Seamus Heaney, are always urged to be more socially specific in their poetry than poets can be. Poets resist this pressure by offering
their own meditations of the social function of the artist, faced with the huge
and varied questions of the world. Imagination, as Stevens says, presses back
against the pressure of reality. I want to quote two poems, one by Milosz, one
by Heaney, which reaffirm the necessarily symbolic nature of the artist's work
and yet repeat its equally necessary connection with social reality.

Milosz's poem, "The Poor Poet," was written in Warsaw, in 1944, during
the last horrors of the war. It recapitulates the passage that we have seen in
the young poet from an aesthetic of joy to an aesthetic of tragedy; it is Mod-
ernist in its hatred of the mutually tormenting relation between the arranged
symbolic order of art and the random tragic sense of life; and it sees the creating of the symbolic order as a form of revenge against the horrors of life. The
poet as a man is deformed by the deformations he witnesses; and for all the
beauty he creates he cannot himself be beautiful but must share the deformi-
ties of the world:

The Poor Poet

The first movement is singing,
A free voice, filling mountains and valleys.
The first movement is joy,
But it is taken away.

And now, that the years have transformed my blood
And thousands of planetary systems have been born
        and died in my flesh,
I sit, a sly and angry poet
With malevolently squinted eyes,
And, weighing a pen in my hand,
I plot revenge.

I poise the pen and it puts forth twigs and leaves,
   it is covered with blossoms.
And the scent of that tree is impudent, for there,
   on the real earth,
Such trees do not grow, and like an insult
To suffering humanity is the scent of that tree.

Some take refuge in despair, which is sweet
Like strong tobacco, like a glass of vodka drunk
   in the hour of annihilation.
Others have the hope of fools, rosy as erotic dreams.

Still others find peace in the idolatry of country,
Which can last for a long time,
Although little longer than the nineteenth century lasts.

But to me a cynical hope is given,
For since I opened my eyes I have seen only the
   glow of fires, massacres,
Only injustice, humiliation, and the laughable
   shame of braggarts.
To me is given the hope of revenge on others
   and on myself.
For I was he who knew
And took from it no profit for myself.
   Selected Poems (Ecco, 1980, 53–54)

Formally, this poem places its one moment of adult "beauty" in one line, recounting the blossoming of the pen and alluding to Aaron's rod. This Keatsian moment (with its promise of fruit to come, following the blossoms), is encapsulated within Milosz's two mentions of revenge: "I plot revenge.... To me is given the hope of revenge." It is also encapsulated within tragedy ("Joy ... is taken away") and the common responses to tragedy, whether despair, hope, or idolatry. The poet's "cynical hope" is his penalty for his creation of poetry, and his revenge is directed not only against others but against himself for daring to "insult" suffering humanity with the perfection of form. Milosz's Manichaean spirit poses the problem of content and form in its most violent aspect, as the serenity of form (even here, in the concentric form of this lyric) tortures the anguish of content ("fires, massacres.... injustice, humiliation, ... shame"). There can be, according to Milosz, no political poetry that does not aim at the aesthetic equilibrium of form. Art, in its social function, thus enacts for us the paradox of our orderly symbolic capacity as it meets the disorder it symbolizes.

A poem by Seamus Heaney about Chekhov traces again the young poet's passage from sensuous pleasure to social obligation. The recognition of social obligation by the poet must pass, the poem suggests, not into social activism but rather into symbolic representation in the poem, as in fact, Chekhov decides to leave his attractive life in Moscow to go to see the penal colony on the faraway island Sakhalin, off the east coast of Russia below Japan. Though Chekhov is a doctor, he does not go to Sakhalin to minister to the convicts, but rather to observe, and to write a book. He even forces himself to stay to watch a flogging in order to see the full reality of life in the colony. And then he has to find the right tone to write about what he has seen—"not tract, not thesis." Once he has admitted the colony to his consciousness, he will never be able to exorcise it; he will carry a second convict-self within him. The parallels with Northern Ireland need no describing; the poet has left Northern Ireland and lives in the Republic, but he writes about the reality he has left behind and must find a symbolic way to enact its truth.

Chekhov's biographer recounts that as he departed for Sakhalin, his friends came to see him off at the railway station and gave him a bottle of cognac to drink when he should have arrived (by rail and boat and troika) at Sakhalin, thousands of miles away. The cognac is Chekhov's last taste of uncomplicated sensual joy; henceforth he will be a symbolic convict:

Chekhov on Sakhalin

So, he would pay his "debt to medicine".
But first he drank cognac by the ocean
With his back to all he travelled north to face.
His head was swimming free as the troikas

Of Tyumin, he looked down from the rail
Of his thirty years and saw a mile
Into himself as if he were clear water:
Lake Baikhal from the deckrail of the steamer.

That far north, Siberia was south.
Should it have been an ulcer in the mouth,
The cognac that the Moscow literati
Packed off with him to a penal colony—

Him, born, you may say, under the counter?
At least that meant he knew its worth. No cantor
in full throat by the iconostasis
Got holier joy than he got from that glass

That shone and warmed like diamonds warming
On some pert young cleavage in a salon,
Inviolable and affronting.
He felt the glass go cold in the midnight sun.

When he staggered up and smashed it on the stones
It rang as clearly as the convicts chains
That haunted him. In the months to come
It rang on like the burden of his freedom

To try for the right tone—not tract, not thesis—
And walk away from floggings. He who thought to squeeze
His slave's blood out and waken the free man
Shadowed a convict guide through Sakhalin.
    Station Island (Farrar, Straus, 1984)

Heaney's poem implies that the truest way to write about the condition of the poet in twentieth-century Ireland is to write about a nineteenth-century Russian incident. The indirection proper to art is reflected thematically here in the repudiation of religious tract and political thesis alike: Chekhov's book is detached, descriptive, the book of a novelist, not an evangelist or social reformer. Heaney's formal insistence here on the suppression of Chekhov's audience enacts the one condition for socially effective art—that it be directed, not to the transformation of its putative audience, but to the transformation of the artist's own self. By acknowledging his own past as the grandson of a serf and the son of a grocer, Chekhov can enter the chains of the convict and write powerfully about them. At the same time, he drinks with full relish and intoxication the brandy of his Moscow self, before he turns to "all he travelled north to face." The self-transformation of Keats's goddess of the corn acknowledged a similar death in the self as the condition of an art that could nourish others.

In separate ways, Milosz and Heaney have retraced the steps toward an analysis of art that we have seen in Keats. It is important to each of them to assert that poetry does perform a social function; it is equally important to them to remove it from a direct and journalistic mimesis. The poet witnesses, constructs, and records; but the creation of symbolic and musical form is the imperative, in the end, which he must serve if his witness is to be believed.

PAUL DE MAN

Time and History in Wordsworth

U p till now, the double-barrelled topic of these lectures[1] has rather prevented us from reading our romantic authors with the kind of receptivity,
the self-forgetting concentration, that we have been describing (in the case
of Rousseau) as the proper state of mind for critical insights. The need to
keep one eye on the text and another eye on the critical commentator has
forced us into the rather tiresome grimace well known to anyone who has
ever played in an orchestra—where one has to keep track simultaneously of
the score and of the conductor. The grimace becomes even more painful
when the directives of the score and those of the interpreter are pulling in
different directions, . . . The result often is that because of the unavoidable
simplifications involved in a polemical discussion, one fails to do justice
to both the writer and the critic. I probably had to overstate the degree of
my disagreement with Girard and Starobinski, critics for whom I have a
great deal of sympathy and admiration—and I was clearly not being critical
enough, to your taste, with Heidegger, when I suggested that there might be
perhaps something of merit in an imaginary figure, one that never existed in
the flesh, who would have approached literature with some of the insights
that appear in *Sein und Zeit*.[2] More distressing are the one-sided readings
given to some of the texts, in order to use them as a rebuttal of methodological assertions. Such over-analytical approaches are certainly not attuned to

From *Diacritics: A Review of Contemporary Criticism* 17, no. 4 (Winter 1987): 4–17. Copyright
© 1987 by the Johns Hopkins University Press.

catch the subtle nuances of temporality and intent that a valid commentary
should bring out.

Fortunately, my topic today will allow for a more relaxed kind of presentation, in which the voice of the poet might come through in a less
garbled manner. Geoffrey Hartman's study of Wordsworth awakens in me
no trace of methodological disagreement.[3] I read whole parts of it with the
profound satisfaction of full agreement, only marred by the slight feeling
of jealousy that I did not write them myself. The much hoped-for synthesis
between the best qualities of American and Continental criticism certainly
begins to come true in a book like this. It is based on a wide knowledge of
the tradition in which the poet is writing, in this case true familiarity with
Wordsworth's antecedents in Milton and in eighteenth-century poetry,
combined with an ear that is finely attuned to the slightest nuances of
Wordsworth's language. Moreover, by interpreting Wordsworth from the
inside, from the phenomenological point of view of his own consciousness,
Hartman can trace a coherent itinerary of Wordsworth's poetic development. His achievement will make it possible for us to limit ourselves to
some indications derived from the reading of a few very short but characteristic texts, thus tracing, in turn, an itinerary through Wordsworth by
means of some of those larger themes that Hartman has pursued. These
themes, in the case of Wordsworth and Wordsworth scholarship, are quite
obvious, and Hartman does not depart from a well-established custom
when he makes the relationship between nature and the imagination into
Wordsworth's central problem. The Arnoldian tradition of reading Wordsworth as a moralist has, for quite a while now, been superseded by a concern for the implicit poetics that are present in his writing, and that have
to be understood prior to the interpretation of a moral statement that
seems conventional. This leads inevitably to such abstractions as nature,
the imagination, self-knowledge, and poetry as a means to self-knowledge,
all of which figure prominently in recent Wordsworth studies, not only
because Wordsworth himself talks at times openly about them, but because
his poetry, even at its most trivial, always seems to be supported by and to
relate back to them.

As will be clear to all of you, the path I'll try to trace by this direct commentary overlaps with that proposed by Hartman in more places than I will
have time to mention. It diverges from it in at least one point of some importance, and I will comment on this disagreement later, as a way to summarize
a tentative view of Wordsworth's poetry.[4]

Let me start out with a very well-known poem to which Hartman
devotes a chapter, the text that Wordsworth placed at the head of the section of his *Collected Poems* entitled "Poems of the Imagination." He later

incorporated it into *The Prelude* and seems to have, in general, attached a special importance to it. It was written in Goslar, during his stay in Germany, together with several other of the childhood memories that went into the two first books of *The Prelude*. "The Winander Boy" is divided into two sections separated by a blank space, and all readers of the poem have been struck by the abruptness of the transition that leads from the first to the second part. Problems of interpretation tend to focus on the relationship between the two parts. (I would add that these problems were solved in a definitive but somewhat peremptory fashion in a fine recent anthology of English literature, in which the second part has simply been suppressed.)

> There was a Boy, ye knew him well, ye Cliffs
> And Islands of Winander! many a time
> At evening, when the stars had just begun
> To move along the edges of the hills,
> 5 Rising or setting, would he stand alone
> Beneath the trees, or by the glimmering Lake,
> And there, with fingers interwoven, both hands
> Press'd closely, palm to palm, and to his mouth
> Uplifted, he, as through an instrument,
> 10 Blew mimic hootings to the silent owls
> That they might answer him.—And they would shout
> Across the watery Vale, and shout again,
> Responsive to his call, with quivering peals,
> And long halloos, and screams, and echoes loud
> 15 Redoubled and redoubled; concourse wild
> Of mirth and jocund din! And when it chanced
> That pauses of deep silence mock'd his skill,
> Then, sometimes, in that silence, while he hung
> Listening, a gentle shock of mild surprise
> 20 Has carried far into his heart the voice
> Of mountain torrents; or the visible scene
> Would enter unawares into his mind
> With all its solemn imagery, its rocks,
> Its woods, and that uncertain Heaven, receiv'd
> 25 Into the bosom of the steady Lake.
>
> This Boy was taken from his Mates, and died
> In childhood, ere he was full ten years old.
> —Fair are the woods, and beauteous is the spot,
> The Vale where he was born; the Churchyard hangs

30 Upon a Slope above the Village School,
   And, there, along the bank, when I have pass'd
   At evening, I believe that oftentimes
   A full half-hour together I have stood
   Mute—looking at the Grave in which he lies.[5]

The first part of the poem introduces us into a world that is, in the words of the text, both "responsive" and, as in the gesture of the hands, "interwoven." Voice and nature echo each other in an exchange of which the exuberance expresses a stability, a firm hold on a universe that has the vastness of rising and setting stars, but nevertheless allows for an intimate and sympathetic contact between human and natural elements. Not the "vaste et profonde unité" of Baudelaire's *Correspondances* should come to mind, but a more innocent, more playful, pleasure at finding responses, satisfying possibilities of relationship even for someone who, like the boy, "stands alone." The "watery Vale" that might separate him from an alien natural presence is easily bridged by the cry of the owls; it is, by itself, an eerie noise enough on a dark night, but little of this eeriness is allowed to enter the poem. If we mimic it well enough to engage the response of its originators, the gulf between ourselves and nature need not be unbridgeable. "The poet . . . considers man and nature as essentially adapted to each other, and the mind of man as naturally the mirror of the fairest and most interesting qualities of nature"—this statement from the Preface to the *Lyrical Ballads* would be a good commentary on the opening scene of the poem.[6] Much Wordsworth criticism, still today, considers this frequently as the fundamental statement, not just of Wordsworth, but of romantic naturalism as a whole, and refuses to go beyond it. Yet, even in this first section of the poem, one finds some strain at keeping up a belief in such an "interwoven" world. "Mimic hootings" is not the highest characterization imaginable for the human voice, and we have somehow to be told explicitly that this is "concourse wild / Of mirth and jocund din . . ." to convince us of the persistent cheer of the scene.

    As soon as the silence of the owls allows for the noise to subside, what becomes audible is poetically much more suggestive than what went before. The deepening of the imaginative level is not announced with any fanfare or pointed dramatic gesture. The "surprises" that Wordsworth's language gives are indeed such "*gentle* shocks of *mild* surprise" that the transition from stability to suspense can be accomplished almost without our being aware of it. Yet certainly, by the time we come to "*uncertain* Heaven," we must realize that we have entered a precarious world in which the relationship between noun and epithet can be quite surprising. Coleridge singled out the line for comment, as being most unmistakably Wordsworth's: "Had I met these lines running wild in the deserts of Arabia, I should instantly have screamed out, 'Wordsworth.'"[7] The line is indeed bound to engender wonder and meditation. The movements of the stars, in the opening lines, had seemed "certain" enough, and their reflection in the lake was hardly needed to steady the majesty of their imperceptible motion. But the precariousness that is here being introduced had been announced before, as when, a little earlier, in lines 18 and 19, it was said that when "pauses of deep silence mock'd his skill, / Then, sometimes, in that silence, while he (the boy) *hung* / Listening, a gentle shock of mild surprise. . . ." We would have expected "stood Listening" instead of the unusual "hung / Listening." This word, "hung," plays an important part in the poem. It reappears in the second part, when it is said that the graveyard in which the boy is buried "*hangs* / Upon a Slope above the Village School." It establishes the thematic link between the two parts and names a central Wordsworthian experience. At the moment when the analogical correspondence with nature no longer asserts itself, we discover that the earth under our feet is not the stable base in which we can believe ourselves to be anchored. It is as if the solidity of earth were suddenly pulled away from under our feet and that we were left "hanging" from the sky instead of standing on the ground. The fundamental spatial perspective is reversed; instead of being centered on the earth, we are suddenly related to a sky that has its own movements, alien to those of earth and its creatures. The experience hits as a sudden feeling of dizziness, a falling or a threat of falling, a *vertige* of which there are many examples in Wordsworth. The nest-robbing scene from Book I of *The Prelude* comes to mind, where the experience is a literal moment of absolute dizziness which disjoins the familiar perspective of the spatial relationship between heaven and earth, in which the heavens are seen as a safe dome that confirms at all times the earth's and our own centrality, the steadfastness of our orientation towards the center which makes us creatures of earth. But here, suddenly, the sky no longer relates to the earth.

> Oh! at that time,
> While on the perilous ridge I hung alone,
> With what strange utterance did the loud dry wind
> Blow through my ears! the sky seem'd not a sky
> Of earth, and with what motion moved the clouds!
>   [1805 *Prelude*, I, 335–39; 291]

Later, when in the Preface to the 1815 edition of his *Poems* Wordsworth gives examples of the workings of the highest poetic faculty, the imagination, as it shapes poetic diction, he chooses three passages, from Virgil, Shakespeare, and Milton, in which the italicized key-word is the same word, "hang,"

not used literally as in the last instance from *The Prelude*, but used imaginatively. The Milton passage begins

> As when far off at Sea a Fleet descried
> Hangs in the clouds, by equinoxial winds
> Close sailing from Bengala . . .
>   . . . so seem'd
> Far off the flying Fiend.
>   [Preface to *Poems* (1815), 248]

Wordsworth comments: "Here is the full strength of the imagination
involved in the word *hangs*, and exerted upon the whole image: First, the
Fleet, an aggregate of many Ships, is represented as one mighty Person,
whose track, we know and feel, is upon the waters; but, taking advantage
of its appearance to the senses, the Poet dares to represent it as *hanging in
the clouds*, both for the gratification of the mind in contemplating the image
itself, and in reference to the motion and appearance of the sublime object to
which it is compared" [248]. This *daring* movement of the language, an act
of pure mind, corresponds to the *danger*, the anxiety of the moment when
the sudden silence leaves the boy *hanging*/listening. In the second part of the
poem, we are told, without any embellishment or preparation, that the boy
died, and we now understand that the moment of silence, when the analogical stability of a world in which mind and nature reflect each other was
shattered, was in fact a prefiguration of his death. The turning away of his
mind from a responsive nature towards a nature that is not quite "of earth"
and that ultimately is called an "uncertain Heaven" is in fact an orientation
of his consciousness towards a preknowledge of his mortality. The spatial
heaven of the first five lines with its orderly moving stars has become the
temporal heaven of line 24, "uncertain" and precarious since it appears in the
form of a pre-consciousness of death.

    The uncertainty or anxiety is not allowed, however, to go unrelieved.
In the prefigurative first section the uncertain heaven is, with a suggestion
of appeasement, "receiv'd / Into the bosom of the steady Lake," and in the
second part, at the moment when we would have expected an elegiac lament
on the death of the boy, we hear instead a characteristically Wordsworthian
song of praise to a particular place, the kind of ode to spirit of place of which
Hartman has traced the antecedents in eighteenth-century nature poetry:

> Fair are the woods, and beauteous is the spot,
> The Vale where he was born; the Churchyard hangs
> Upon a Slope above the Village School,

And, there, along that bank, when I have pass'd
At evening, I believe that oftentimes
A full half-hour together I have stood
Mute—looking at the Grave in which he lies.

The dizziness revealed in the "hung / Listening . . ." has indeed resulted in a fall, has been the discovery of a state of falling which itself anticipated a fall into death. Now become part of earth in the graveyard, the boy is part of an earth that is itself falling into a sky that is not "of earth." But the movement is steadied, the fall cushioned, as it were, when the uncertain heaven is received into the lake, when sheer dizziness is changed into reflection. The corresponding moment in the second part is the meditative half-hour which introduces a long, extended period of continuous duration that exists outside of the ordinary time of daily activity, at the moment of a privileged encounter with a scene that merges the youth of the village school with the death of the graveyard, as boyhood and death merged in the figure of the Winander boy.

We understand the particular temporal quality of this slow half-hour better when we remember that the earliest version of this poem was written throughout in the first person and was referring to Wordsworth himself as a boy. The text went: "When it chanced / That pauses of deep silence mocked *my* skill. . . ." The poem is, in a curious sense, autobiographical, but it is the autobiography of someone who no longer lives written by someone who is speaking, in a sense, from beyond the grave. It would be banal and inadequate to say that Wordsworth is praising and mourning, in the poem, his own youth, the boy he used to be. The movement is more radical, more complex. The structure of the poem, although it seems retrospective, is in fact proleptic. In the second part, Wordsworth is reflecting on his own death which lies, of course, in the future, and can only be anticipated. But to be able to imagine, to convey the experience, the consciousness of mortality, he can only represent death as something that happened to another person, in the past. Dead men,[8] as we all know, tell no tales, but they have an assertive way of reminding us of mortality, of bringing us eventually face to face with our own finitude. Wordsworth is thus anticipating a future event as if it existed in the past. Seeming to be remembering, to be moving to a past, he is in fact anticipating a future. The objectification of the past self, as that of a consciousness that unwittingly experiences an anticipation of its own death, allows him to reflect on an event that is, in fact, unimaginable. For this is the real terror of death, that it lies truly beyond the reach of reflection. Yet the poem names the moment of death in a reflective mood, and it is this reflective mood that makes it possible to transform what would otherwise be an experience of terror into the relative appeasement of the lines

that uncertain Heaven, receiv'd
Into the bosom of the steady Lake.

Another way of putting it is that what Wordsworth strives to conquer, on
the relentless fall into death, is the time, the surmise that would allow one
to reflect upon the event that, of all events, is most worth reflecting upon
but hardest to face. This time is conquered at the end of the poem, in the
curiously exact full half-hour that becomes available to him, a purely meditative time proportionate to the time it takes us to understand meditatively
Wordsworth's own poem. But the strategy that allows for this conquest is
temporally complex: it demands the description of a future experience by
means of the fiction of a past experience which is itself anticipatory or prefigurative. Since it is a fiction, it can only exist in the form of a language,
since it is by means of language that the fiction can be objectified and made
to act as a living person. The reflection is not separable from the language
that describes it, and the half-hour of the end also clocks the time during
which Wordsworth, or ourselves, are in real contact with the poem. Hartman is quite right in saying that the poem "becomes an . . . extended epitaph" [20], though one might want to add that it is the epitaph written by
the poet for himself, from a perspective that stems, so to speak, from beyond
the grave. This temporal perspective is characteristic for all Wordsworth's
poetry—even if it obliges us to imagine a tombstone large enough to hold
the entire *Prelude*.[9]
     Wordsworth himself gives us sufficient evidence to defend this kind
of understanding. The first of the *Essays upon Epitaphs* describes, in prose,
insights that are very close to what we have found in "The Winander Boy."
What seems to start out as a simply pious statement about the consolatory
power of a belief in the immortality of the soul turns very swiftly into a
meditation on the temporality that characterizes the consciousness of beings
capable of reflecting on their own death. The first characteristic of such a consciousness is its power to anticipate: "The Dog or Horse perishes in the field,
or in the stall, by the side of his Companions, and is incapable of *anticipating*
the sorrow with which his surrounding Associates shall bemoan his death, or
pine for his loss; he cannot *pre-conceive* this regret, he can form no thought of
it; and therefore cannot possibly have a desire to leave such regret or remembrance behind him" [605]. And Wordsworth characterizes a human being
that, not unlike the Winander boy at the beginning of the poem, would have
chosen to remain in a state of nature by an "inability arising from the imperfect state of his faculties to come, in any point of his being, into contact with
a notion of death; or to an *unreflecting* acquiescence in what had been instilled
in him" [606]. Very soon in the same essay, however, it becomes clear that the

power to anticipate is so closely connected with the power to remember that it is almost impossible to distinguish them from each other. They seem like opposites, and are indeed at opposite poles if we think of time as a continual movement from birth to death. In this perspective, the source is at a maximal remove from the final point of destination, and it would be impossible to reach the one by way of the other. In a more reflective, more conscious concept of temporality, however, the two poles will, in Wordsworth's phrasing, "have another and finer connection than that of contrast" [608]. "Origin and tendency are notions inseparably co-relative" [606], he writes, and the essay develops this notion in an extended voyage image: "As, in sailing upon the orb of this Planet, a voyage, towards the regions where the sun sets, conducts gradually to the quarter where we have been accustomed to behold it come forth at its rising; and, in like manner, a voyage towards the east, the birthplace in our imagination of the morning, leads finally to the quarter where the Sun is last seen when he departs from our eyes; so, the contemplative Soul, travelling in the direction of mortality, advances to the Country of everlasting Life; and, in like manner, may she continue to explore those cheerful tracts, till she is brought back, for her advantage and benefit, to the land of transitory things—of sorrow and of tears" [608]. Stripped of whatever remnants of piety still cling to this language,[10] the passage summarizes the temporality of the "Winander Boy" poem. In this poem, the reflection on death takes on the form, at first sight contradictory, of a remembrance of childhood. Similarly, in Wordsworth, evocations of natural, childlike, or apocalyptic states of unity with nature often acquire[11] the curiously barren, dead-obsessed emptiness of non-being.[12] The poetic imagination, what is here called the contemplative soul, realizes this and thus encompasses source and death, origin and end within the space of its language, by means of complex temporal structurizations of which we found an example in "The Winander Boy."[13]

Another brief poem of Wordsworth's will allow us to take one further step in an understanding of his temporality; it may also make the concept less abstract by linking it to its more empirical mode of manifestation, namely history. The poem belongs to the later sonnet cycle entitled *The River Duddon* that appeared in 1820.

> Not hurled precipitous from steep to steep;
> Lingering no more mid flower-enamelled lands
> And blooming thickets; nor by rocky bands
> Held;—but in radiant progress tow'rd the Deep
> 5 Where mightiest rivers into powerless sleep
> Sink, and forget their nature; now expands
> Majestic Duddon, over smooth flat sands,

Gliding in silence with unfettered sweep!
Beneath an ampler sky a region wide
10 Is opened round him;—hamlets, towers, and towns,
And blue-topped hills, behold him from afar;
In stately mien to sovereign Thames allied,
Spreading his bosom under Kentish downs,
With Commerce freighted or triumphant War.
    [699]

The *Essay upon Epitaphs* had already suggested the image of a river as
the proper emblem for a consciousness that is able to contain origin and end
into a single awareness. "Origin and tendency are notions inseparably co-
relative. Never did a Child stand by the side of a running Stream, pondering
within himself what power was the feeder of the perpetual current, from what
never-wearied sources the body of water was supplied, but he must have been
inevitably propelled to follow this question by another: 'Towards what abyss
is it in progress? what receptacle can contain the mighty influx?'..." [606]. In
this poem, we have what seems at first sight like a progression, a continuous
movement that flows "in radiant progress" towards the triumphant ending:

In stately mien to sovereign Thames allied,
Spreading his bosom under Kentish downs,
With Commerce freighted or triumphant War.

Equally convincing seems to be the movement that leads, in the
poem, from the idyllic setting of "flower-enamelled lands / And blooming
thickets..." to the political, historically oriented language at the end. The
progression from nature to history, from a rural to an urban world seems
to be without conflict. We move from a relationship between the personified river Duddon and its pastoral banks, to a relationship that involves
human creations such as "hamlets, towers, and towns," or human historical
enterprises such as "commerce and war." And this gliding passage, similar
to what is called in *The Prelude* "love of nature leading to love of man"
[title of 1850 Book VIII, cf. 395], appears as a liberation, an expansion
that involves a gain in freedom. The river is no longer restricted "by rocky
bands" and now flows "with unfettered sweep." The order of nature seems to
open up naturally into the order of history, thus allowing the same natural
symbol, the river, to evoke the connection between both. The poem seems
to summarize the "growth of a mind" as espousing this movement, and to
prove, by the success of its own satisfying completeness, that language can
espouse poetically this very movement.

Some aspects of the language, however, prevent the full identification of the movement with natural process and put into question an interpretation of the River, which a subsequent poem in the same series addresses as "my partner and my guide" ["Conclusion," 1, 699], as a truly natural entity. The beginning of the poem, for instance, casts a curious spell over the subsequent progression. It describes what the river no longer is in such forceful and suggestive language that we are certainly not allowed to forget what the river *has been* by the time we encounter it in its expanded form. The opening line, for example, cannot cease to haunt us, and no matter how strongly the italicized *now* (in "*now* expands") takes us to the present, so much has been told us so effectively about what came before that we can only seize upon this present in the perspective of its past and its future. The past is described as successive motions of falling and lingering. The dizziness of the Winander Boy poem and of the childhood scenes of *The Prelude* is certainly present in the image of the river "hurled precipitous from steep to steep," which introduces, from the start, a powerful motion that dominates the entire poem, and that the various counterforces, including the initial *not*, are unable to stem. For the idyllic stage that follows, among flowers and blooming thickets, is a mere lingering, a temporary respite in a process that is one of steady descent and dissolution. The implications of this movement become clearer still when the radiant progress is said to be " . . . tow'rd the Deep / Where mightiest rivers into powerless sleep / Sink, and forget their nature." This description of the sea is certainly far removed from the image of a pantheistic unity with nature that one might have expected. It is presented instead as a loss of self, the loss of the *name* that designates the river and allows it to take on the dignity of an autonomous subject. The diction of the passage, with the antithetical balance of "mightiest" and "powerless" is all the stronger since the apparent strategy of the poem does not seem to demand this kind of emphasis. It makes the forgetting of one's nature that is here mentioned into a movement that runs counter to the original progression; this progression, which first seemed to lead from nature to history while remaining under the dominant sway of nature, now becomes a movement away from nature towards pure nothingness. One is reminded of a similar loss of name in the Lucy Gray poems where death makes her into an anonymous entity

Roll'd round in earth's diurnal course
With rocks and stones and trees!
["A slumber did my spirit seal," 7–8, 165]

Similarly, the river Duddon is first lost into a larger entity, the Thames, which in turn will lose itself in still larger anonymity. There is no cycle here by means of which we are brought back to the source and reunited with it by natural means. No prospect of natural rebirth is held out, and the historical achievement at the end seems caught in the same general movement of decay.

Nevertheless, the poem can overcome the feeling of dejection that this irrevocable fall might suggest; it ends on a statement of assertion that is not ironic. Not altogether unlike the uncertain heaven in "The Winander Boy" that was steadied in reflection, the fall here is not prevented, but made tolerable this time by the assertion of historical achievement. There seems to be an assertion of permanence, of a duration in what seems to be an irrevocable waste, a falling away into sheer nothingness. It is based on a certain form of hope, on the affirmation of a possible future, all of which made it possible for man to pursue an enterprise that seems doomed from the start, to have a history in spite of a death which Wordsworth never allows us to forget.

In this poem, the possibility of restoration is linked to the manner in which the two temporalities are structurally interrelated within the text. If taken by itself, the progression towards history would be pure delusion, a misleading myth based on the wrong kind of forgetting, an evasion of the knowledge of mortality. The countertheme of loss of self into death that appears in the first and second quatrain introduces a temporality that is more originary, more authentic than the other, in that it reaches further into the past and sees wider into the future. It envelops the other, but without reducing it to mere error. Rather, it creates a point of view which has gone beyond the historical world of which we catch a glimpse at the end of the poem, but which can look back upon this world and see it within its own, relative greatness, as a world that does not escape from mutability but asserts itself within the knowledge of its own transience. We have a temporal structure that is not too different from what we found in "The Winander Boy." Instead of looking back upon childhood, upon an earlier stage of consciousness that anticipates its future undoing, we here look back on a historical consciousness that existed prior to the truly temporal consciousness represented by the river. This historical stage is named at the end of the poem, but this end is superseded by the authentic endpoint named in line 5. We see it therefore, with the poet, as destined to this same end. Like the boy experiencing the foreknowledge of his death, history awakens in us a true sense of our temporality, by allowing for the interplay between achievement and dissolution, self-assertion and self-loss, on which the poem is built. History, like childhood, is what allows recollection to originate in a truly temporal perspective, not as a memory of a unity that never existed, but as the awareness, the remembrance of a precarious condition of falling that has never ceased to prevail.[14]

Hence, in the concluding sonnet of the same cycle, the emphasis on the italicized word *backward* in

> For, *backward*, Duddon! as I cast my eyes,
> I see what was, and is, and will abide.
> ["Conclusion," 3–4, 699]

As a mere assertion of the permanence of nature, the poem would be simply pious and in bad faith, for we know that as soon as we think of the river as analogous to a self, as a consciousness worthy of engaging our own, that it only reveals a constant loss of self. Considered as a partner and a guide, it has indeed "past away" [line 2] and never ceases to do so. This is the Function it fulfills in the line

> The Form remains, the Function never dies
> [line 6]

in which the Form corresponding to this function is the trajectory of a persistent fall. The entire poignancy of the two sonnets is founded on the common bond between the I of the poem and its emblematic counterpart in the Duddon, which makes the river into something more than mere nature. Instead of merely letting ourselves be carried by it, we are able to move backwards, against the current of the movement.[15] This backward motion does not exist in nature but is the privilege of the faculty of mind that Wordsworth calls the imagination; asserting the possibility of reflection in the face of the most radical dissolution, personal or historical. The imagination engenders hope and future, not in the form of historical progress, nor in the form of an immortal life after death that would make human history unimportant, but as the persistent, future possibility of a retrospective reflection on its own decay. The 1850 version of *The Prelude* makes this clearest when it defines the imagination as being, at the same time, a sense of irreparable loss linked with the assertion of a persistent consciousness:

> I was lost
> Halted without an effort to break through;
> But to my *conscious soul* I now can say
> "I recognise thy glory."
> [1850 *Prelude*, VI, 596–99]

The restoring power, in Wordsworth, does not reside in nature, or in history, or in a continuous progression from one to the other, but in the persistent power of mind and language after nature and history have failed. One wonders what category of being can sustain the mind in this knowledge and give it the future that makes imagination dwell, in the later version of *The Prelude*, with "something evermore about to be" [VI, 608].

This may be the moment at which a return to Hartman's book is helpful. Like all attentive readers of Wordsworth, he reaches a point at which the nature of this restorative power has to be defined as the main assertive power in Wordsworth's poetry. And the understanding he has of Wordsworth's own mind allows him to give a very full and penetrating description of the complexities involved. He has noticed, more clearly than most other interpreters, that the imagination in Wordsworth is independent of nature and that it leads him to write a language, at his best moments, that is entirely unrelated to the exterior stimuli of the senses. He has also noticed that there is a kind of existential danger connected with this autonomy, and that when Wordsworth speaks about the daring of his imagery in the 1815 Preface, this risk involves more than mere experimentation with words. Hartman refers to this danger as an apocalyptic temptation, in his words, "a strong desire to cast out nature and to achieve an unmediated contact with the principle of things" [x]. Carried by the imagination, Wordsworth would at certain privileged moments come close to such visionary power, although he reaches it without supernatural intervention and always in a gradual and gentle way. Still, in the climactic passages of *The Prelude*, and in the main poems generally, the evidence of a moving beyond nature is unmistakable. What characterizes Wordsworth, according to Hartman, and sets him apart from Milton, for instance, and also from Blake, is that the apocalyptic moment is not sustained, that it is experienced as too damaging to the natural order of things to be tolerated. Out of reverence, not out of fear, Wordsworth feels the need to hide from sight the vision he has glimpsed for a moment; he has to do so, if his poetry is to continue its progression. And he finds the strength for this avoidance of apocalyptic abandon in nature itself—a nature that has been darkened and deepened by this very insight, and that has to some extent incorporated the power of imagination. But it has naturalized it, re-united it with a source that remains in the natural world. "The energy of imagination enters into a natural cycle though apart from it" [69], writes Hartman. The return to a natural image at the end of the famous passage on Imagination in Book VI of *The Prelude* "renews the connection between the waters above and the waters below, between heaven and earth. Towards this marriage of heaven and earth the poet proceeds despite apocalypse. He is the matchmaker, his song the spousal verse" [69]. The road apparently beyond and away from nature in fact never ceased to be a natural road, albeit nature in a negative form, the "via naturaliter negativa."

We cannot follow him in speaking of an apocalyptic temptation in Wordsworth. The passages that Hartman singles out as apocalyptic never suggest a movement towards an unmediated contact with a divine principle.

The imagination [in Book VI, 371–72] is said to be "like an unfather'd vapour" [527] and is, as such, entirely cut off from ultimate origins; it gives sight of "the invisible world" [536], but the invisibility refers to the mental, inward nature of this world as opposed to the world of the senses; it reveals to us that our home is "with infinity" [538–39], but within the language of the passage this infinity is clearly to be understood in a temporal sense as the futurity of "something evermore about to be" [542]. The heightening of pitch is not the result of "unmediated vision" but of another mediation, in which the consciousness does not relate itself any longer to nature but to a temporal entity. This entity could, with proper qualifications, be called history, and it is indeed in connection with historical events (the French Revolution) that the apostrophe to Imagination comes to be written. But if we call this history, then we must be careful to understand that it is the kind of history that appeared at the end of the Duddon sonnet, the retrospective recording of man's failure to overcome the power of time. Morally, it is indeed a sentiment directed towards other men rather than towards nature, and, as such, imagination is at the root of Wordsworth's theme of human love. But the bond between men is not one of common enterprise, or of a common belonging to nature: it is much rather the recognition of a common temporal predicament that finds its expression in the individual and historical destinies that strike the poet as exemplary. Examples abound, from "The Ruined Cottage" to "Resolution and Independence," and in the various time-eroded figures that appear throughout *The Prelude*. The common denominator that they share is not nature but time, as it unfolds its power in these individual and collective histories.

Nor can we follow Hartman in his assertion of the ultimately regenerative power of nature. His argument returns to passages like the passage on Imagination in Book VI of *The Prelude* in which, according to him, after having shown the "conscious soul" as independent, Wordsworth has to return to a natural image. The soul is said to be

Strong in herself and in beatitude
That hides her, like the mighty flood of Nile
Poured from her fount of Abyssinian clouds
To fertilize the whole Egyptian plain . . .
[1850 *Prelude*, VI, 613–16; Hartman 69]

Perhaps enough has been said about the river Duddon to suggest that Wordsworth's rivers are not to be equated with natural entities. We don't even have to point to the further distancing from nature suggested by the exotic reference to an entity richer in mythological and literary than in natural associations; the abyss in "Abyssinian" maintains the source far beyond our reach, at a dizzying distance from ordinary perception and certainly not in "any mountain-valley where poetry is made" [69], as Hartman would have it. The fertile plain at the end occupies the same position that the historical world occupies in the last lines of the Duddon sonnet, and is thus not a symbol of regeneration. Hartman reads the "hiding" as naturally beneficial, as the protective act of nature that makes possible a fertile continuation of the poem and of life, in contrast to the "unfathered vapour" that rejects the source in a supernatural realm. The hiding rather refers to the invisibility, the inwardness, the depth of a temporal consciousness that, when it reaches this level, can rejoice in the truth of its own insight and find thoughts "too deep for tears." If rivers are, for Wordsworth, privileged emblems for the awareness of our mortal nature, in contrast to the natural unity of echoes and correspondences, then the use of an allegorical river at this point can hardly be the sign of a renewed bond with nature.

Hartman speaks of the need for Wordsworth "to respect the natural (which includes the temporal) order" if his poetry is to continue "as narrative" [46]. The equation of natural with temporal seems to us to go against Wordsworth's most essential affirmation. He could well be characterized as the romantic poet in which the separation of time from nature is expressed with the greatest thematic clarity. The narrative order, in the short as well as in the longer poems, is no longer[16] linear; the natural movement of his rivers has to be reversed as well as transcended if they are to remain usable as metaphors. A certain form of narrative nevertheless persists, but it will have to adopt a much more intricate temporal movement than that of the natural cycles. The power that maintains the imagination, which Hartman calls nature returning after it has been nearly annihilated by apocalyptic insight, is time. The key to an understanding of Wordsworth lies in the relationship between imagination and time, not in the relationship between imagination and nature.

A late poem of Wordsworth's that appears among the otherwise truly sterile sequence of the *Ecclesiastical Sonnets* can well be used as a concluding illustration. Like all other romantic poets, Wordsworth claims a privileged status for poetic language—a formula which was most legitimately put into question during our last session[17] as standing in need of closer explanation. In Wordsworth, the privileged status of language is linked with the power of imagination, a faculty that rates higher than the fancy, or than rhetorical modes such as imitation, which, unlike the imagination, are dependent on correspondence with the natural world and thus limited by it. The language of imagination is privileged in terms of truth; it serves no empirical purposes or desires other than the truth of its own assertion:

> The mind beneath such banners militant
> Thinks not of spoils or trophies, nor of aught

That may assert its prowess, blest in thoughts
That are its own perfection and reward
Strong in itself . . .
    [1805 *Prelude*, VI, 543–47; 372]

This truth is not a truth about objects in nature but a truth about the self; imagination arises "before the eye and progress of my Song" [526], in the process of self-discovery and as self-knowledge. A truth about a self is best described, not in terms of accuracy, but in terms of authenticity; true knowledge of a self is knowledge that understands the self as it really is. And since the self never exists in isolation, but always in relation to entities, since it is not a thing but the common center of a system of relationships or intents, an authentic understanding of a self means first of all a description of the entities towards which it relates, and of the order of priority that exists among these entities. For Wordsworth, the relationships towards time have a priority over relationships towards nature; one finds, in his work, a persistent deepening of self-insight represented as a movement that begins in a contact with nature, then grows beyond nature to become a contact with time. The contact, the relationship with time, is, however, always a negative one for us, for the relationship between the self and time is necessarily mediated by death; it is the experience of mortality that awakens within us a consciousness of time that is more than merely natural. This negativity is so powerful that no language could ever name time for what it is; time itself lies beyond language and beyond the reach of imagination. Wordsworth can only describe the outward movement of time's manifestation, and this outward movement is necessarily one of dissolution, the "deathward progressing" of which Keats speaks in *The Fall of Hyperion*. To describe this movement of dissolution, as it is perceived in the privileged language of the imagination, is to describe it, not as an actual experience that would necessarily be as brusque and dizzying as a fall, but as the generalized statement of the truth of this experience in its universality. Dissolution thus becomes mutability, asserted as an *unfailing* law that governs the natural, personal, and historical existence of man. Thus to name mutability as a principle of order is to come as close as possible to naming the authentic temporal consciousness of the self. The late poem entitled "Mutability" comes as close as possible to being a language that imagines what is, in essence, unimaginable:

Mutability

From low to high doth dissolution climb,
And sinks from high to low, along a scale

Of awful notes, whose concord shall not fail;
A musical but melancholy chime,
Which they can hear who meddle not with crime,
Nor avarice, nor over-anxious care.
Truth fails not; but her outward forms that bear
The longest date do melt like frosty rime,
That in the morning whitened hill and plain
And is no more; drop like the tower sublime
Of yesterday, which royally did wear
Its crown of weeds, but could not even sustain
Some casual shout that broke the silent air,
Or the unimaginable touch of Time.
   [780]

NOTES

1. This essay is transcribed by Tom Keenan from a photocopy of the manuscript. It is the fourth in a series of six lectures on *Contemporary Criticism and the Problem of Romanticism* that de Man delivered at the Christian Gauss Seminar in Criticism at Princeton University in April and May 1967. The manuscript has been transcribed with almost no editing other than the addition of bibliographical information and all footnotes, minor grammatical changes, and the correction of quoted texts and titles. A few of de Man's more interesting deletions have been restored in the footnotes. All emphases and (parentheses) are de Man's; [square brackets] mark added material. The passages from the "second layer" of de Man's text quoted in footnotes 4, 9, 13, 14, and 16 were transcribed by Andrzej Warminski. A critical edition of the essay will be published along with the other Gauss lectures and other unpublished texts in a volume forthcoming from the University of Minnesota Press.

2. De Man refers here to the previous lectures in his Gauss series.

3. References to Hartman's text throughout this essay follow the pagination of *Wordsworth's Poetry 1787–1814* (New Haven and London: Yale UP, 1964).

4. The opening paragraphs seem to have been left out when de Man gave this lecture again (around 1971 or 1972). The new lecture began with some more informal remarks about what it means to read based on a version of the following notes:

   reading

      not declaim it—pure dramatic, vocal presence
      not analyze it structurally—as in Ruwet
         semantic, thematic element remains present in
         Jakobson/Riffaterre
      but read, which means that the thematic element remains
         taken into consideration

we look for the delicate area where the thematic, semantic field and the rhetorical structures begin to interfere with each other, begin to engage each other

they are not necessarily congruent, and it may be (it is, as a matter of fact, it *is* the case) that the thematic and the rhetorical structures are in conflict and that, in apparent complicity, they hide each other from sight

in truth, there are no poems that are not, at the limit, about this paradoxical and deceptive interplay between theme and figure; the thematization is always the thematization of an act of rhetorical deceit by which what seems to be a theme, a statement, a truth-referent, has substituted itself for a figure

I can't begin to prove this, but want to hint at what I mean by reading two Wordsworth poems

Wordsworth, because he is the anti-rhetorical, natural poet (i.e. thematic) par excellence, not only because he explicitly attacked the use of figure as *ornatus*, but also because the thematic seduction is particularly powerful, in its transparency and clarity—one gets very far very quickly by meditative participation

no one has reached the point where this question of Wordsworth's rhetoricity can begin to be asked, except Hartman.—

5. *Wordsworth: Poetry and Prose*, selected by W. M. Merchant (Cambridge: Harvard UP [The Reynard Library], 1955) 352–53. 1805 *Prelude*, V, 389 ff. Merchant prints only the 1805 edition of *The Prelude*. All quotations from Wordsworth and page references, unless otherwise noted, are from this edition (which de Man used) and will be included in the text.
6. Preface [1800]," in Wordsworth and Coleridge, *Lyrical Ballads 1798*, ed. W. J. B. Owen (London: Oxford UP, 1967), 150–79 at 167. De Man quotes from a section Wordsworth added for the 1802 addition.
7. Quoted in *The Norton Anthology of English Literature*, gen. ed. M. H. Abrams (New York: Norton, 1962), 2:152n5.
8. De Man's manuscript reads "Death men." Restoring portions crossed out in the manuscript, the sentence fragment reads: "Death men, as we all know from Western movies, tell no tales, but the same is not true of Western romantic poetry, which knows that the only interesting tale is to be told by a man who."
9. In the second version of the lecture, the final sentences of this paragraph seem to have been replaced by the following passage:

It is always possible to anticipate one's own epitaph, even to give it the size of the entire Prelude, but never possible to be both the one who wrote it and the one who reads it in the proper setting, that is, confronting one's grave as an event of the past. The proleptic vision is based, as we saw in the poem, on a metaphorical substitution of a first person subject by a third person subject, "the boy" for "I." In fact, this substitution is, of all substitutions, the one that is, thematically speaking, a radical impossibility: between the living and the dead self, no analogical resemblance or memory allows for any substitution whatever. The movement is only made possible by a linguistic sleight-of-hand in which the order of time is reversed, rotated around a pole called self (the grammatical subject [first and third persons] of the poem). The posterior events that are to occur to the first person, I, (usually death) are made into anterior events that have occurred to a third person, the boy. A pseudo-metaphorical and thematically inconceivable substitution of persons leads to a temporal reversal in which anteriority and posterity are inverted. The structural mechanics of metaphor (for, I repeat, the substitution of the dead he for the living I is thematically, literally, "unimaginable" and the metaphor is not a metaphor since it has no proper meaning, no *sens propre*, but only a metaphorical structure within the sign and devoid of meaning)—the structural mechanics of metaphor lead to the metonymic reversal of past and present that rhetoricians call metalepsis. The prolepsis of the Winander boy, a thematic concept— for we all know that we can proleptically anticipate empirical events, but not our death which is not for us an empirical event—is in fact metalepsis, a leap outside thematic reality into the rhetorical fiction of the sign. This leap cannot be represented, nor can it be reflected upon from within the inwardness of a subject. The reassurance expressed in the poem when the "uncertain" heaven is received in the lake or when the meditative surmise seems to promise the reflective time of the meditation is based on the rhetorical and not on thematic resources of language. It has no value as truth, only as figure. The poem does not reflect on death but on the rhetorical power of language that can make it seem as if we could anticipate the unimaginable.

This would also be the point at which we are beginning to "read" the poem, or to "read" Wordsworth according to the definition I gave at the start, namely to reach the point where the thematic turns rhetorical and the rhetorical turns thematic, while revealing that their apparent complicity is in fact hiding rather than revealing meaning.

10. A crossed-out clause here reads: "and with the understanding that what is here called immortality stands in fact for the anticipated experience of death."

11. Reading uncertain.

12. A sentence crossed out here reads: "Being the father of man, the child stands closer to death than we do."

13. In the second version, the final sentences of this paragraph (from "Stripped of whatever remnants . . .") seem to have been replaced by the following transitional passage:

The metaphor of the voyage, with its vast stellar and heliotropic movements of rising and setting suns and stars, here makes the link between life and death, origin and end and carries the burden of the promise. But this is precisely the metaphor that was "deconstructed" in the Winander boy, in which this kind of analogism is lost from the start and never recovered; as is often, but not always, the case, a poetic text like the Boy of Winander takes us closer to an actual "reading" of the poet than discursive statements of philosophical convictions and opinions, especially when these statements are themselves heavily dependent on metaphor.

Another brief poem by Wordsworth may make the movement we are trying to describe less abstract.

14. In the second version, the final sentences of this paragraph (beginning with "We see it therefore . . .") seem to have been replaced by the following passage:

Middle and end have been reversed by means of another metonymic figure in which history, contained within a larger dimension of time, becomes, in the poem, the container of a temporal movement that it claims to envelop, since it is present at the end of the text. But, again, as in the Boy of Winander, this metonymy of a content becoming a container, of an "enveloppé" becoming an "enveloppant," is a rhetorical device that does not correspond to a thematic, literal reality. When Wordsworth chooses to name mutability for what it is, in one of his most suggestive poems, the Mutability sonnet from the Ecclesiastical Sonnets, no historical triumphs are mentioned but only decay. It would take us a great deal more time and effort than we have available tonight to reveal the de-constructive rhetoricity of the Mutability poem; though it could be done. It would take us closer to an actual reading of Wordsworth, for which these remarks are only introductory exercises.

My entire exposition could be seen as a gloss on a sentence in Hartman's admirable book on Wordsworth in which he speaks of the need, for Wordsworth, "to respect the natural (which includes the temporal) order" if his poetry is to continue "as narrative." The narrative (which is itself metonymic) depends indeed on making the natural, thematic order appear as the container, the enveloppant, of time rather than as its content; the narrative is metonymic not because it is narrative but because it depends on metonymic substitution from the start. I can therefore totally subscribe to Hartman's reading of Wordsworth's strategy. The only thing I might

[Note that in this interpolated passage de Man seems to be re-reading his own metaphor of "enveloping" above (the more authentic temporality "envelops the other" in the fourth sentence of the paragraph), that is, is reading his own text rhetorically. Ed.]

15. The remainder of the sentence, crossed out here, reads: "and thus to become aware of the persistence of the movement that can then be asserted as an eternal truth, almost regardless of its negative connotation."

16. In the second version, the following passage was inserted (directly after the words "no longer") to replace the rest of the sentence:

a natural metaphor but a veiled metonymy. Wordsworth's most daring paradox, the claim to have named the most unnamable of experiences, "the unimaginable touch of time," is still based on a metonymic figure that, skillfully and effectively, appears in the disguise of a natural metaphor. In this least rhetorical of poets in which time itself comes so close to being a theme, the theme or meaning turns out to be more than ever dependent on rhetoric.

17. A lecture on Hölderlin as read by Heidegger.

JONATHAN WORDSWORTH

The Secret Strength of Things

And what were thou, and earth, and stars, and sea,
If to the human mind's imaginings
Silence and solitude were vacancy? (ll. 142–44)

Shelley concludes *Mont Blanc* not with a rhetorical gesture like the end of
the *West Wind*—"If winter comes, can spring be far behind?"—but with a
leading question that one tends to think of as requiring the answer, "nothing."
The single best-known fact about him, of course, is his atheism. Not only was
he sent down from Oxford for proclaiming it in a pamphlet, but in the summer of 1816—the period of *Mont Blanc*—he amused himself by writing "*a eos*"
after his name three times in different Alpine visitors'-books. Shocking as it
was to Byron and others, the word (or its English equivalent) didn't have quite
the modern implication of total disbelief. In Shelley's case atheism consisted of
a Blakean abhorrence of institutionalized Christianity, plus a scepticism that
refused steadfastly to worship a Divinity whose existence cannot be proved.
As he put it in a note to *Queen Mab* (1813): "God is an hypothesis, and, as
such, stands in need of proof. . . . From the phenomena, which are the objects
of our senses, we attempt to infer a cause, which we call God. . . . we invent
this general name, to conceal our ignorance of causes and essences . . ." (p. 51:
all citations refer to the Norton Critical Edition, ed. Donald H. Reiman and
Sharon Powers). The note concludes in a four-page quotation from Holbach's

From *The Wordsworth Circle* 18, no. 3 (Summer 1987): 99–107. Copyright © 1987 by Marilyn
Gaull.

Système de la Nature (1781), and Holbach had earlier made his way into both text and notes of *Queen Mab* under the heading of "necessity"—the hypothesis which alone can be proven from experience. Of the many different forms of necessitarianism that were current, Shelley's (and Holbach's) was the most drab. The various Calvinist sects of the period worshipped a God who had from eternity divided the human race into the elect and the damned, Priestleyan Unitarians looked forward (in Coleridge's words) to "the passing away of this earth and . . . our entering the state of pure intellect, when all Creation shall rest from its labours"; Godwin, on whom Shelley as a social reformer often depended, had been at different stages a minister in both Calvinist and Priestleyan congregations, and emerged in *Political Justice* (1793) with an allegedly secular millennium based on a most unreasonable faith in human reason. Shelley, by contrast, for all his social ideals, could allow himself nothing more exciting than the necessity of cause and effect: "He who asserts the doctrine of Necessity means that, contemplating the events which compose the moral and material universe, he beholds only an immense and uninterrupted chain of causes and effects, no one of which could occupy any other place than it does occupy . . ." (*Norton*, p. 50).

If one returns with these notes in mind to the conclusion of *Mont Blanc*, everything seems to fall into place: the final question, it would seem, undercuts any transcendental interpretations of the landscape, relegating not just God, but all perception of the numinous, to "the human mind's imaginings." Shelley, the atheist, is aghast at the guidebook eulogies, and the more sophisticated tradition of the religious sublime (on which Angela Leighton in *Shelley and the Sublime* [1984], pp. 1–24, has written so well). He has designed a poem that will flout the standard responses, just as he had written his pamphlet flouting Christianity while still an undergraduate. There was much provocation to do so. As early as 1739, Gray had written of the Alpine landscape, "Not a precipice, not a torrent, not a cliff, but is pregnant with religion and poetry. There are certain scenes that would awe an atheist into belief . . ." (Gray to West, Nov. 16, 1739), and it is fairly certain that Shelley had with him in Switzerland a copy of Coleridge's *Friend*, containing the ecstatic *Hymn Before Sunrise in the Vale of Chamouni*:

> Motionless torrents! silent cataracts!
> Who made you glorious, as the Gates of Heaven . . . ?
> GOD! let the torrents, like a shout of nations,
> Answer! and let the ice-plains echo, GOD!

In the face of such euphoria Shelley might be forgiven for wishing to assert the opposite view, and it may well have been his original intention to do so. But the poem itself (necessarily, no doubt) becomes rather more complex. Even the final signing-off is worth looking at in greater detail:

> The secret strength of things
> Which governs thought, and to the infinite dome
> Of heaven is as a law, inhabits thee!
> And what were thou, and earth, and stars, and sea,
> If to the human mind's imaginings
> Silence and solitude were vacancy?

Donald Reiman comments in his notes to the *Norton* Shelley: "The clause, [The secret strength of things / That governs thought, and to the infinite dome / Of heaven is as a law] states that the *Power* that generates *things* and is the law of nature, also *governs thought*—that mind is ultimately subordinate to the *remote, serene and inaccessible* force that originates the amoral cycles of Necessity."

Notes have a way of denuding poetry of its mystery—and as an editor I must often have been guilty of doing so—but it seems to me that this note destroys both the larger meanings and the balance of Shelley's lines. "The *Power* that generates *things*" seems a reductive translation, and has the effect of identifying "the secret strength" too completely with references to "Power" earlier in the poem—Shelley could have repeated himself, but he didn't, he invented a phrase that was strange and new. His philosophical statements make no concessions; the purpose of the poem seems to have been the flouting of Christian assumptions; and the last lines imply that qualities and values perceived in the natural world are the result merely of projection. And yet the language is full of numinous possibility, and the sources from which it derives imply a concern in the poet that he would surely have denied.

"If one no longer believes in God (as truth)," Wallace Stevens wrote in August, 1940, "it is not possible merely to disbelieve; it becomes necessary to believe in something else. . . . A good deal of my poetry recently has concerned an identity for that thing. . . . In [*Asides on the Oboe*] I say that one's final belief must be in a fiction. I think that the history of belief will show that it has always been in a fiction." To which he adds, two months later, "The major poetic idea in the world is and always has been the idea of God. . . . The poetry that created the idea of God will either adapt it to our different intelligence, or create a substitute for it, or make it unnecessary" (*Letters*, ed. Holly Stevens [1981], pp. 370 and 378). Shelley is clearly incapable of making the idea of God unnecessary: like Stevens he no longer believes in the Divinity "as truth," and finds it "necessary to believe in something else." Presumably, however, he would have agreed that "the major poetic idea in the world . . . [has always] been the idea of God," and much of his writing shows him concerned to identify the "something else" adapted to his own different intelligence. Yet, despite the final lines of *Mont Blanc*, he would hardly have accepted that "one's final belief *must* be a fiction." Stevens, as an atheist in the more modern sense of the word, and writing 124 years later, can value as fact what to Shelley—for all the bravado—is still an appalling thought. Like *The Prelude* (which he knew only in small fragments, printed in *The Friend*), Shelley's poetry tests and extends the possibilities of belief, pushing it sometimes very close to wish-fulfillment, but never consciously fictionalizing it in the sense that Stevens intends. If he cannot accept the personal God of his contemporaries, it is *as truth* that the "something else" will have to be believed in.

Shelley's definition of "the secret strength *of things*" takes us back to "The everlasting universe *of things*" in the opening line, and beyond that to the Wordsworth whom he did know—the poet who had written not merely of a human power to "see into the life *of things*," but of a world permeated by the presence of the One Life:

> A motion and a spirit that impels
> All thinking things, all objects of all thought,
> And rolls through all *things*. (*Tintern Abbey*, 101–03)

Standing on his bridge over the River Arve on 22 July—or, more probably, writing in Geneva a few days later—Shelley fastens on the Wordsworthian use of "things." At the same time he takes the river-image that is implied in "rolls through all things" back to its source in the opening lines of *Tintern Abbey*:

> Five years have passed, five summers with the length
> Of five long winters, and again I hear
> These waters *rolling* from their mountain springs
> With a sweet inland murmur . . . (ll. 1–4)

Shelley's purpose, one assumes, is to deny (or replace) the Wordsworthian God in Nature, and nothing could be further from the "sweet inland murmur" than a vast Alpine torrent that "Over its rocks ceaselessly bursts and raves." We do not, however, confront the Arve directly at the beginning of *Mont Blanc*; the river in its actuality emerges through a ramifying series of metaphors which have as their subject not landscape, but the human mind:

> The everlasting universe of things
> Flows through the mind, and rolls its rapid waves
> (Now dark, now glittering; now reflecting gloom,

Now lending splendour) where from secret springs
The source of human thought its tribute brings
Of waters—with a sound but half its own . . . (ll. 1–6)

Political condemnation in Shelley's sonnet *To Wordsworth* and *Upon Receiving a Celandine* has obscured the fact that his admiration for the earlier poetry of Wordsworth was at its height in this period. He had not merely been reading the 1815 *Collected Poems*, but (as Medwin reports) "dosing" Byron with them—and it is of course *Tintern Abbey* that interfuses Canto III of *Childe Harold*. Given what Neville Rogers has described as Shelley's "natural Platonism," it is likely that he saw in Wordsworth's early pantheism an enviable certainty—the expression of a faith to which he was instinctively drawn, but which intellectual scepticism made it impossible fully to accept.

The immanent God who is both "motion" and "spirit," and who for the Wordsworth of July, 1798, had "roll[ed] through all things" ("thinking" and otherwise), is replaced in the opening lines of *Mont Blanc* by a river of sense-experience flowing through the individual mind. Such experience may be either dark or glittering, but is as capable of reflecting gloom as it is of lending splendour. Logically, gloom reflected by the surface of the river of experience seems likely to be the "sober colouring" of the eye, or mind, through which it passes, and Shelley's third major borrowing from *Tintern Abbey*—the "sound but half its own"—shows him, as one would expect, to be pondering Wordsworth's reference to

the mighty world of eye and ear,
Both what they half-create, and what perceive . . . (ll. 106–07)

In the opening of *Mont Blanc* he has achieved, more successfully even than Wordsworth himself, the interchange of natural and symbolic that is the appropriate image (or poetic reflection) of the half-way state between creation and perception. As Coleridge had defined it in the *Shakespeare Lectures* of 1811–12, there is "a middle state of mind more strictly appropriate to the imagination than any other, when it is, as it were, hovering between images" (ed. Raysor [1930], pp. ii and 138). As "the source of human thought" brings its "tribute" of waters to merge into the great river of experience (which must itself flow through the mind), the reader is at first delighted by the power of analogy. Almost at once, however, the analogy becomes engulfed in the immediacy of the visual image. Only for it to emerge in the opening of Section Two that Shelley has been using his metaphor to establish the actuality of the scene in which he stands—to all intents and purposes, the vast metaphorical river *is* the Ravine of Arve:

> where from secret springs
> The source of human thought its tribute brings
> Of waters—with a sound but half its own,
> Such as a feeble brook will oft assume
> In the wild woods, among the mountains lone,
> Where waterfalls around it leap for ever,
> Where woods and winds contend, and a vast river
> Over its rocks ceaselessly bursts and raves.
>   *Thus thou*, Ravine of Arve, dark deep ravine . .

Though figurative from the outset, Shelley's language has established the landscape of his poem. It has established too the role of the mind as meeting-place of experience and thought—at once percipient of "The everlasting universe of things," and capable of bringing its own independent tribute. Representing individuality, the brook is inevitably "feeble," but though the implied observer standing on its banks will hear a noise that belongs partly to the nearby torrent and its surroundings, the waters of human thought do have a voice of their own: they well up from "secret springs" within the self, and astonishingly they contribute half of the total sound.

F. R. Leavis, who had a way of noticing the qualities of a piece of writing, then drawing unwarranted moral conclusions, commented in *Revaluation* (1936) on the opening lines of *Mont Blanc*: "The metaphorical and the actual, the real and the imagined, the inner and the outer, could hardly be more unsortably and indistinguishably confused. The setting, of course, provides special excuse for bewildered confusion; but Shelley takes eager advantage of the excuse, and the confusion is characteristic" (pp. 212–13). To which he added grudgingly, "what might be found unusual in *Mont Blanc* is a certain compelling vividness." Leaving aside the talk of excuses, the word that stands out in these comments as especially misguided is "unsortably"—"*unsortably* and indistinguishably confused." Shelley has suffered more than most from those who think that poetry should be sorted. In its boldest, most imaginative effects, *Mont Blanc* cannot be categorized:

> Thus, thou, Ravine of Arve—dark deep ravine—
> Thou many-coloured, many-voiced vale
> Over whose pines, and crags, and caverns sail
> Fast cloud-shadows and sunbeams: awful scene
> Where Power in likeness of the Arve comes down
> From the ice gulphs that gird his secret throne,
> Bursting through these dark mountains like the flame
> Of lightning through the tempest . . .

If we were offered the Arve coming down in the likeness of an abstract Power, it would be a conventional simile; as it is Power (capitalized as a personification, and crowned in the following line by the possession of a "secret throne") comes down in likeness of the river, which nonetheless maintains its actuality, ceaselessly raving at the foot of the mountain. There is no confusion. Shelley's reversal of expectation allows the reader to create the simile if he chooses (and hang onto the expected meaning), but at the same time it asserts a larger and stranger possibility which the poetry does not seek, or need, to define.

Though there have been important counter-attacks—notably Spencer Hall's in *Studies in Philology* (1970), pp. 199–221—an orthodoxy has been created by Earl Wasserman's *Subtler Language* (1959) that reads *Mont Blanc* in terms of the *Essay on Life*. According to the variant of Berkeley described in the *Essay* as "the Intellectual Philosophy," there can be no inherent difference between thoughts and things. To put it in Shelley's own words: "Nothing exists but as it is perceived. The difference is merely nominal between those two classes of thought which are vulgarly distinguished by the names of ideas and of external objects." "Pursuing the same thread of reasoning," he continues (moving across to what may seem to the rest of us a decidedly *different* train of thought),

> the existence of distinct individual minds similar to that which is employed in now questioning its own nature, is likewise found to be a delusion. The words 'I', 'you', 'they', are not signs of any actual difference subsisting between the assemblage of thoughts thus indicated, but are merely marks employed to denote the different modifications of the one mind. (*Norton*, pp. 477–78)

Individual human minds are, to use the Christian terms of Coleridge's *Religious Musings*, "parts and proportions of one wond'rous whole." Shelley in the final sentences of his *Essay*, however, makes it clear that his "one mind" is *not* the Unitarian God (Coleridge's "one omnipresent Mind / Omnific, [whose] most holy name is Love"), *not* the creator of life—in fact, *not* to be seen as an active force within the universe at all: "Mind, as far as we have any experience of its properties—and beyond that experience, how vain is argument—cannot create, it can only perceive" (*Norton*, p. 478).

Wasserman's view of *Mont Blanc* is beautifully argued, and in its own terms extremely persuasive:

> By means of a river, a stream of thought, the valley of the mind, and the attendant scenic images, the poet calls into symbolic form the

Intellectual Philosophy, the essence of which is that mind and world, thought and thing, are meaningless distinctions, since they are only biased and partial versions of a unity, but that in order to give this unity linguistic form it is necessary to express it from both biases simultaneously. . . . The poem is the product of the poet's urge so to reconstitute his available language that it will, not express, but inherently contain that philosophy, and thereby open the otherwise closed doors to the dark corridors of thought that lie beyond ordinary conception. By creating the language of the Intellectual Philosophy, the poet can think *with* it. (*The Subtler Language* [rpt. 1979], p. 208)

Once Wasserman's basic premises are granted, his argument is irrefutable: the message of *Mont Blanc* is the message of the *Essay on Life*; the poetry is an attempt to reconstitute language and think beyond the barriers of prose; and if at times the poem seems to imply a dualism that is denied by the *Essay*, that is because unity is to be given its symbolic form through the simultaneous expression of opposing ways of thought.

But perhaps the premises need not be granted. The Norton editor (who, it should be said, accepts Wasserman's reading) offers late 1819 as the date of the *Essay on Life*, it would surely be odd that the Intellectual Philosophy should find its expression three years earlier in *Mont Blanc*, and scarcely at all in the interim? Could Wasserman, one wonders, ever have arrived at his subtle language without a knowledge of the *Essay*? The first line-and-a-half of the poem must be the test case: "The everlasting universe of things / Flows through the mind." If Shelley had intended us to see the mind in question as the One Mind, wouldn't he have made it a little more obvious? In effect Wasserman wishes us to rearrange the line, and read, "The universe of things flows through / The everlasting mind," but that is not what Shelley wrote. Spencer Hall points out that Wasserman had his precursors, but I can't believe that many readers have leapt to his conclusions. It is so much easier to see the mind as human, and regard it as the meeting-place of the external world experienced through the senses, and the thought (in Coleridge's or Wordsworth's terms, the imagination) that wells up within the individual to modify his perception. Because his local criticism is so good, and his probing of language so meticulous, Wasserman's chapter stands as by far the most impressive discussion of *Mont Blanc*, and his conclusions, though couched in terms of a preoccupation with the *Essay on Life* are frequently just. But there is a level of complexity—of super-subtlety—in his argument that is made necessary by his will to see the poem as denying the reality of the landscape with which the poet's mind is shown to be interacting. "Even though the independent existence of an objective world," he writes at one point, has been only pretended, that world insists upon acting out symbolically the ontology of the Intellectual System, and thereby denies its own exclusive reality. (p. 218)

Well, maybe.

There is a sameness about philosophical interpretation that responds very little to mood, tones, pleasure, within the poetry, and after a while becomes decidedly humourless. Dr. Johnson, for one, would have found amusement in a poet *pretending* that the world in which he lives has a separate existence—and worlds that deny their own exclusive reality by *insisting* on acting out symbolic ontologies seem a fairly extreme form of the pathetic fallacy. Shelley could be humourless too, of course, but *Mont Blanc* is a poem of delightfully changing mood; often it is quite as relevant to speak of fantasy being acted out, as ontology. Shelley's first attempt to create a god for the mountain had been at once powerful and openly whimsical, tailored to the "sci.fic." determinism of Peacock, to whom he was writing: "Do you who assert the supremacy of Ahriman [the spirit of evil] imagine him throned among these desolating snows, among these palaces of death and frost, sculptured in this their terrible magnificence by the unsparing hand of necessity, and that he casts around him as his first essays of his final usurpation avalanches, torrents, rocks and thunders—and above all, these deadly glaciers, at once the proofs and the symbols of his reign?" (*Letters*, ed. Jones [1964], p. 499).

Two days later—while still at Chamouni, and still writing the letter to Peacock that would become part of the *Six Weeks Tour* and lead up to the first publication of his poem—Shelley produced a far more terrible, and more imaginative fantasy. This time, the mountain itself became animate: "One would think that Mont Blanc was a living being, and that frozen blood forever circulated slowly through his stony veins." It is the writer of this letter, not the author of the *Essay on Life* (or, for that matter, of the footnotes to *Queen Mab*), who describes the

> awful scene,
> Where Power in likeness of the Arve comes down
> From the ice-gulphs that gird his secret throne,
> Bursting through these dark mountains like the flame
> Of lightning through the tempest . . . (ll. 15–19)

Shelley, it seems, is not so appalled by the Arve's more obvious display of force, as by the power of the glaciers, beautifully symbolised in the blood that is frozen yet circulating still (and forever) through the veins of the mountain. His image of kingship in the lines quoted is closer to the fantasy of Ahriman, "throned among these desolating snows"; but where Ahriman casts around him torrents, rocks and thunders like Jove of old, the Power that comes down "in likeness of the Arve" is at once less personal and more numinous. He has his throne (and his gender), but at the same time he is present as an abstraction of the power which the Ravine embodies—diffused, one might say, as an immanent yet undivided God, Wordsworth's "motion and . . . spirit" which both "impels," and "rolls through," two different orders of Creation. One cannot know whether it is intended to do so, but Shelley's idiom guards him against the solemn critical assumptions. He cannot be held to *believe* in a Power seated on a secret throne girded by ice-gulphs, and it is anyone's guess how great is the wish that his fantasy hides, or reveals.

Mont Blanc is not about the Universal Mind and the Intellectual Philosophy—for all his subtlety and acumen, Wasserman has misled his readers; and the Norton editor, by adopting his position so singlemindedly in the notes, has misled many thousands more—it is about imagination, the human power that in response to human need invests the material world with spiritual significance. Shelley does not make Coleridge's firm distinction between imagination and fancy: for him, as for Wordsworth, fancy shades into the higher power. In his account of the Ravine of Arve, we have at first a viewpoint that is openly fanciful—thrones girded by ice-gulphs, pines that (like Tolkien's tree-people, the *ents*) are "children of elder time," winds that come in religious devotion to savour the incense of the pines and respond to their "old and solemn harmony." Already in this last phrase, however, the poetry is felt to be merging into fantasy that is, in a fuller sense of the word, imaginative: the "unsculptured image" behind the veil of the waterfall, that speaks of undefined potential, and the "strange sleep" which, replacing the mysterious "voices of the desert," has power to "wrap all in its own deep eternity." Shelley is to be seen externalising—first whimsically, then with increasing seriousness—the moods and powers of his own mind. The "strange sleep" of line 27 will reappear as the "trance sublime and strange," the reverie in which the poet turns the Ravine of Arve into an image of his "own separate phantasy."

Reiman's note at this point instructs us to see "the poet explor[ing] the relationship of his own seeming individual identity . . . to the Universal or One Mind, of which all minds are parts" (*Norton*, p. 89). I suspect, however, that Shelley uses the phrase "My own separate fantasy" to make a quite ordinary distinction, not between his own mind and a higher one, but between his own in two different aspects: as creator/perceiver on the one hand, and observer on the other. In his reverie he turns the Arve, which had first been presented as an image of superhuman power, into an image of his own mental process, as seen from a position of detachment.

One could say that for a moment he takes on the kingly, or godlike, role, sending forth his imagination to dominate the landscape of the mind, as the Arve dominates the physical scene that surrounds him. But this implication is subdued by the musing tones of the verse, and by the stress that is laid on passivity in the lines that follow:

> when I gaze on thee,
> I seem as in a trance sublime and strange,
> To muse on my own separate phantasy,
> My own, my human mind, which passively
> Now renders and receives fast influencings,
> Holding an unremitting interchange
> With the clear universe of things around . . . (ll. 35–40)

Standing back from his mind—not willing it to do, or be, anything, but watching it in complete detachment—Shelley sees it as passive not just in its reception, but in its rendering, of influence. To use the terms of the opening lines of the poem, he is watching a river whose waters are composed both of "the everlasting universe of things" (sense experience), and of the tributary of human thought. Now, however, it seems that the "feeble brook" of human individuality lays claim to rather more than half the total volume of sound. Except to the eye of the observer, the mind is in no sense passive. "Renders" noticeably, and rightly, takes prominence over "receives." The poetry enacts the dominance of imagination which it also portrays.

The question preoccupying Shelley, the observer of his own creative process, is the relation, not of the individual to the Universal Mind, but of art and truth—as Keats would have it, of truth and beauty. In apposition to "My own separate phantasy" and "my own, my human mind" is a third, less flattering phrase, "one legion of wild thoughts." Shelley's lines are a good deal simpler than one might assume from reading his commentators, but do need to be read with attention:

> One legion of wild thoughts, whose wandering wings
> Now float above thy darkness, and now rest
> Where that, or thou, art no unbidden guest
> In the still cave of the witch Poesy . . . (ll. 41–44)

"The witch Poesy," we are told in the Norton footnote, "personifies the imagination; only in the stillness of her cave—within the mind—can the individual communicate with 'that' [i.e.] 'the clear universe of things', or 'thou' [i.e.] the Universal Mind." "Note," the editor continues, heaping

confusion upon confusion, "that the syntax is ambiguous, leaving the possibility that these [the 'clear universe' and the Universal Mind] may be either
two separate entities, or only one" (*Norton*, p. 90).

The idea that Shelley in his use of the pronoun "thou" is addressing
the Universal Mind has no basis in the poem: it is perfectly clear, indeed,
from lines 12, 15, 19, 25, 30, 32, 33, and 35, that in this section he is consistently addressing the Ravine. So much for "thou" in line 43—"Where that,
or thou, art no unbidden guest"—what of the "that"? Reiman's answer takes
us back three lines to "the clear universe of things," because this can be made
to square with the Wasserman reconstruction. It also strains the syntax, and
ignores "thy darkness" in the previous line, which is Shelley's obvious referent:

> Now float above *thy darkness*, and now rest
> Where *that* . . .

Why then the darkness, and why should it, or the Ravine, be "no unbidden
guest"?

The Ravine has by this time been a guest in the poet's cave for 45 lines;
but "darkness" is a new element. The "wild thoughts" float above it, seemingly
unable to penetrate, and the word surely has both its normal associations—
of mystery, or the unknown—and a more specific reference to the darkness
which for Plato characterises human vision. In his version of the Cave from
The Republic, Shelley seeks among poetic visions that are ghosts of a higher
reality for "some phantom" or "faint image" that will tell him about the Power
of which the Ravine is symbolic:

> Seeking among the shadows that pass by,
> Ghosts of all things that are, some shade of thee,
> Some phantom, some faint image, till the breast
> From which they fled recalls them, thou art there! (ll. 45–48)

Intent on reading the final "thou art there" as an allusion to the Universal
Mind, Reiman and others take "they" and "them" to refer to the "shadows"
that are "Ghosts of all things that are." They therefore have to think in
terms of a supernatural source, from which they fled, and which is anthro-
pomorphised by the poet as a breast. As usual, there is a simpler explanation:
the breast is Shelley's; "they" refers to the "legion of wild thoughts" that float
above the darkness of the Arve. Till he recalls the wild thoughts (by coming
out of his reverie), the Ravine that he has throughout been addressing, and
the mystery that surround it, are to be found within the Cave of Poesy; that
is, they are subject to the imagination—half, perhaps, created by it.

In simple terms, such as could never be true to the poem itself, Shelley is claiming that his art bears the same relation to truth as the shadows in Plato's Cave. Through it the incomprehensible may to some extent be comprehended, the ideal glimpsed. In this Wordsworthian/Coleridgean poem, reverie (later disparaged in the *Essay on Life*) is associated with poetry as a means to the perception of truth. It is analogous too to the "gleams of a remoter world" which have been thought by some to visit the soul in sleep. As Shelley begins his third section it is clear that he has in mind not just Plato, but Wordsworth's most Platonic poem. He is writing about intimations of immortality—not so much intimations of an afterlife, as those visionary glimpses that help to show the present one in its relation to the eternal:

> Some say that gleams of a remoter world
> Visit the soul in sleep—that death is slumber,
> And that its shapes the busy thoughts outnumber
> Of those who wake and live. I look on high;
> Has some unknown omnipotence unfurled
> The veil of life and death? Or do I lie
> In dream, and does the mightier world of sleep
> Spread far around and inaccessibly
> Its circles? (ll. 49–57)

The central myth of *Intimations* had shown sleep as oblivion—"Our birth is but a sleep and a forgetting"—but the numinous alternative view had already been beautifully evoked in stanza three: "The winds come to me from the fields of sleep." Shelley's development of this central metaphor has been ignored by commentators anxious to have their say about the veil of life and death. Early in the poem there is the "strange sleep" of l. 27, that "Wraps all in its own deep eternity," together with its personal equivalent, the "trance sublime and strange" of 35; now the association of sleep with higher truth is taken a step further as it comes to be equated with death.

It may be useful to spell out in detail the stages of Shelley's analogy. Basically, they are five: (1.) In his reverie at the end of Section Two, the poet seeks amid the shadows, ghosts, phantoms that inhabit the creative mind, for an image of the higher reality which the voice and power of the Ravine have seemed to embody. (2.) Adopting a speculative tone reminiscent of Coleridge's *Eolian Harp*—

> And what if all of animated Nature
> Be but organic harps diversely framed . . . (ll. 44–45)

—Shelley introduces the analogy of the soul visited in sleep by gleams of otherworldly truth. (3.) Death is offered as the extreme example of this active sleep, a state that is inherently more creative (more capable, that is, of imaginative "shaping") than the living and waking mind. (4.) Looking up for the first time in the poem to Mont Blanc, Shelley asks whether the veil of mortality, seemingly lifted during his earlier reverie, has now again descended to obscure his vision. (5.) Alternatively, is he surrounded by the world of sleep and truth, yet himself in a dream (like Albion's dream in *Vala*) that renders truth inaccessible, separates him from the eternal?

If Section Two belongs to the Ravine, and to the mind of which it becomes the image, Section Three presents a takeover by the mountain, and a corresponding abasement of the mind, "Driven like a homeless cloud from steep to steep." Power and kingship, earlier associated with the Ravine (though carefully never said to belong to it), are now seen to be vested in the mountain:

> Far, far above, piercing the infinite sky,
> Mont Blanc appears, still, snowy and serene.
> Its subject mountains their unearthly forms
> Pile around it, ice and rock; broad vales between
> Of frozen floods, unfathomable deeps
> Blue as the overhanging heaven . . . (ll. 60–65)

Ice-gulphs once said to gird the throne of Power, now reappear as part of a landscape subject to the mountain. Mont Blanc, meanwhile, "piercing the infinite sky," is in touch with the eternal from which the poet has been excluded, and even its subject mountains take on unearthly forms. The whimsical voice, heard in parts of Section Two, returns as Shelley evokes the force (and perhaps the caprice) needed in the past to shape the scene that is now serene and still:

> Is this the scene
> Where the old Earthquake Demon taught her young
> Ruin? Were these her toys? Or did a sea
> Of fire envelope once this silent snow?
> None can reply. All seems eternal now. (ll. 71–75)

The "seems" in this last phrase is important: Shelley is tentative. And yet it is at this point that he feels able to make his largest, and oddest, claim. The mysterious voice of the wilderness can teach either doubt or faith—*faith* which (whatever the difficulties of the text) is clearly Wordsworthian in reconciling man and Nature, or *doubt*, which is no less "awful," and which we assume to represent Shelley's own position. To what extent a distinction is being made between the mountain and its surrounding wilderness it is impossible to know, but it is to *Mont Blanc* itself that Shelley returns with the climactic words:

> Thou hast a voice, great mountain, to repeal
> Large codes of fraud and woe—not understood
> By all, but which the wise, and great, and good
> Interpret, or make felt, or deeply feel. (ll. 80–83)

Among the codes that Shelley is certain to have in mind are the twin "testaments" of Christianity, both associated with the special sanctity of the mountain: the Ten Commandments, brought down by Moses from his meeting with the Voice of God on Mount Sinai, and their replacement in Christ's Sermon on the Mount. Repealing these established codes, responsible in his view (as in Blake's) for many centuries of fraud and woe, Shelley offers a voice that belongs not to God, or to the Son of God—or even to man—but to the mountain itself. It may not be understood by all, but it is nonetheless accessible to those who have ears to hear, and its message can be passed on to others. Scholars who interpret this poem as a philosophical tract should take note of its central statement: "which the wise, and great, and good / Interpret, or *make felt*, or *deeply feel*." The assumptions are purely Wordsworthian:

> Love now an universal birth,
> From heart to heart is stealing,
> From earth to man, from man to earth
> It is *the hour of feeling*.
>   (*Lyrical Ballads*, 1798)

>   in all things
> He saw one life, and *felt* that it was joy.
>   (*Excursion* Book I, 1814)

The reader cannot be too often reminded that poetry is passion: it is the history or science of *feelings* (Preface to *Lyrical Ballads*, 1800).

In his emphasis on feeling as the mode of perception, and the means of sharing truth, Shelley may or may not have been taking up a consciously Wordsworthian position; but there can be no doubt that as he moves on into Section Four, Wordsworth is in his thoughts. Twelve lines at the opening of the section are used to evoke different aspects of the changeful world, natural and human, and come to a climax in a version of *Tintern Abbey*'s "All thinking things, all objects of all thought":

> All things that move and breathe, with toil and sound,
> Are born and die, revolve, subside and swell. (ll. 94–95)

Though there is a full stop at this point in both the printed text of 1817 and the manuscript, no main verb has been included. The whole passage carries forward to depend on "dwells" in the line that follows: "Power *dwells* apart in its tranquility." "And I have *felt* / A presence," Wordsworth had written in *Tintern Abbey*,

> that disturbs me with the joy
> Of elevated thoughts—a sense sublime
> Of something far more deeply interfused,
> Whose *dwelling* is the light of setting suns,
> And the round ocean, and the living air,
> And the blue sky, and in the mind of man . . . (ll. 94–100)

In place of the Wordsworthian "presence," we have precisely absence— "Power dwells apart"—but there is the same anthropomorphism, and the reappearance of "dwelling" is important as Shelley moves on to assert his contrary message:

> Power dwells apart in its tranquility,
> Remote, serene, and inaccessible;
> And *this*, the naked countenance of earth,
> On which I gaze—even these primaeval mountains—
> Teach the adverting mind. The glaciers creep
> Like snakes that watch their prey, from their far fountains,
> Slow rolling on . . . (ll. 96–102)

"Slow *rolling* on": the verb seems an odd one for masses of ice that crunch and inch their way along. The snaky glaciers, however, provide a godless necessitarian alternative to the "motion and spirit" which in *Tintern Abbey* "impels / All thinking things . . . And *rolls* through all things." Shelley's use of italics to emphasize the wisdom he has learned—"And *this* the naked countenance of earth . . ."—quietly draws attention to the message that Wordsworth's gazing might have extracted from primeval mountains. For once, Shelley has been willing to "Let Nature be [his] teacher," but he has deduced a very different moral. With Wordsworth still in mind, he takes us next into "A city of death," that first solidifies the cloudscape New Jerusalem of *Excursion*, Book II, turning the airy promise of eternal life into "dome, pyramid and pinnacle . . . distinct with many a tower / And wall impregnable of beaming ice," and then astonishingly liquefies the "wall[s] impregnable" so that he may return to his image of the mighty, and *rolling*, river:

> Yet not a city, but a flood of ruin
> Is there, that from the boundaries of the sky
> Rolls its perpetual stream . . . (ll. 102–04)

Like almost every part of this extraordinary poem, the apocalyptic lines that follow are worth looking at in detail—not least for their Blakean reworking of *The Ruined Cottage* (*Excursion*, Book I)—but I have time only to draw attention briefly to the curious re-entry of Coleridge, who alongside Wordsworth is the support of Shelley's unspoken redemptive implications:

> Below, vast caves
> Shine in the rushing torrents' restless gleam,
> Which from those secret chasms in tumult welling

[*Kubla Khan* had presumably been introduced to Shelley by Byron.]

> Meet in the vale, and one majestic river,
> The breath and blood of distant lands, for ever
> *Rolls* its loud waters to the ocean waves,
> Breathes its swift vapours to the circling air. (ll. 120–26)

Wordsworth had been transformed to a city of death, Coleridge is positively revived, as the Alph, no longer sinking in tumult to a lifeless ocean, turns into the Rhone, source of fertility in distant France. It too "rolls," of course, linking us back not just to *Tintern Abbey*, but to the opening lines, as for the last time in the poem "The everlasting universe of things" *flows* through the poet's mind.

Stanzas Three and Four both evoke the destructive powers at work shaping the Alpine landscape. Three deals with the past, replacing a Christian teleology of mountains formed by the departing waters of the Flood, with an old Earthquake Demon and a fantasy of Pagan caprice. Four deals with the present, evoking a Necessity that is at first dispassionate, then malignant (in the strangely disproportionate image of the snakes), then unexpectedly beneficent. But however comforting it may be that death-dealing glaciers are doers of distant good, this great poem of the imagination cannot end with social reflections. If it is to have a conclusion, it has to be about a way of seeing. We return therefore to the mountain, left "piercing the infinite sky" at line 60:

> Mont Blanc yet gleams on high: the power is there,
> The still and solemn power of many sights,
> And many sounds, and much of life and death. (ll. 127–29)

The "visionary gleam" persists, but what claims is Shelley finally able to make? The words "and much of life and death" seem a little desperate, and it is by no means clear how the "still and solemn power" of Mont Blanc will link through to the concluding lines from which this lecture started:

> And what were thou, and earth, and stars, and sea,
> If to the human mind's imaginings
> Silence and solitude were vacancy? (ll. 142–44)

We are brought, it seems, to the edge of the void—to what Blake would have called "the margin of non-entity." But in fact, despite his use of the belittling plural, "Imaginings," Shelley has made it impossible that at this stage in the poem silence and solitude should be taken for vacancy. All three words are defined by their opposites, by what they are not, but whereas vacancy—the absence of matter itself—is the ultimate horror of solipsism, the absence of sound, and the absence of human life, have been invested by the poetry with power and mystery:

> In the calm darkness of the moonless nights,
> In the lone glare of day, the snows descend
> Upon that mountain; none beholds them there,
> Nor when the flakes burn in the sinking sun,
> Or the star-beams dart through them. Winds contend
> Silently there, and heap the snow with breath
> Rapid and strong, but silently! (ll. 130–36)

"Coleridge is in my thoughts," Shelley had written to Peacock a week before (on 17 July), and it is nowhere more evident than in this concluding section of *Mont Blanc*. There can be no doubt that he is specifically recalling the use of repetition in *Hymn Before Sunrise*:

> but thou, most awful form!
> Risest from forth thy *silent* sea of pines
> How *silently* . . . (ll. 5–7)

But the movement of the verse, and the flakes that burn in the sinking sun, also take us appropriately to the central lines of *This Lime-Tree Bower My Prison*:

> Ah, slowly sink
> Behind the western ridge, thou glorious sun!
> Shine in the *slant beams of the sinking orb*
> Ye purple heath-flowers! *richlier burn ye clouds!*
> Live in the yellow light, ye distant groves,
> And kindle thou blue ocean! (ll. 32–37)

Shelley recollects the passage in lines that value—or attempt to value—the total self-sufficiency of Nature. His language, however, is rich with the associations that he is apparently hoping to suppress. The winds are a case in point. They may contend, but unlike the "Winds thwarting winds, bewildered and forlorn" of Wordsworth's *Simplon Pass*, they do so amid a Coleridgean sense of purpose, heaping the snow in silence, and at the same time performing a "secret ministry" akin to that in *Frost at Midnight*. Brooding over the snow, the "voiceless lightning" is another symbol of power tamed to a purpose:

> Its home
> The voiceless lightning in these solitudes
> Keeps innocently, and like vapour broods
> Over the snow. The secret strength of things
> That governs thought, and to the infinite dome
> Of heaven is as a law, inhabits thee! (ll. 136–41)

Shorn of its thunder, and taking on the purity that is associated with the snow, the lightning is a version of the lion lying down with the lamb. Christian reference is coming close to the surface of the poetry. The "breath / Rapid and strong" that enabled the winds to perform their silent priestlike function had been linked through the *Eolian Harp* and *Kubla Khan* to the breath of God; and now the lightning (traditionally connected with the destructive power of Jove) broods innocently over the mountain-slopes, as Milton's Holy Spirit broods over Chaos in the moment of Creation.

What then is being created? On one level—the level of Wallace Stevens's remarkable comments—the answer has to be God. It is wonderment that is chiefly apparent as Shelley's rhythms, and his claims, mount towards their final stress, "inhabits thee!" A sort of Incarnation is taking place as the ruler of "the infinite dome / Of heaven" becomes an inhabitant of earth. As in the *Hymn to Intellectual Beauty*—companion-piece to *Mont Blanc*—Shelley has created an abstraction which will satisfy his imaginative need for a personal, or near-personal, God. No dogma has been put forward, and the existence of the Secret Strength of Things does not have to be proved; yet Shelley's position at this stage in the poem is not really so very far from that of Coleridge in the *Hymn Before Sunrise*. As perhaps one should expect, the God whom he creates has many of the attributes—power, mystery; even, in some sense, beneficence—of the God whom he rejects.

How much then is undercut by the concluding lines? It is a small point with which to end, but may I just remark how different it would be if Shelley had written "But" instead of "And": "*But* what were thou ... ?" "And" permits the previous implications to be carried forward—permits us to feel that silence and solitude are conditions of imaginative truth. Like the Coleridge of *Dejection, An Ode*—

> O Lady! we receive but what we give,
> And in our Life alone does Nature live ...
>   (ll. 47–48)

—Shelley fears that his perceptions and intuitions may be merely projection (the human mind's "imaginings," with an "s"), and as in *Dejection* the poetry wins through to a confidence which the poet does not initially possess. It is this resilient hopefulness that places *Mont Blanc* among the very greatest Romantic poems.

JEAN HALL

The Evolution of the Surface Self: Byron's Poetic Career

In 1814 Byron wrote in his journal, "When I am tired—as I generally am—out comes this, and down goes every thing. But I can't read it over;—and God knows what contradictions it may contain. If I am sincere with myself (but I fear one lies more to one's self than to any one else), every page should confute, refute, and utterly abjure its predecessor."[1] The personal inconsistency he confesses to here was frequently commented on by others. Lady Blessington, who knew Byron well during his later years in Italy, gives a particularly vivid account of it:

> Byron seems to take a peculiar pleasure in ridiculing sentiment and romantic feelings; and yet the day after will betray both, to an extent that appears impossible to be sincere, to those who had heard his previous sarcasms: that he is sincere, is evident, as his eyes fill with tears, his voice becomes tremulous, and his whole manner evinces that he feels what he says. All this appears so inconsistent, that it destroys sympathy, or if it does not quite do that, it makes one angry with oneself for giving way to it for one who is never two days of the same way of thinking, or at least expressing himself. He talks for effect, likes to excite astonishment, and certainly destroys in the minds of his auditors all confidence in his stability of character.[2]

From *Keats–Shelley Journal* 36 (1987): 134–57. © 1987 by the Keats–Shelley Association of America.

Lady Blessington can feel no assurance of Byron's "stability of character." She suggests that his inconsistency includes not only a puzzling changeability of mood but also an unpredictable alteration of attitude from sincerity to performance, and from true belief to sarcasm or irony. Byron's personality appears to be a dazzling succession of parts that do not cohere.

This conspicuous lack of personal wholeness is reflected in his poetry, which throughout his career displays a huge variety of postures and tones. Byron's incessant mobility seems to place him apart from the other Romantic poets, who value personal consistency and identity and work to achieve a sense of wholeness in their poetry. Indeed, the difference is so marked that Byron sometimes has been considered not a Romantic poet at all.[3] I shall argue for Byron as a Romantic, albeit a perverse one, on the grounds that he shares categorical assumptions about wholeness with his contemporaries. Briefly put, Byron as well as the others assumes that personal identity results from the turn toward innerness, the creation of an interior poetic world that builds the core of selfhood. In this view personality becomes an affair of depth, not surface; of integrity, not display. Where the other Romantics believe that this turn toward innerness is both possible and desirable, Byron tends to doubt both the feasibility and attractiveness of the interior self. He tends to avoid self-exploration because it appears to him a futile process, an exercise in self-delusion. If the true interior self is an impossibility, then he prefers to turn his efforts outward and at least enjoy the pleasures of activity in the world. By tracing Byron's attempts to establish selfhood in some of the major poems of his career, this essay will sketch the main outlines of the Byronic surface self.[4]

Byron frequently sees adult innerness as impossible because he assumes that as children we were originally whole but we experience growth as an inevitable loss of this integrity. Wordsworth too sees the child's growth into adulthood as a kind of loss, but he regards the making of poetry as a satisfactory adult compensation. Poetry reconstitutes the child's active, exterior wholeness in a profound and powerful inner form. Here Byron demurs: for him poetry is usually not an integrative activity but a diversion, a form of escape from self. Unlike the other Romantics Byron often does not want to turn within himself, for he fears he will not like what he finds there. As he said of his versifying, "To withdraw *myself* from *myself* ... has ever been my sole, my entire, my sincere motive in scribbling at all; and publishing is also the continuance of the same object, by the action it affords the mind, which else recoils upon itself."[5] But if poetry can offer the pleasures of self-escape, it does so at the price of increased personal fragmentation. For the more Byron evades himself, the more completely he is lost. And this becomes the penalty of any kind of activity: when the fragmented self is roused to action, the outcome must be accelerated fragmentation, in the form of increased superficiality. In *Childe Harold's Pilgrimage*

Byron images this degenerative process in the form of a shattered mirror that multiplies the reflection of an originally single image, splintering the whole into a proliferating series of parts. The mirror

> makes
> A thousand images of one that was,
> The same, and still the more, the more it breaks;
> And thus the heart will do which not forsakes,
> Living in shattered guise.[6]

Thus, as the self becomes more various it also becomes more superficial. The image of one surface is exchanged for the reflection of untold thousands. At times Byron can live with this condition cheerfully, taking delight in the virtuosity of his poetic performances and scoffing at writers who aspire to meaningfulness and profundity. But in Canto III of *Childe Harold's Pilgrimage* he tries to achieve depth by writing Wordsworthian nature poetry. Of course, this attempt at profundity may be superficially motivated, for he is both mimicking another poet's style and responding to pressures from the outside—at the time Shelley was urging him to write this sort of poetry.[7] Nevertheless, for a person of Byron's temperament the poetry of depth may have held a great attraction: meditative innerness and its literary form, the self-contained organic poem, could have provided boundaries that organized the self and stilled its incessant, confusing mobility. If he could not bear to look into himself, possibly he could achieve coherence by looking into Wordsworthian nature. Perhaps "true Wisdom's world will be / Within its own creation, or in thine, / Maternal Nature!" (III, 46).

The embodiment of these hopes becomes Lake Leman, a perfectly still, mirrorlike body of water which, like Thoreau's Walden Pond, is centered in the heart of nature. By its shores,

> All heaven and earth are still—though not in sleep,
> But breathless, as we grow when feeling most;
> And silent, as we stand in thoughts too deep:—
> All heaven and earth are still.

In this place of quiet fullness, motion is suppressed to create the soul of poet and of nature.

> All is concentered in a life intense,
> Where not a beam, nor air, nor leaf is lost,
> But hath a part of being. (III, 89)

The parts unite in the whole, brought together by a meditative centering of everything in the world which works toward the realization of spirit. "Then stirs the feeling infinite" (III, 90).

Byron is deeply attracted to this version of infinity, for it transcends not only the individuality of leaf, beam, and air, but also that of the poet's mind. The moment of being "purifies from self" (III, 90), breaks the bonds of egotism to create a transpersonal, all-uniting reality. For Byron the achievement of depth offers an escape from self, an annihilation that converts Wordsworthian innerness into yet another form of Byronic surface. And even if he had found it possible to center self in nature, the Lake Leman passage suggests that Byron would have experienced this still profundity not as fulfilling, but as boring. Transcendental stillness permeates Lake Leman but a moment; almost immediately Byron finds it necessary to shatter this quiet by imagining a splendid storm approaching over the Alps. Wordsworthian calm has constrained his native mobility, and he must find relief through a vision of unsuppressed energy. The tempest is "wondrous strong, / Yet lovely in your strength . . . let me be / A sharer in thy fierce and far delight" (III, 92–93). But he cannot help realizing the flaw in the storm's magnificence: "But where of ye, oh tempests! is the goal?" (III, 96). The storm's drive, like the poet's own energies, is superficial motion, a splendid display without an interior purpose. And Byron reflects on his own ceaseless flow of words—"Could I embody and unbosom now / That which is most within me . . . into *one* word, / And that one word were Lightning, I would speak" (III, 97). The self-containment of the organic poem might center the self and allow it to utter its identity in one word—but this is an achievement impossible for Byron.

Transcendental stillness having proven unsatisfactory, Byron considers the opposite posture—heroic mobility. Canto III of *Childe Harold's Pilgrimage* mediates on the fate of great men, men of action who make an impact upon the world. Like the superb storm over Lake Leman, such men seem to him splendid forces of nature. Napoleon becomes Byron's prime example. A man of mobility, an inconsistent "spirit antithetically mixt" and "Extreme in all things" (III, 36), Napoleon bestrides the world but finds that he cannot rule his self:

> An empire thou couldst crush, command, rebuild,
> But govern not thy pettiest passion, nor,
> However deeply in men's spirits skill'd,
> Look through thine own, nor curb the lust of war. (III, 38)

Napoleon's energy recoils against itself because his heroic mobility makes self-knowledge impossible. The same energy that fuels his victories becomes a "fever at the core, / Fatal to him who bears," a "fire / And motion of the soul . . . once kindled, quenchless evermore" (III, 42). Unable to look into himself, Napoleon becomes a driven soul, a compulsive activist who moves on helplessly from conquest to conquest, finally turning his heroism to villainy, his creative social effort to destruction. In his hands revolution degenerates into reaction; and now the vast European populations he has stirred up turn on him, reciprocating his aggressions with a popular outpouring of wrath. "He who surpasses or subdues mankind, / Must look down on the hate of those below" (III, 45). The collisions that fragment the great soul disease the social fabric and produce the mob, the "hot throng" that jostles and collides in endlessly irritating motion, causing the mind to "overboil" so that we "become the spoil / Of our infection . . . / In wretched interchange of wrong for wrong / 'Midst a contentious world" (III, 69). To be a man of action is to be an infected soul, and to be in collision with others. They all "join the crushing crowd, doom'd to inflict or bear" (III, 71).

The turn toward the outside represented by Napoleon's heroic activism produces chaos. Personal mobility gives rise to social collision, demonstrating that great spirits "antithetically mixt" can destroy not only themselves, but also the world. To contain these dangers and yet preserve the option of heroic mobility, Byron contemplates the notion of poetic heroism. His example is Rousseau, a hero of the imagination who glorified "ideal beauty" (III, 78). But in confining his activism to the realm of the imaginary, Rousseau does not succeed in protecting either himself or his audience. Quite the contrary: instead of satisfying human passions, Rousseau's flights of imagination artificially inflate desire, build up a terrific longing that makes any human satisfaction impossible. Instead of liberating man from life and preserving his peace, Rousseau's poetry of eternal pursuit and eternal unfulfillment drives him mad. It exaggerates the disruptive process of ordinary living, producing a disease larger than life. Like Napoleon, Rousseau becomes a carrier of infection, a poet whose words precipitate dreadful actions—they "set the world in flame, / Nor ceased to burn till kingdoms were no more: / Did he not this for France?" (III, 81). Rousseau inspires his audience with revolutionary desires so tremendous as to be unfulfillable, and the result is a bloodbath. In spite of himself he becomes a man of action working in concert with Napoleon, and the readers of his poetry become the mob. Far from preventing violence, the case of Rousseau suggests that poetry may fuel it.

In drawing a parallel between Napoleon and Rousseau, Byron recognizes that poetry is not always the harmless, escapist activity he often wishes it to be. Nevertheless the conclusion of Canto III reverts to the escapist posture, suggesting that "these words" may be "a harmless wile,—/ . . . Which I would seize, in passing, to beguile / My breast, or that of others, for a while"

(III, 112). Perhaps, then, the perfect solution for Byron's contradictory needs is a poetry of maximum mobility and forcefulness and yet minimum effect—a poetry that appears to be powerful but actually has no impact on the world. These requirements could be met by a poetry of superficial power, a dazzling poetry that implies the existence of innerness and depth without actually creating it. And thus the Byronic hero is born. This figure is repeated over and over again in the Turkish Tales, which are escapist works because they present a hero who feigns profound innerness without actually possessing it. Like Napoleon and Rousseau, and like Byron himself, the Byronic hero is always a figure "antithetically mixt," a man of extraordinary but self-confounding energy whose personal wholeness has been shattered by some dark action in the past. He responds to fragmentation by displaying a cold, firm, silent posture toward the world. "Prometheus" conveniently summarizes this attitude: Byron sees in the Titan "A silent suffering, and intense," a "patient energy," the "endurance, and repulse / Of thine impenetrable Spirit" (lines 6, 40–42). [8]

Byron creates a poetry of glittering surface, a heroic rigidity that exists for the purpose of being seen. He feigns interior resonance through a clenched posture, an attitude that identifies heroism with the resolve to never change. Militant implacability, not growth of the mind, becomes the value promoted by Byron's heroism. By his spectacular suffering the Byronic hero elevates himself above the throng, so that he can be properly wondered at. His armored public posture isolates him, suggests his superiority, creates an outlet for the energy of his hostilities—but it does not produce innerness, soul.

But if the Byronic hero is a superficial figure, at any rate he does share one characteristic with the Romantic poetry of depth: both Byronic heroism and the organic poem establish boundaries in order to produce identity. The self-containment of the organic poem permits the creation of Romantic wholeness, and it is this wholeness that the rigidly isolated Byronic hero mimics. The Byronic hero exaggerates normal Romantic practices by an absolute separation of innerness from outerness. Where the Wordsworthian poem is bounded but nevertheless permeable, allowing interchange between the poet's mind and nature, Byronic innerness is impermeable—and, therefore, conveniently inaccessible. The Byronic hero can only be observed from the outside, and so his inner life can only be inferred. In this figure Byron has discovered a superficial method of feigning depth, a kind of inversion of the organic poem.

"The Prisoner of Chillon" becomes an important commentary on the Turkish Tales, for it seriously explores the effects of absolute self-containment. This poem departs from the glorification of Byronic heroism by turning Byron's isolated hero into a wretched prisoner confined in a dungeon. Like the Byronic hero or the organic poem, Bonnivard, the prisoner of Chillon, is isolated from the world. He is imprisoned along with his brothers, but they die one by one, at last leaving him entirely alone. The result is not the creation of his depth and character, as might be expected from the normal constitution of the Byronic hero, but the very opposite: the prisoner's personality is annihilated, rendering his innerness a void.

Bonnivard and his two brothers are lively men—for them, imprisonment is a torture, for it blocks their expression of energies. These men of natural mobility are forced to be still, and Byron is outraged by the constraint. Emphatically, their stillness does not build Wordsworthian resonance of soul. Because they are deprived of the opportunity to react to the world's stimuli they grow weak in body, they become "rusted with a vile repose" (line 6); and eventually, this lack of exercise, this decline in physical feelings, leads to the loss of feeling in the heart. Bonnivard's energy is replaced by a coldness, a stillness of spirit, an inability to respond. He ends in a quiet that is tantamount to the death of the soul.

The prisoner's ordeal climaxes with the death of his second and last brother, the only remaining companion in his dungeon world. This "last—the sole—the dearest link / . . . Which bound me to my failing race" (lines 215–217) now becomes a part of the prison's stillness; and as Bonnivard clasps "that hand which lay so still" he realizes that "my own was full as chill; / I had not strength to stir, or strive" (lines 221–223). The loss of all life, all motion, in Bonnivard's world leads to a corresponding stillness in his soul—not a peaceful quiet, but a horrifying blankness.

> First came the loss of light, and air,
> And then of darkness too:
> I had no thought, no feeling—none—
> Among the stones I stood a stone. (lines 233–236)

In this moment of negative vision, everything disappears:

> There were no stars—no earth—no time—
> No check—no change—no good—no crime—
> But silence, and a stirless breath
> Which neither was of life nor death;
> A sea of stagnant idleness,
> Blind, boundless, mute and motionless! (lines 245–250)

This annihilation becomes a negative version of the organic poem—it solves the problems of mobility and variousness by expunging everything so that the world, insofar as it still can be said to exist, lies in a homogenous state of profound calm. Here is a whole and consistent universe, but one without life.

In this crisis Byron explores the possibilities for an organic innerness that could fill the void of Bonnivard's soul. But the forms of organic focus contemplated by the prisoner turn out to be fallacious. The first is a bird that perches in the dungeon window and begins its song. Similar circumstances stimulate Keats's narrator into poetry in "Ode to a Nightingale," and for a moment it appears that this also will happen to Bonnivard. As he listens to the melody, "by dull degrees came back / My senses to their wonted track, / I saw the dungeon walls and floor" (lines 259–261). As he begins to perceive the world again he also begins to regain his capacity for feeling. And it seems to him that the bird links him to life, sings a "song that said a thousand things, / And seemed to say them all for me!" (lines 269–270). Perhaps this bird even "might be / My brother's soul come down to me" (lines 287–288). But this illusion of purpose, the impression that human feelings and natural events are significantly related, evaporates for Bonnivard when the bird suddenly flies away. After all, the song was not meant for him. The bird's appearance and disappearance do not manifest meaning, they merely embody the incessant mobility of nature. The bird turns out to be a creature of surface, not depth.

Next Bonnivard climbs up to his dungeon window, and for the first time since his imprisonment sees the world outside—a beautiful vista of Lake Leman and the Alps. Here is the world of nature, the landscape of Wordsworthian poetry, which perhaps may revitalize his feeling. But the view does not elicit a Wordsworthian poem. Quite the contrary: it acts ironically and disassociatively, for the life of nature brings home to Bonnivard the death of his own soul. The eternal organic forms of the mountains "were the same, / They were not changed like me in frame" (lines 332–333). The unchanging aspect of nature, which links Wordsworth to life and leads him to intuitions of eternity, only serves to alienate Bonnivard. So nature's stillness emphasizes man's mobility and degeneration, and Bonnivard's meditative sequence reverses the normal progression of Wordsworthian nature poetry from surface event to the creation of spiritual innerness.

Having failed to revitalize his soul through organic forms of focus, Bonnivard at last comes to find blankness a comfort. He avoids the view from his window, he avoids activity, he protects himself from any kind of stimulation—for to bring his feelings alive is to live in a world of pain. The dungeon becomes his chosen home; protective isolation and voided feeling become his chosen mode of selfhood. When the prisoner eventually is freed he makes peace with his life by turning the entire world into a replication of his prison. He has "learn'd to love despair" (line 374), and so he avoids action as much as possible. Bonnivard ends as an extremely inner being, but Byron shows this to be a pathological state. The dazzling trappings of Byronic heroism recede here, to reveal absolute isolation as a pathetic rather than a heroic condition.

The possibility raised by "The Prisoner of Chillon" is that effective selfhood may actually be an affair of surface, not of depth. Perhaps the poets of innerness are incorrect in suggesting that it is the meditative activation of organic poetry that builds the self—for what Bonnivard needs is not increased innerness, but rather the courage to reach outside himself and become involved in the activities of life.

"The Prisoner of Chillon" suggests that a case can be made for the surface personality. Perhaps the profound innerness, consistency, and integrity promoted by the poets of organic unity are not the only possible human values. In Canto IV of *Childe Harold's Pilgrimage* the poem's narrator sings a hymn to the ocean, which suggests the values made possible by a surface approach to life. The depths of this Byronic ocean certainly do exist, but they are made evident only as surface effects—the pitch and roll of the waves. Where the prisoner of Chillon imagined his voided world as "a sea of stagnant idleness, / Blind, boundless, mute and motionless!" (lines 249–250), this lively ocean is "boundless, endless, and sublime—/ The image of Eternity" (IV, 183). The petty ravages of man "mark the earth with ruin" (IV, 179) but ocean lifts him up and dashes him to pieces, "Spurning him from thy bosom to the skies, / [Thou] send'st him, shivering in thy playful spray / And howling, to his Gods" (IV, 180). But where other men die in the depths, the narrator of *Childe Harold's Pilgrimage* loves the ocean's rolling surface and learns to skim over it; he was "a child of thee, / And trusted to thy billows far and near, / And laid my hand upon thy mane" (IV, 184). The risk of riding the breakers creates a "pleasing fear" (IV, 180), transforms ocean's destruction into the singer's exhilaration. He knows life's wholeness, but he knows it as a surface; what he experiences is not profound innerness, but the stimulus of the waves' challenge and the pleasure of his own mastery.[9]

And so the Byronic vision of infinity converts innerness to surface, which in turn implies the conversion of action to reaction. Byron finds it more congenial to adapt to events than to initiate them, for the kind of focus needed to control activity requires a purposeful inner self, a core of identity that he lacks. The Byronic hero cannot really organize action; his firmness is limited to the capacity for heroic resistance. But the kind of reactive flexibility demonstrated by the rider of the sea in *Childe Harold's Pilgrimage* is exploited by the Byron of *Don Juan*. This poem abandons the heroic posture of resistance for the comic posture of adaptation. Just as the rider learns to stay mounted on the ocean's billows, appropriating the power of the waves by adjusting himself to it, the narrator of *Don Juan* adapts to his poem's flow of events and thereby masters them. He does not originate the power of infinity, but by becoming a creature of surface and learning to stay afloat, he appropriates powers that far exceed the capacity of Byronic heroism.[10]

Where the Byronic hero remains in one rigid posture, adopts a hyperbolic consistency meant to authenticate his innerness, the mobile narrator of *Don Juan* blithely announces his poem has no plan or purpose. And indeed, *Don Juan* abounds in contradictions, chance collisions, abortive episodes, incongruous juxtapositions, sudden reversals. These fragmentations, these testaments to man's inability to maintain purpose, become the motive power of the poem—the force that propels it randomly onward. Byron's Juan is tossed ahead by the surging ocean of life, and this becomes comic because he cannot sink; he is a superficial creature and he continually bobs up like a cork. Juan learns very little from his experience, which is why he can happily continue his experiencing.[11]

And so *Don Juan* becomes the great Romantic poem of surface, as *The Prelude* is the great Romantic poem of depth. *The Prelude* is the autobiography of a man who examines his past in search of an inner self that is latent there and needs to be brought into present awareness. Thought and speech are vital to Wordsworth's procedure, for he is reflecting upon himself, examining the apparently incomplete events of his past to bring out the fullness of their meaning, the manner in which these parts have contributed to the development of his whole self. In making his poem he both recounts and extends his own self-development; the inwardness initiated by his childhood experiences is continued and expanded by his ongoing poetic interpretations. But while Wordsworth's procedure creates an immense field of inner activity, it also does pose problems. He must see all the events of his life through the focus of his self-development, a focus that validates not only the significance of his own life but the way in which all parts lead to the whole, all episodes partake of infinity, all things of the world rest in God. Therefore, to affirm the harmony of the world he also needs to assert the success of his own self-development.

In contrast, Byron's poem of surface denies all claims to unity and focus. The author of *Don Juan* gives up the attempt to make complete sense of his experience. His is a poem of middle age, a stream of words that begins to flow when "I / Have spent my life, both interest and principal, / And deem not, what I deem'd, my soul invincible" (I, 213). He writes because he is losing the physical capacity to act, and he believes that the next best thing to sensuous experience is the imagination of it. So Byron splits his self between the mindless but cheerful physicality of the young Juan, who learns nothing from his experiences and never grows up, and the incessant verbal flow of the poem's middle-aged narrator, who exists to escape Wordsworthian interpretation—to avoid looking into himself by constantly searching for new external stimuli, new diversions. Wordsworth and Byron become contraries: where Wordsworth's poem is halted by his middle age, Byron's begins there. Wordsworth's poetry of spontaneous overflow is inhibited and finally cut off by his immense need to have the spontaneous reveal design, to have utterance in the present embody the significance of the entire past life. But it is Byron who truly practices poetry as spontaneous overflow: "I write what's uppermost, without delay," and the words become "a straw, borne on by human breath," a self-created but meaningless plaything that evokes the enthusiasm to produce an additional rush of words (XIV, 7–8). The openness, the inconsistency of *Don Juan* allow it to become endless. As long as Byron's life continues, his poem also is free to proceed. As an alternative to the focus of the organic poem, he offers the delights of extension—the indefinitely prolonged unfurling of new surfaces, new stimuli.[12]

So Byron manages to write an autobiographical poem that is the polar opposite of *The Prelude*: instead of going into himself, he turns himself inside out and becomes the world. For him youth is the time of innerness, the time when one believed in one's dreams and subscribed to the proposition that the self is its own universe. But at thirty, the poet cries, "No more—no more— Oh! never more, my heart, / Canst thou be my sole world, my universe!" Now "The illusion's gone forever" (I, 215) and the poet is left "To laugh at all things—for I wish to know / *What* after *all*, are *all* things—but a *Show?*" (VII, 2). Byron himself becomes this show of life by unleashing an incessant flow of words that cause a world to appear.

It is his most effective way of fulfilling the desire expressed in 1813, "To withdraw *myself* from *myself* . . . has ever been my sole, my entire, my sincere motive." The poetic shows of *Don Juan* become a form of self-escape. They lead not to the growth of the poet's mind, but to displacement from selfhood, to entertainment. In *Childe Harold's Pilgrimage* Byron had criticized Rousseau for making his audience believe in the illusion of a poetic idealism that created havoc in the actual world. His own poetry does not promote the willing suspension of disbelief that can lead to this unfortunate result; he constantly deflates his performances by his own narrative intrusions, which become yet another kind of amusing show. We are never allowed to forget for long that everything in this poem is surface. Given these procedures, the compulsive force of a Rousseau simply cannot build up. Like the poem's narrator, who fails to develop a consistent center of self, *Don Juan* may lack a central purpose—but reading it certainly is a pleasure.[13]

But if the poem attempts to escape innerness, its superficiality cannot be branded as wholly escapist. It is the Turkish Tales that offer true escape, for their heroes are designed to create the illusion of power without its actual impact. In his completely escapist moods Byron wants poetry to be "a harmless wile," but *Don Juan*, as well as seeking pleasure, has one item of real business—to attack the notion of the inner personality and to debunk the poetry of innerness, on the grounds that the imagination of inner selfhood is the only dangerous illusion. Where the poet of *Don Juan* brings illusion to the surface, constantly unmasking his own performances, those who believe in innerness create an illusion that they mistake for truth.

As the narrator of *Don Juan* claims, "For me, I know nought; nothing I deny, / Admit, reject, contemn" (XIV, 3). Apparently it is not this speaker but the people who aspire to innerness who are constantly denying, admitting, rejecting, contemning—using words to proclaim a truth they then proceed to impose on themselves and on others. But if interpretations are merely another form of appearance, then they have no special claim to authority. They should be worth neither more nor less than any other show. Wordsworth particularly draws Byron's fire because of all contemporary poets he is the strongest advocate of interpretation, of the word as a guide to meaning, innerness, and reality. Byron did not have the opportunity to read *The Prelude*, but an acquaintance with "Tintern Abbey" and the other *Lyrical Ballads* would have been enough to give him a feeling for Wordsworth's methods of building innerness. In "Tintern Abbey" childhood action is exchanged for the adult's poetic interpretations—the body's activity is succeeded by the authority of the word. Wordsworth's exchange of the body for the word, of action for interpretation, builds an innerness that Byron is moved to discredit. What he notices is not the Wordsworthian soul, but the willing surrender of body that has produced it. Why should soul be valued over body, innerness over surface?

Juan's first experience of love dramatizes these issues. When he begins to have feeling for Julia, it registers as thoughts "unutterable" (I, 90), an unfocused, restless affect that creates the need for definition, outlet, activity, the drive toward some kind of goal. But Juan cannot find relief in action because he does not know what troubles him. In his perplexity he becomes a naive Wordsworth, wandering in nature and hearing "a voice in all the winds" (I, 94), thinking great thoughts and pursuing "His self-communion with his own high soul." He turns "without perceiving his condition, / Like Coleridge, into a metaphysician" (I, 91). Juan interprets his restlessness through the use of words, but this is not a case of unveiling reality. On the contrary, it is the transposition of energy from one form to another—not a higher form, merely a different one. The body's urges and the mind's metaphysics both are forms of appearance; the only sure thing is that interpretation fails to soothe Juan's restlessness. His naive poetry formulates his energies, but does not terminate them. This inner focus cannot bring stillness, for it neglects to notice the original source of restlessness in the human body itself. "If *you* think it was philosophy that this did, / I can't help thinking puberty assisted" (I, 93). Finally Juan finds relief in sexual activity with Julia, but this is not a lasting answer either—it leads to an imbroglio with her husband that forces his exile from home and begins the wanderings recounted in *Don Juan*. Mobility may be channeled through various forms of appearance, but it never can be finally centered or stilled. Wordsworthian sacrifice of the body therefore strikes Byron as a form of repression, of authoritarianism. As the contrary of Wordsworth, Byron stands for the liberation of all appearances, the free play of energies through whatever forms they may take. In unbinding the life force Byron releases delight and vitality, which he feels is surely preferable to the deadliness of Wordsworth's interminable explanations. If life is purposeless, at least it might as well be enjoyed.

Although Byron rejects the claim of the word to meaning and authority, he by no means condemns verbal behavior. To do so would be to repeat Wordsworth's error in inverted form, by authorizing body over word. Words and bodies both are forms of appearance that incarnate energy, and Byron recognizes that in some situations words may do the better job. Middle age is one example; the body's decreased capacity gives way to the lightning of the mind, which produces *Don Juan*. Another example is the intrigue hatched by the Duchess of Fitz-fulke. Her story of the ghostly Black Friar, who walks the halls outside Juan's bedroom every night, employs the conventions of the Gothic novel to stir up Juan's interest and apprehension. She maneuvers him into a state of mind where his supernatural frisson can be converted into an expression of sexual energies, as he finally reaches out to touch the ghostly Black Friar but instead finds his hand upon the Duchess. In using fiction to create the conditions that give her sexual possession of Juan, Fitz-fulke is engaging in a manipulative process that compares to the audience manipulations incessantly attempted by the narrator of *Don Juan*. For this speaker, manipulation is an amusing, enlivening process.

The poets of innerness cannot adopt Byron's cheerful attitude toward manipulation because their business is to create the illusion of innerness, not only for their audiences but for themselves. The creation of innerness involves a necessary element of self-deception, a problem that is salient in Julia's developing responses to her lover Juan. Juan himself first felt the physical restlessness of love and then transposed it into Wordsworthian verbalizing, and similarly, Julia sublimates her physical feeling into the terminology of Platonic love. By adopting the language of Platonism she seeks to create love on the spiritual plane, the realm of innerness and soul. But in focussing on Platonic visions she neglects the sexual energy they sublimate and allows herself to be overpowered by the force hidden within her own expressions. In becoming Juan's lover she at last does what she has really wanted to do all along, but her satisfaction must be prepared for by what Byron sees as a complicated and ridiculous process of self-deception. Those who believe in innerness must elaborately manipulate themselves before they are able to do anything at all. The narrator of *Don Juan* himself proposes to be more direct, and more active. He wants to be the master rather than the pawn of his own words; they will do things for him, rather than the other way around. By denying innerness, by bringing everything to the surface, he liberates words as an effective form of energy. The rider of the sea who writes *Don Juan* also must become the rider of the word—the poet who has the skill to use words to his own advantage.

Since life is an affair of power not purpose, the narrator really can see no way out of manipulation. He himself undoubtedly manipulates by using words as a form of power, but then so do the interpretationists. Interpretation is simply another form of appearance, and since it is constantly rearranging its own appearances, interpretation itself must be a manipulation. Therefore, the only difference between the poet of *Don Juan* and the Lake poets must be in the gravity of their operations. The Dedication to *Don Juan* condemns these Laker interpretationists because not only are they manipulators, they are also long-winded and distinctly boring. Where Byron offers vitality and entertainment, Wordsworth writes "a rather long 'Excursion'" ... "the vasty version / Of his new system to perplex the sages" (Dedication, 4). Coleridge, the "hawk encumber'd with his hood" is forever "Explaining metaphysics to the nation—/ I wish he would explain his Explanation" (Dedication, 2). Like Julia, these poets conceal their motives behind a massive smokescreen of sanctimonious words, which stuns the audience. But putting people to sleep is exactly what the British government wants its poets to do—for a slumbering populace cannot revolt. By diverting people into a dull semblance of action through writing and reading the poetry of innerness, of a self-contained world, Wordsworth and his colleagues help preserve the status quo. A grateful government, relieved of the necessity to directly suppress its citizens, rewards its poets with sinecures and respectability.

Byron charges that the poetry of innerness deadens feeling, the sense of individuality, and the capacity for response. Far from contributing to the growth of the mind, it suppresses and atrophies human powers. His audience relationships will aim at the opposite effect—to wake people up. The narrator of *Don Juan* does this by releasing his aggressive feelings, which can assume a positive role in the poem. His tendency to irritate, to jolt, to collide with people, functions to startle his audience into awareness. This adversary relationship with the audience minimizes the morally suspect aspects of manipulation and maximizes its possibilities for liberation, for by jarring people the poet forces them to become alert and think for themselves. As he says, "I wish men to be free / As much from mobs as kings—from you as me" (IX, 25).

Before *Don Juan* Byron had maintained a collaborative rather than an adversary audience relationship. He wrote of the Byronic hero again and again not only to feign his hero's innerness, but also his audience's. For through reading the Turkish Tales every man could imagine himself a hero and every woman could experience romance. The spiritual collusion in this arrangement had as its physical analogue the exchange of cash. Byron's poetry sold well; flattery turned out to be a viable commodity. In *Don Juan* Byron casts the Lakers in this pandering role, remarking that "You have your salary; was't for that you wrought?" (Dedication, 6). Manipulation, it turns out, is not practiced only by poets—audiences too can manipulate, by paying for what they like to hear and encouraging the poet to produce more of it. But this mutually manipulative relationship falsely enriches both parties at the same time it really demeans everyone. In *Don Juan* Byron rejects such an exchange by rudely calling attention to its suppressed basis: he hails us as his "gentle reader! and / Still gentler purchaser!" (I, 221).[14]

We are forced to see that the relationship between poet and reader always threatens to become mutually manipulative, an exchange of cash for an inflated sense of self-importance. The author of the Turkish Tales certainly knows what he is talking about here; but as his youth gives way to middle age Byron ceases to see any point in taking cash in exchange for poetic flattery. He imagines his past life as an analogue of money, and realizes that "I / Have squander'd my whole summer . . . I / Have spent my life, both interest and principal" (I, 213). His past is spent, and no amount of money can recover it or offer adequate compensation for the loss of his youth. Still:

> I *have* succeeded
> And that's enough; succeeded in my youth,
> The only time when much success is needed:
> And my success produced what I in sooth
> Cared most about; it need not now be pleaded—
> Whate'er it was, 'twas mine. (XII, 17)

Recovery of the past is impossible, and so the only wisdom must be to live as fully as one can in the present. Byron cheerfully squandered his energies in his youth, and he continues to do so in middle age by openly speaking his mind, squandering his credit with his audience. He is the spendthrift, but the spendthrift is the only truly wise man—he realizes he cannot save anything, and so he throws everything away, tries to use all his energies before he loses them. Generosity becomes the best adaptive posture toward the inevitable decline of life.[15]

By spending his energies Byron becomes the antithesis of Wordsworth, who tries to conserve his. *The Prelude* is written in the faith that one's past is not lost, that it can be recovered and compounded in value through the process of interpretation. Like Byron, Wordsworth practices an economy of the word. Because he believes in focus, in the possibility of the organic poem, he finds it possible to gather his life's energies and compress them into the intensity of poetic speech. The analogy between poetry and money, suppressed in Wordsworth, is brought to the surface in *Don Juan*. But where Wordsworth would have thought of himself as a prudent investor, Byron sees conservative poets as misers. Or rather, he sees the miser as "your only poet;—passion, pure / And sparkling on from heap to heap, displays / *Possess'd*, the ore" (XII, 8). Like the recollective poet, the miser turns to hoarding money when his youth is spent, and he is no longer able to physically exert power in the world. He becomes a parody of the interpretive poet, a man who despises "every sensual call, / Commands—the intellectual lord of all" (XII, 9). In possessing the world the miser cannot truly enjoy it, but he certainly can exert intellectual domination by owning everyone and everything possible. In *Don Juan* money and worldly power finally buy the heroes and the lovers; the Empress Catherine purchases the victors of war for her bed, and English society turns love into a marriage market. The miser carries these tendencies to the extreme by sacrificing all sensuous enjoyment to his intellectual lust for absolute domination. He is the ultimate, the pure manipulator, and his heaps of pure gold are the analogue to the pure compression of the self-contained poem.

The analogy between money and poetry remains only an analogy for Byron; as with the other analogies in *Don Juan* it never is granted symbolic status. For symbolism is an assertion of identity, a claim that the part indeed is the whole. Byron cannot move from part to whole symbolically, for although he does identify one great whole in life—the eternal ocean of surging energy—he also believes that the whole manifests itself only variously, appearing now as money, now as love, now as physical power, now as verbal dexterity, and so on. There is never a great moment of meaningful unity, of reality focussing all the appearances, such as is expressed by the symbol. Instead, "The eternal surge / Of time and tide rolls on, and bears afar / Our bubbles; as the old burst, new emerge, / Lash'd from the foam of ages" (XV, 99). Given this state of affairs, the fiscal conservatism of symbolic poets is misplaced. For life becomes a moving surface requiring the economics of risk and liquidity. The poet must become a speculator; he must learn to play fast and loose with the appearances.[16]

In the final cantos of *Don Juan* Byron shows English society behaving in just this way. The marriage mart in which Juan finds himself enmeshed is a "sweepstakes for substantial wives," a "lottery" in which the speculator may "draw a high prize" (XII, 37); and the women who are the prizes carefully tend their "floating balance of accomplishment" (XII, 52). In this society every relationship is in a speculative key, "For good society is but a game . . . / Where every body has some separate aim, / An end to answer, or a plan to lay" (XII, 58). The poet of analogy sees manipulation surfacing everywhere, in the financial ventures and in the games of relationship that people forever play to get the better of each other.

Once again the narrator's adaptation to life threatens to dissolve, for he knows that this English shell game of appearances is cold—it lacks heart, interior. He can cheerfully disregard his own lack of inner identity, but when he looks at English society he can see only meaningless motion and vacant quiet. In this superficial and sensation-mad society, life speeds on at a terrifying rate until "Change grows too changeable, without being new" (XI, 82), motion accelerates until it becomes a vapid stillness. At that point "Society is now one polish'd horde, / Form'd of two mighty tribes, the *Bores* and *Bored*" (XIII, 95).

But the solution cannot be to develop interior being, for the narrator feels no sense of inner existence. His only option is to take bigger risks, to play the inevitable game with even greater verve. And this, finally, is why poetry is important for him—not because it means anything, but because it is the best game of all. The insular and self-contented English think their world is everything, just as the poets of innerness believe their poems are worlds—but Lord Byron in exile looks back on "that microcosm on stilts, / Yclept the Great World" (XII, 56) and knows its insignificance. He resists it not by setting up poetry as a rival, a source of the significance society lacks; instead, poetry becomes valuable because it is the best device for keeping the poet afloat in a treacherous but boring world. To counterpoint the financial speculations of the English, the narrator floats his own kind of paper; "I'm serious—so are all men upon paper; / And why should I not form my specu-lation, / And hold up to the sun my little taper?" (XII, 21). The notion that poetry is a cultural resource, that poems link the generations and provide a kind of immortality, is ridiculous to him. Poetry simply cannot harbor and conserve meaning in this way. Asked why he publishes, the narrator replies, "why do you play at cards? / Why drink? Why read?—To make some hour less dreary." The fallible and perishing results of his labor "I cast upon the stream, / To swim or sink" (XIV, 11).

But if he finds no solutions, at least he is brought alive by his poetic game—for it involves risk. Where Wordsworth values spontaneous overflow because it reveals the latent meaning of his life, Byron enjoys it because it results in happy accidents, marvellous recoveries, spectacular fabrications. These bringings together of appearance are comic, not symbolic; the organic fusive power that truly reconciles opposites is no part of Byron's experi-ence. Instead, he delights in taking great risks and winning tremendous, but temporary, resolutions. He constantly threatens to drown in the sea of life, but yet once more he resurfaces. In poetry, "I think that were I *certain* of success / I hardly could compose another line: / . . . In play, there are two pleasures for your choosing—/ The one is winning, and the other losing" (XIV, 12).

Poetry gives him the power to adapt, the power to remain ebullient, not only when he considers English society, but when he reflects on life itself. For if the English are incessant manipulators, their devices are nothing compared to the world's. It is life's energy and not the poet which is the original manipulator of us all—for it fuels a restlessness, an unremitting mobility, that suddenly can turn love to hate, honesty to deception, good to evil. A prime example of this occurs in the war cantos of *Don Juan*, which climax in a vision of Juan as "Love turned a Lieutenant of Artillery!" (IX, 44). We see that if it is Juan's extraordinary energy that makes him an ardent lover, it is this same energy that fuels his lust to kill. Energy surfaces in contradictory forms that can be suddenly reversed. Byron responds to this confusing situation by attempting to out-manipulate life. His poetry becomes a creative adaptation that plays fast and loose with the facts in order to avert destruction. As he says, his muse is "the most sincere that ever dealt in fiction" (XVI, 2), for by the sudden reversals of poetry the false can become true and the contradictory consistent—or the other way around. He makes this remark as prologue to the story of Fitz-fulke and Juan, which indeed does demonstrate how the manipulations of fiction can creatively rearrange the facts of life. We marvel at the Byronic mobility that can change faster than life itself, beat life at its own game. The poet of surface becomes the great trickster, the saver of appearances who preserves our capacity for laughter and keeps us afloat on the ocean of eternity. Byron's achievement is essentially manipulative. In *Don Juan* the rider of the sea converts the lack of inner identity and of consistency of purpose that had vexed his early career from tragedy into comedy, from his loss into his triumph over life.[17]

But by inverting the normal Romantic assumptions, perhaps Byron does manage in some sense to confirm their desirability. He repudiates the inner self, consistency of character and purpose, the organic poem—the great Romantic postulates of wholeness. To replace them *Don Juan* exfoliates an endless world of incessantly mobile surfaces that is at once an escape and an exile from the central self. Byron struggles for equilibrium in the absence of any fundamental organizing principle in self or in society. He can conceive of wholeness only as a form of anarchy—anarchy manipulated and temporarily bested by the poet's improvisational art.

Notes

1. *Byron's Letters and Journals*, ed. Leslie A. Marchand, III, 1813–1814 (Cambridge: Harvard University Press, 1974), 233: entry for Monday, 6 December 1814.

2. *Lady Blessington's Conversations of Lord Byron*, ed. Ernest J. Lovell, Jr. (Princeton: Princeton University Press, 1969), p. 33.

3. M. H. Abrams excludes Byron from his discussion of Romanticism in *Natural Supernaturalism: Tradition and Revolution in Romantic Literature* (New York: W. W. Norton, 1971), because Byron "in his greatest work . . . speaks with an ironic counter-voice and deliberately opens a satirical perspective on the vatic stance of his Romantic contemporaries" (p. 13). See also "On Byron," *Studies in Romanticism*, 16 (1977), 563–587. This exchange between George M. Ridenour, for the Romantic Byron, and Jerome J. McGann for the anti-Romantic, was stimulated by Ridenour's reaction to McGann's *Don Juan in Context* (Chicago: University of Chicago Press, 1976).

4. Critics disagree over the question of Byron's identity, or lack of it. Three of the best arguments for Byron's personal hollowness are Paul West's *Byron and the Spoiler's Art* (London: Chatto and Windus, 1960), John Wain's "Byron: the Search for Identity" in his *Essays on Literature and Ideas* (London: Macmillan, 1963), and Philip W. Martin's *Byron: a poet before his public* (Cambridge: Cambridge University Press, 1982). Two approaches that trace the evolution of Byron's poetic identity are Jerome J. McGann's *Fiery Dust: Byron's Poetic Development* (Chicago: University of Chicago Press, 1968) and Robert F. Gleckner's *Byron and the Ruins of Paradise* (Baltimore: Johns Hopkins Press, 1967).

5. *Byron's Letters and Journals*, III, 225: entry from Byron's journal, Saturday, 27 November 1813.

6. Canto III, stanza 33. The poetry is quoted from *Lord Byron: The Complete Poetical Works*, ed. Jerome J. McGann (Oxford: Clarendon Press, 1980), except for *Don Juan*, where I cite Leslie Marchand's edition (Boston: Houghton Mifflin, 1958).

7. For an analysis of Byron's employment of Wordsworth, Shelley, and Rousseau in *Childe Harold's Pilgrimage*, Canto III, as a diversion from his sense of personal hollowness rather than as an approach to authentic Romantic identification with nature, see Philip Martin's discussion of the canto in *Byron: a poet before his public*. Wordsworth himself seems to have felt that Byron's enthusiasm for nature was derivative. In his *Memoirs*, Moore tells of a visit Wordsworth paid to him in October 1821: Wordsworth "spoke of Byron's plagiarisms from him; the whole third canto of 'Childe Harold' founded on his style and sentiments. The feeling of natural objects which is there expressed, not caught by B. from nature herself, but from him (Wordsworth), and spoiled in the transmission. 'Tintern Abbey' the source of it all; from which same poem too the celebrated passage about Solitude, in the first canto of 'Childe Harold,' is (he said) taken, with this difference, that what is naturally expressed by him, has been worked by Byron into a laboured and antithetical sort of declamation" (ed. John Russell [Boston: Little, Brown, 1853], III, 161).

8. There is disagreement over the literary merit of Byron's heroic poetry. For a defense of the Turkish Tales see Robert F. Gleckner's *Byron and the Ruins of Paradise* and Jerome J. McGann's *Fiery Dust: Byron's Poetic Development*. For a sympathetic approach to the Byronic hero, see McGann's *Don Juan in Context*, Chaps. 2, 3, and 4; also Peter L. Thorslev, Jr.'s *The Byronic Hero: Types and Prototypes* (Minneapolis: University of Minnesota Press, 1962). Attacks on Byronic heroism include John Jump's chapter on "Heroes and Rhetoric, 1812–1818" in his *Byron* (London and Boston: Routledge, 1972), and Andrew Rutherford's chapter on the Turkish Tales, "Romantic Fantasy," in *Byron: A Critical Study* (Stanford: Stanford University Press, 1961). The most interesting criticism of the Turkish Tales is Philip W. Martin's

chapter in *Byron: a poet before his public*, which sees the heroic poetry as providing a sense of gentility for the rising middle-class Regency public at the same time that it gives Byron a sense of independence from middle-class values. Daniel P. Watkins suggests that *The Giaour* offers an attack on idealism "for its absolutist element that cannot accommodate the changes, contradictions, and transience of everyday life." See "Idealism in Byron's 'The Giaour,'" *The University of Southern Florida Language Quarterly* 19 (1981), 32–33. Although I do not find Watkins' notion convincing in the case of the Turkish Tales, his position seems much stronger in relation to Byron's history plays. In a series of articles Watkins argues that the plays criticize idealism and Romantic individualism by rendering a historical analysis of ideology and class struggle: see especially "Byron and the Poetics of Revolution," *Keats-Shelley Journal*, 32 (1985), 95–130. See also "Violence, Class Consciousness, and Ideology in Byron's History Plays," *ELH*, 48 (1981), 799–816, and "The Ideological Dimensions of Byron's *The Deformed Transformed*," *Criticism*, 25 (1983), 27–39.

    9. The sense in which Ocean is taken by the narrator of *Childe Harold's Pilgrimage* is shared by Byron himself, as is suggested by a letter of 26 September 1813 to Anabella Millbanke: "You don't like my 'restless' doctrines—I should be very sorry if *you* did—*I* can't *stagnate* nevertheless—if I must sail let it be on the ocean no matter how stormy—anything but a dull cruise on a level lake without ever losing sight of the same insipid shores by which it is surrounded" (*Byron's Letters and Journals*, III, 119).

    10. For a superb analysis of *Don Juan* which regards "the two master symbols of the poem" as "fire and ocean" (p. 181), see Alvin B. Kernan's chapter on the poem in *The Plot of Satire* (New Haven: Yale University Press, 1965). Where I shall approach the Byronic ocean as an opposition between surface and depth, Kernan emphasizes the aspect of onward flow

    11. See Jerome J. McGann's anti-Romantic analysis of the poem, *Don Juan in Context*: Chap. 6, "Form," is particularly important. McGann argues that Byron proceeded not on organic models of poetry but by the order he discovered in Horace, who offered a tradition "rhetorical and functional" (p. 109). The poem becomes a series of rhetorical experiments that reveal the multiple contexts and uses of language—so that variety, not organic unity, must become the central linguistic technique of the poem. For critical accounts that argue for the unity of the poem, see Ernest J. Lovell's "Irony and Image in *Don Juan*" in *The Major English Romantic Poets: A Symposium in Reappraisal*, eds. Clarence D. Thorpe, Carlos Baker, and Bennett Weaver (Carbondale: Southern Illinois University Press, 1957), George Ridenour's *The Style of Don Juan* (New Haven: Yale University Press, 1960), and Robert F. Gleckner's chapter on *"Don Juan* and *The Island"* in *Byron and the Ruins of Paradise*.

    12. For an interesting stylistic comparison of *Don Juan* and *The Prelude*, see pp. 89–99 of Jerome J. McGann's *Don Juan in Context*. McGann suggests that Wordsworth's need to integrate mind and nature, to "transform landscape into either interior or apocalyptic categories" (p. 90) creates problems of stylistic transition that often are poorly solved in *The Prelude*. Since Byron is not committed to integration, he "can manage such shifts and transitions because the whole point of the style of *Don Juan* is to explore the interfaces between different things, events, and moods. *Don Juan* is a poem that is, in fact, always in transition—not in the Wordsworthian sense of 'something evermore about to be,' but in the Byronic sense that 'there woos no home nor hope, nor life, *save what is here*' (*Childe Harold* IV, 105, my italics). And

for Byron, 'what is here' is a vast spectacle of incongruences held together in strange networks between the poles of sublimity and pointlessness. Transitions between styles, lines, stanzas, and tones not only do not present a problem for Byron, they are the locus of all his opportunities" (p. 95).

13. For a discussion of *Don Juan* as a meaningless poem, see Brian Wilkie's "Byron and the Epic of Negation" in his *Romantic Poets and Epic Tradition* (Madison and Milwaukee: University of Wisconsin Press, 1965).

14. For the most sustained analysis of Byron's relations with his audience see Philip W. Martin's *Byron: a poet before his public*. In addition, see Andrew Rutherford's short history of Byron's lifetime reception in his Introduction to *Byron: The Critical Heritage* (New York: Barnes and Noble, 1970), pp. 3–12. Edward Bostetter offers a history of the composition and reception of *Don Juan* in his Introduction to *Twentieth Century Interpretations of Don Juan* (Englewood Cliffs, New Jersey: Prentice Hall, 1979), as does Elizabeth French Boyd in her chapter "Against the Wind" in *Byron's Don Juan: A Critical Study* (1945; reprint, The Humanities Press, 1958). The most complete history of Byron's composition of *Don Juan*, and of his relations with his publishers and the friends who read the manuscript of *Don Juan* is volume I of Truman Guy Steffan's *Byron's Don Juan, The Making of a Masterpiece* (Austin: University of Texas Press, 1957, 1971).

15. For an analysis of the economics of *Don Juan* which identifies Byron with the misers rather than the men of generosity, see Frank D. McConnell's "Byron's Reductions: 'Much Too Poetical',", *ELH*, 37 (1970), 415–432.

16. Jerome J. McGann acutely discusses normal Romantic symbolic techniques and Byron's evasion of them in Chap. 6 of *Don Juan in Context*. As McGann says, "To know by symbols is to make up for what Wordsworth calls 'the sad incompetence of human speech'" (*The Prelude*, IV, 592). Byron opposes a discourse ruled by symbols, which drive into silence and ecstatic revelation, with a discourse of 'conversational facility' (XV, 20). The structure of *Don Juan* is based upon the structure of human talk, which is dialectical without being synthetic" (p. 111).

17. Although I recognize the tragic undertones in *Don Juan*, it seems to me that the narrator's ebullience, his pleasure in his manipulations, dominates. But several critics emphasize the tragic tone of the poem. For Alvin Kernan it is part of a mingling of genres—comic, satiric, and tragic. The tragic element emerges "When viewed from the angle of the solitary man"; for "the movement of life which flows through *Don Juan* darkens to a tragic setting in which while Life rolls on, the individual is fated to stillness and obliteration"—*The Plot of Satire* (p. 213). Ridenour sees a dark *Don Juan* that continually exfoliates repetitions of the Fall, and Robert F. Gleckner carries this interpretation farther in *Byron and the Ruins of Paradise*.

JOHN L. MAHONEY

"We Must Away": Tragedy and the Imagination in Coleridge's Later Poems

And thus he sang: "Adieu! Adieu!
Love's dreams prove seldom true.
The blossoms, they make no delay:
The sparkling dew-drops will not stay
Sweet month of May,
We must away;
Far, far away!
Today, to-day!"

Song from *Zapolya* (2.1.74–81)

It has been almost a commonplace of Coleridge criticism to think of his greatest poetry as largely the work of the years before 1800, the years of the Conversation poems and of the great imaginative trio—*Christabel, The Rime of the Ancient Mariner, Kubla Khan*—poems of the wondrous worlds of preternatural and supernatural. These are poems not always unqualifiedly joyous—witness the disturbing presence of "pensive Sara" in *The Eolian Harp*, the eerie and distressing violation of the lovely and innocent Christabel by the tormented serpent-woman Geraldine—yet ultimately and with few exceptions they celebrate the power of mind, of imagination to shape diversity into harmony, to achieve a sympathetic oneness with the beauty of nature. So also do they capture the nuances and shadings as well as the divinity-bearing

From *Coleridge, Keats, and the Imagination: Romanticism and Adam's Dream*, edited by J. Robert Barth, S. J., and John L. Mahoney, pp. 109–34. Copyright © 1990 by the Curators of the University of Missouri.

135

power of "the one Life within us and abroad"; of "the whole World . . . imag'd in" the "vast circumference" of "the stony Mount"; of "This little lime-tree bower," its "broad and sunny leaf," "that walnut-tree," "the ancient ivy . . . fronting elms" that an accident has prevented him from sharing with his friends, but that imagination has enabled him to see and to "lift the soul, and contemplate / With lively joy the joys we cannot share."[1] These poems generally move toward triumphal conclusions of blessing and redemption, of acclaim for the poet who "on honey-dew hath fed, / And drunk the milk of Paradise," even conclusions that hint at the possibility of rescue for the magical Christabel from the savage spell of the serpentine Geraldine.

In discussing *Dejection: An Ode* with its terrifying descriptions of "A grief without a pang" and "the smothering weight" on "my breast," there has been a notable tendency in critical writing about Coleridge to see the early stages of a tragic valedictory to the great creative period. The poem *To William Wordsworth* is seen as a further example as the mournful and respectful speaker, having heard Wordsworth recite *The Prelude*, views his predicament "as Life returns upon the drowned, / Life's joy rekindling roused a throng of pains" (63–64), and views genius and knowledge as "but flowers / Strewed on my corse, and borne upon my bier / In the same coffin, for the self-same grave!" (73–75). Such a tendency, while providing certain superficial advantages of chronology and ordering, seems to undermine the artistic achievement of these early nineteenth-century poems, and the extension of the view that decline characterizes the large body of poetry after 1810 simply worsens the problem.

What is intriguing about this valedictory approach to the later or even latest Coleridge poems is that it fails to make key connections between these and the pre-1800 poems and—a crucial point—to see them in the larger context of Coleridge's ideas about literature as the work of imagination. This is not to say that these late poems have not received full and perceptive treatment. Anyone familiar with the work of Patricia Adair, W. J. Bate, James Boulger, Kathleen Coburn, Angela Dorenkamp, Beverly Fields, Edward Kessler, Paul Magnuson, Marshall Suther, George Watson, and others knows from what a number of fruitful angles they have been examined.[2] Especially interesting is J. Robert Barth's observation in his recent study concerning Coleridge's ideal of love. Speaking of *Constancy to an Ideal Object* and other late poems, he sees no affirmation, no positive resolution, yet there are for him "times of hope and even moments of joy, for even in the darkest times there was always love in Coleridge's life." Eschewing the easy dismissal of the late poems as a dramatic falling-off after the turn-of-the-century triumphs, he argues, "Both in substance and style they have a life of their own."[3]

Many of these considerations of this body of poetry have been necessarily brief, treating the works quite understandably as a relatively minor part of the larger Coleridge repertoire. Others—and Barth's new book is a good example—have been more concerned with relating the poetry to matters biographical, philosophical, or theological. Molly Lefebure, in her fine study of the fullness of Coleridge's opium addiction, sees the poet practically admitting in 1811–1812 that he could only transcribe, not create.[4] George Watson sees a great deal that is right in the later poetry, arguing that it would be redundant to debate all the things that went wrong. Praising Coleridge, the post-1802 "occasional poet," especially for poems like *The Delinquent Travellers, Work without Hope*, and *The Garden of Boccaccio*, he nevertheless chooses the single-theme approach, the theme for him being "unrequited love."[5]

Patricia Adair, finding that Coleridge's "unusual proneness to reverie and daydream, in which the conscious and unconscious powers of the mind are merged, is the secret of his greatest poetry," argues that as the dream faded, the poetry declined, and she concludes quite remarkably with a thesis very different from our own: "No one understood better than Coleridge himself that the loss of joy meant also the death of his imagination."[6] Specifically, she contends that "*Dejection* ... lacks the power of Coleridge's greatest poetry" and that at Highgate, cared for but hopeless, wandering from place to place, a slave to increasing doses of opium, "It is no wonder that the little poetry he wrote is an expression of despair."[7] Her analysis of individual later poems is perceptive if, I think, somewhat beside the mark, as in her contention that the images are "all too obviously fixed," their meaning "so confined and definite as almost to approach the method of allegory," "another sign of the death of the imagination."[8]

James Boulger, in his *Coleridge as Religious Thinker*, sees the poet of the later years as "the poet in prose of the post-Christian Kantian ontology." Regarding the early poetry as the work of the imagination, he notes that "the later may with some justice appear as that of the higher or religious reason." And because of the emotional failure of the late poetry, Coleridge is "not remembered as a great Christian poet."[9]

W. J. Bate, using 1817 as a beginning point for the late poems, sees poems like *Limbo, Ne Plus Ultra*, and *Fancy in Nubibus* as "intensely personal," as "what a poet may write when he no longer conceives of himself as a poet at all." Yet Bate finds in the best post-1817 poems "a denseness of thought often embodied in an odd original imagery, frequently homely, occasionally even grotesque," abstractions "thick with emotion and meaning." Coleridge, he says, "creates a mode of poetry entirely his own."[10] Norman Fruman, who sees the poems generally as "almost all short, personal statements, often revealing a fitful energy quickly exhausted," regards the decade following *Dejection: An Ode* as "the blackest of his unhappy life, ten years of almost complete failure and personal demoralization" and the period following as offering the image "of a great artist adrift on a wide, wide sea, without sextant or compass or rudder, but still capable of moments of brilliant seamanship."[11]

All of the above is not to say that the late poems have not had their admirers and advocates, although at times the admiration and advocacy seem to stem from considerations of subject matter—philosophy and theology especially—rather than from those of poetic achievement. I. A. Richards finds poems like *Youth and Age, Phantom and Fact, Self-Knowledge*, and *Epitaph* "more taut and self-sustaining" than the later prose and finds the poetry of *Phantom and Fact* and *Constancy to an Ideal Object* "highly distinctive."[12] Kathleen Coburn sees some of the later works as "too much neglected now" and argues that "Coleridge continued to the end to think and feel like a poet."[13] She is especially interesting in her remarks on Coleridge's use of the mirror as "the image of the inward self" as well as something that "distances the self from itself," inspiring "with whatever of fear or awe it is capable, the need to bridge the gap, whether by philosophy or by poetry, between the percipient and the perceived." The bridge is built occasionally, she argues, "not by any consistent system of thought, but by brilliant aperçus touching both the knower and the world to be known."[14]

George Whalley, who has done so much with the ordering of the composition of Coleridge's poems, bemoans the lack of a "full-scale discussion of these [late] poems and of their place in the development of Coleridge's poetic art." He takes to task those who hold a view of Coleridge "as a poet who squandered and neglected his poetic faculties and took to philosophy and theology *faute de mieux*."[15] While not denying Coleridge's intense and lifelong interest in philosophy and theology, he sees these disciplines as "correlate to, and not hostile to, poetry."[16] Interestingly, in what he calls the late "metaphysical" poems of Coleridge—*Human Life, Limbo, Ne Plus Ultra, Constancy to an Ideal Object*, and others—he takes as criteria "ingenuity of metaphor, violence of conceit, and the tendency to conduct argument through a train of images rather than by logical sequence."[17]

In *Coleridge's Nightmare Poetry*, Paul Magnuson argues that while *Dejection: An Ode* has the tone of a "last poetic utterance," there is rich evidence that Coleridge "is not totally devoid of feeling and imagination," that his "still active imagination may project an image of its own destruction," that "his imagination is not totally unresponsive."[18] And in his perceptive *Coleridge's Metaphors of Being*, Edward Kessler has a special concern with the late poems. He is particularly illuminating in his discussion of the philosophical reverberations of the poems, although he underplays the workings of the poetic imagination and the success of the late poetry as poetry. For him the late poetry is not so much the record of Coleridge's poetic quest as the fulfillment of a long struggle through the metaphors of poetry to realize the potential of

Being; "physical imagery must be cast aside before Being can emerge as itself, substantial and not illusory. His own poetic evolution moves away from the 'concrete', the particular, the individual—elements that most modern readers expect to find in poems."[19]

Summarizing a body of scholarship on any group of poems is dangerous, of course, but what seems clear from the above perhaps general survey is a pronounced tendency to treat the late poems of Coleridge as inferior poems after the great years, as minor works of a major poet, as good examples of the poet as philosopher, or—more sharply negative—as signs of poetic or imaginative decline or even demise after the poet, plagued by physical and psychological suffering, found less inspiration for his art and turned increasingly to the firm foundations of philosophy and theology. Yet for some readers—and I am one of them—many of these poems dramatize imaginatively a yearning for the world of people and the power of nature, and simultaneously a feeling of alienation and isolation. While an essay of this length cannot explore fully the range of possibilities in these poems, it can perhaps suggest some new directions in reading them, some fresh ways of seeing the Coleridgean imagination at work within them.

The major argument of this essay is that Coleridge remained a poet almost to the end of his life, even though he produced an enormous amount of literary theory and philosophical and theological speculation during his last twenty-five years. The all-important corollary of this argument is that the poet's central ideas on imagination and its workings did not radically change even though the materials of his experience and the rhythms and patterns of his inner life did, and even though—ironically—he protested that he had lost his capacity to feel and to imagine. The frequent and, it seems, easy argument that he turned from art to the higher disciplines needs to be examined in the light of several factors. First, from his earliest days, as his letters and notebooks reveal, Coleridge had been interested in all kinds of philosophy. The most confident and successful efforts of the great years reveal the creative artist articulating a vision nourished by his reading in Hartley, Kant, Schelling, the Schlegels, and many others. In this connection George Whalley's contention is telling. Coleridge, he contends, "had been fascinated by philosophy and theology almost from childhood. As his precocity settled into mature interest and concern, the philosophy and theology were still important to him though changed. His poetic imagination, specialized at times in the production of verse, commanded and unified the whole ambience of his mind."[20]

A word about chronological strategies. Beginning points for the so-called late poems are at best arbitrary and in the eye and ear of the beholder. Some would find convenient the period beginning with *Dejection: An Ode*; others would start with the so-called Highgate period. I have found

Whalley's delineation of Coleridge's poetic career sensible and convenient for my purposes. "The poems," Whalley suggests, "fall into three clearly defined periods: from *Lyrical Ballads* to 'Dejection' (1797–1802); from 'Dejection' to 'To William Wordsworth' (April, 1802, to January, 1807), and from January, 1807 to 1834."[21] In the rest of this essay, I will use the poems of the second period, so fully and, richly treated by a number of critics, as springboards for a fuller discussion of the post-1807 poems. The major concern will be close attention to certain key poems (and less close attention to others), with a view to providing new insight into the dominant themes and techniques of the poetry of the third period and offering a foundation for a later and more extensive study.

Returning to our central argument, there was rapid development in the poetry during the 1790s, development in poetic technique and in the unfolding of certain dominant concerns that would continue throughout Coleridge's life and work—the need for unity, for the full and active expression of that vital power of synthesizing, sympathizing, and creating called imagination. The Conversation poems evince that blend of description and rumination emerging from a solitary speaker. A silent listener—present or absent—serves as a vital force. The landscape plays a prominent part in the drama. The meter is a free-flowing blank verse; the manner relaxed and idiomatic; the language concise, rich, sensuous; the subject matter the probing of complex psychological states.[22] In "The Eolian Harp," the speaker, in the presence of a seemingly orthodox and cautious listener, moves from a description of a quiet, warm, comforting cottage setting—"How exquisite the scents / Snatch'd from yon bean-field! and the world *so* hush'd!" (9–10)—to a daring speculation on the lute in the casement—"its strings / Boldlier swept, the long sequacious notes / Over delicious surges sink and rise" (17–19)—to a powerful question rooted in an imaginative vision of the lute—"And what if all of animated nature / Be but organic Harps diversely fram'd, / That tremble into thought, as o'er them sweeps / Plastic and vast, one intellectual breeze, / At once the Soul of each and God of all?" (44–48)—to an awareness of the listener's dissatisfaction with such pantheistic talk, to a final statement about his "unregenerate mind" (55) and a prayer for God's gift of faith to "A sinful and most miserable man, / Wilder'd and dark" (62–63).

There is, on the one hand, the matter-of-factness of the opening of *This Lime-Tree Bower My Prison* as the speaker records the bad fortune that has kept him at home as his friends, especially Charles Lamb, to whom he addresses the poem, walk through dazzling natural settings. There is, on the other hand, that moving statement of confidence that, even though absent, he can share imaginatively, sympathetically with his sauntering friends the joys of "walnut tree," "ancient ivy," "late twilight." The underpinnings are clearly

Coleridge's developing ideas of the power of mind, the linking of man and nature, yet philosophy seems always to be in the service of poetry:

> Henceforth I shall know
> That Nature ne'er deserts the wise and pure;
> No plot so narrow, be but Nature there,
> No waste so vacant, but may well employ
> Each faculty of sense, and keep the heart
> Awake to Love and Beauty! and sometimes
> 'Tis well to be bereft of promis'd good,
> That we may lift the soul, and contemplate
> With lively joy the joys we cannot share. (59–67)

The poems of the so-called great trio also reveal their share of poetic preoccupation with philosophical and religious motifs. There is the great moment of imaginative vision when the Mariner, having shot the albatross and brought death and sterility to his world, sees and blesses intuitively, imaginatively the water snakes:

> Within the shadow of the ship
> I watched their rich attire:
> Blue, glossy green, and velvet black,
> They coiled and swam; and every track
> Was a flash of golden fire.
>
> O happy living things! no tongue
> Their beauty might declare:
> A spring of love gushed from my heart,
> And I blessed them unaware:
> Sure my kind saint took pity on me,
> And I blessed them unaware. (277–87)

And there are, of course, the almost Dionysiac lines of *Kubla Khan*, lines that celebrate the visionary poet whose imaginative creations can outrival the greatest human creations:

> Could I revive within me
> Her symphony and song,
> To such a deep delight 'twould win me,
> That with music loud and long,
> I would build that dome in air,

That sunny dome! those caves of ice!
And all who heard should see them there,
And all should cry, Beware! Beware!
His flashing eyes, his floating hair!
Weave a circle round him thrice,
And close your eyes with holy dread,
For he on honey-dew hath fed,
And drunk the milk of Paradise. (42–54)

Undoubtedly the growing physical and psychological pain—especially unhappy marriage, unrequited love, the prison of opium—that characterized Coleridge's life after 1800, the search for meaning as joy seemed to vanish, triggered a more intense quest for the method and consolation of philosophy and theology in an effort to understand and to articulate, as Richard Haven has argued, the patterns of his consciousness. Haven observes, "When philosophy replaced poetry as Coleridge's primary activity, the language and symbols of philosophy came to serve some of the same functions that had earlier been served by the language and symbols of poetry."[23] One can, of course, question Haven's distinction between "symbols" of philosophy and poetry— and I do—but that seems like another matter here. Coleridge, it is true, wrote less poetry after 1800; indeed he wrote a good deal less poetry throughout his career than Wordsworth or Byron or Shelley, for example. In no sense did he abandon poetry. He continued to write a variety of poems in a variety of manners, not only those of tragic disillusionment that are relatively well known and occasionally anthologized, but also those less well known expressions of joy, however transitory, and those more overtly religious poems of prayer and resignation. As in his earlier work, some of these poems are little more than pious, abstract moralizing. In others, however, and these are the chief interest in this essay, the creative impulse seems alive and free in the midst of sadness and loss, and the imagination brings the whole soul into unified action, capturing the moods of the spirit—bright and dark—with vividness and intensity.

Expressions of joy, of communion with nature, are never completely absent, indeed are cherished deeply and expressed lovingly in later poems like *To Nature* that must be kept in mind when examining the later Coleridge repertoire. There is, of course, in *To Nature* the note of self-deprecation, the turning to nature for evidences of love and unity:

It may indeed be phantasy, when I
Essay to draw from all created things
Deep, heartfelt, inward joy that closely clings;

And trace in leaves and flowers that round me lie
Lessons of love and earnest piety. (1–5)

Yet one senses here a hesitancy (Wordsworth's "If this / Be but a vain belief")
comes to mind) to attribute complete authenticity to the imagination, to
the emotion that transcends abstract dogma. However, the poet continues
(again with echoes of Wordsworth), let the world mock. He will conquer
"fear," "grief," "vain perplexity"; he will offer not the formulaic prayer, but a
different kind of present to God, one alive with the fresh and vibrant natural phenomena that pervade an early poem like *Frost at Midnight*, one that
links natural and supernatural—"fields," "blue sky," "wild flower," "God,"
"even me":

So will I build my altar in the fields,
    And the blue sky my fretted dome shall be,
And the sweet fragrance that the wild flower yields
    Shall be the incense I will yield to Thee,
    Thee only God! And thou shalt not despise
    Even me, the priest of this poor sacrifice. (9–14)

What interesting if muted echoes of a deeply religious commitment are
expressed in a letter to Thomas Meuthen from 2 August 1815. Desirous of
the esteem of good men, Coleridge fears that many may say that he seems
interested in the Gospel, that he has talents revealed in political essays, in
plays, "'but what has he sacrificed on the altar?' To this, before God, I dare
not answer; for I ought to have chosen the better part, and have *trusted*." If
he were more gifted, he claims, he "most gladly and willingly would, with
divine grace, have devoted all my faculties to one object, both in verse and
prose." And he does plan such art. "Till the whole mind is given to God, no
man can be happy; and who gives a *part, and only* a part, cannot even have
quiet—that sad boon of lethargy—which the utterly unawakened enjoy."[24]
     There is some of the same hopeful quality in the sonnet *Fancy in Nubi-
bus*, significantly subtitled "The Poet in the Clouds." Written, according to
Charles Lamb, on the seacoast, it isolates moments of joy close to nature,
but, more interesting, these are moments of creativity when the imagination
can shape natural beauties according to one's hopes and desires. The speaker
echoes Keats's urbanite's exclamation, "'Tis very sweet to look into the fair
/ And open face of heaven," and revels in the joys of the mind when it can
make images from beauty and happiness as they quickly pass. "O! it is pleas-
ant, with a heart at ease, / Just after sunset, or by moonlight skies, / To make
the shifting clouds be what you please" (1–3), he begins, skillfully painting an

evening sky in which ever-moving clouds can be shaped to suit the energy and inventiveness of his imagination. Or in the same mood, he can be stirred by the creations of a fellow poet; he can "let the easily persuaded eyes / Own each quaint likeness issuing from the mould / Of a friend's fancy" (4–6). Or, even more venturesome, he can exercise that sympathetic aspect of the imagination, can become part of the scene he creates. In pictures of rich color and swift movement, he imagines himself "with head bent low / And cheek aslant see rivers flow of gold / 'Twixt crimson banks; and then, a traveller, go / From mount to mount through Cloudland, gorgeous land!" (6–9).

The joyous moment or condition can also be one of love for a person or a state of the spirit that renders it open and receptive to all creation. In the dramatic piece called *The Improvisatore*, Coleridge assumes the title role and deals with the question of what is true love posed by two young ladies, Katherine and Eliza. The core of his response moves beyond personal anecdote to the more philosophical dimension of sympathy in love, of the outward manifestations betokening a deeper power within the soul. Love, he tells the young ladies in his discursive response, is "a constitutional communicativeness and *utterancy* of heart and soul; a delight in the detail of sympathy, in the outward and visible signs of the sacrament within—to count, as it were, the pulses of the life of love" (1.464). Fascinated by the Improvisatore's response, the girls teasingly wonder whether one who speaks so beautifully of love in the abstract can have truly experienced it. His answer is a song of affirmation qualified: he loved in his imagination, which for a time created an ideal embodiment, but "She missed her wonted food" (15). "Fancy must be fed" (12); hope, the cardinal Coleridgean virtue, must be kept alive, but was not. Images of stormy sea, castaway, and bewilderment, images that recur in the later poetry, dominate Coleridge's self-portrait. In a mood reminiscent of Wordsworthian remembrance, he traces the decline of love's intensity, of hope, but speaks of new gifts that surpass all others. In richly figurative language that ironically anticipates the tragic later poem *Work without Hope*, he pictures a new calm, "Late Autumn's Amaranth, that more fragrant blows / When Passion's flowers all fall or fade" (56–57).

There are few more powerful evocations of joy revived in the midst of dejection, imagination reactivated in the midst of the dull ache of spiritual and physical pain, than *The Garden of Boccaccio*. A dream vision, the situation, rhythm, diction, and imagery of the opening lines recall *Dejection*. The mood is "dreary"; life seems "emptied of all genial powers"; the poet sits "alone" (1–4). All prayers for help seem to fail; the past cannot be revived. The "dull continuous ache" (8) seems the only vital sign as he hovers at the brink. Then the "Friend" of the poem, Anne Gilman, leaves at his side a striking illustration of Boccaccio's "First Day" from an edition of the *Decamerone* by Thomas Stothard, a contemporary painter and engraver. Again, as elsewhere in the poems being discussed, the theme is not rebirth or return to youthful sensuous awareness. The joy is vivid but not lasting; it is remembrance in its highest form, the product of the artist's ability to evoke and stir imaginative response. Wordsworth's "The picture of the mind revives again" is echoed. The idle eye becomes busy; the inward power is recharged; language and image are freshly recovered:

> Like flocks adown a newly-bathed steep
>   Emerging from a mist: or like a stream
> Of music soft that not dispels the sleep,
>   But casts in happier moulds the slumberer's dream. (19–22)

The process is progressive. "The picture stole upon my inward sight" (24), and "one by one (I know not whence) were brought / All spirits of power that most had stirr'd my thought / In selfless boyhood" or "charm'd my youth" or "lent a lustre to the earnest scan / Of manhood" (24–34). The delights of Boccaccio move him to sing again, to hope until that "sober" matron reappears "Whom as a faery child my childhood woo'd / Even in my dawn of thought—Philosophy; / Though then unconscious of herself, pardie, / She bore no other name than Poesy" (46–51). There is here the intriguing implication that poetry and philosophy have, in spite of their obvious differences, a special kinship, that poetry, active in the creation of a youthful, realizable ideal, later becomes philosophy for some artists, but that philosophy can never completely divorce itself from the need to concretize, to vivify abstractions and make them real to the heart. The poem's conclusion is dramatic and stirring. Thanks to Boccaccio the poet is, at least for a time, "all awake!" There is a new immediacy to his life: "I see no longer! I myself am there, / Sit on the groundsward, and the banquet share" (59–65).

Such poems are, of course, not fully representative of the work of the last twenty-five years. The basic argument of the essay to this point has been that Coleridge's career cannot be neatly divided into a phase during which he produced his most memorable poetry and another in which, imagination and poetry failing, he turned to the solace of philosophy and theology. The key corollary of the argument is that Coleridge remained a poet to the end, that the controlling image of the later poetry, a poetry of uneven quality, is the ideal unity, a state in which the imagination discovers in nature analogues of an interior joy. If the analogues become fewer and fewer, if some seem abstract and lifeless, if disillusionment dominates at times, the triumphs still remain. The ideal for Coleridge may seem evanescent, but it still remains a goal to be pursued and cherished, and the imagination provides an extraordinary access route.

Yet the pain and sadness of so much of the later poetry are inescapable. The poems of this period and after catch a strongly tragic spirit. At times— and invariably the poetry suffers—he openly doubts the creative power and seeks the more solid foundations of philosophy or theology, or, like the fideist, throws himself totally on God's mercy. The result, as in earlier poems when intensity of religious zeal and strength of philosophical argument dominate, is an abundance of heavy-handed moralizing, a strong reliance on conventional poetic diction, and a rigidly regular, almost singsong, rhythm. Lines like the following from *A Hymn*, with their commonplace plea of the guilty man to an all-powerful God, illustrate the fideistic posture and the poetic effects described above:

> Great God! thy works how wondrous fair!
> Yet sinful man dids't thou declare
>   The whole Earth's voice and mind!
> Lord, ev'n as Thou all-present art,
> O may we still with heedful heart
>   Thy presence know and find! (11–16)

Similar characteristics are seen in his translation *Faith, Hope, and Charity: From the Italian of Guarini*. They can be seen all too strikingly in the lackluster didacticism of *Love, Hope, and Patience in Education* with its distrust of the joys of spontaneity and its presentation of a new and stiffly personified heroine of comfort:

> When overtask'd at length
> Both Love and Hope beneath the load give way.
> Then with a statue's smile, a statue's strength,
> Stands the mute sister, Patience, nothing loth,
> And both supporting does the work of both. (22–26)

But the failure of such poems should not be allowed to hide a considerable number of triumphs, poetry still responsive to the predicament of the artist who creates from the exploration of human alienation and loss complex, abruptly expressed, and vividly realized images in free-flowing rhythms that seem modern. Coleridge's imagination is still at work, albeit its range is widened to include the tragic as well as the joyous, to catch the multifaceted nuances of human emotion. Coleridge was, of course, theorizing more about the imagination during these years—in *Biographia Literaria*, the notebooks, *The Statesman's Manual*, and other prose works touching on aesthetic questions. He was describing his vision of nature in greater detail, not as the "one, clear, unchanged, and universal light" of Pope, but as a process, a living force in which universal forms and concrete particulars are constantly interacting. He was offering his idea of imagination as the root of genius in the arts, the great completing power mediating between and reconciling opposites to create unity and, in words from his celebrated definition in *The Statesman's Manual*, giving "birth to a system of symbols, harmonious in themselves, and consubstantial with the truths, of which they are the *conductors*."[25] Symbol, far from a simple image, is a translation of a complex reality, capturing what is essential within the creative activity of nature.

Imagination, then, is not simply the faculty of triumph, of joyous unity with nature. It is also at home capturing the tragic notes of human experience, the sense of human suffering, loss, alienation. Nothing that is human can be foreign to imagination. Just as the great tragedians capture the predicaments of men and women who suffer and yet endure, who cry out against injustice, who achieve a kind of grandeur in spite of battles lost but fought nevertheless, so to a lesser extent Coleridge captures imaginatively sadness and struggle. Yet, as in great tragedy, he catches it in such a way that we feel, sympathize with, pity, but do not despair; "all disagreeables evaporate," as Keats says of the stark intensity of King Lear's loss of everything and his discovery of himself. There is, in Aristotle's words, a catharsis, not an avoidance of pain or an easy solution, but a genuine purging of the tragic emotions, a putting into perspective of the individual predicament so that those who read or watch feel their experience widened, their sense of the range of human possibility enlarged.

Michael Friedman offers an illuminating way of thinking about the tragic imagination. Writing about Wordsworth's pamphlet *The Convention of Cintra*, he argues, "Wordsworth suggests that the true sorrow of life is that reality offers so few experiences that are correlative 'to the dignity and intensity of human desires.'" Wordsworth, according to Friedman, saw the Convention as evoking only shame and sorrow and yet as offering "an opportunity for the release of emotions that would not be beneath the dignity and intensity of human desires. The sorrow of human life would be overcome in the experience of true shame and sorrow. A catharsis would have been achieved." Friedman concludes his analysis with the contention that the "discharge of emotion may well lessen the emotional tension in the sorrowing individual's psychic economy. The diminution of psychic tension is felt as a form of pleasure."[26]

Coleridge himself had been interested in the tragic and the purgation of tragic emotion. "The communicativeness of our nature leads us," he wrote, "to describe our own sorrows; in the endeavour to describe them, intellectual activity is exerted; and from intellectual activity, there results a pleasure, which is gradually associated, and mingles as a corrective, with the painful subject of the description."[27] He alerts his readers to the dark side of his spirit: "If any man expect from my poems the same easiness of style which he admires in a drinking song, for him I have not written." And carrying aesthetic theory into the realm of theology, he explains, "Poetry has been to me its own 'exceeding great reward': it has soothed my afflictions; it has multiplied and refined my enjoyments; it has endeared solitude; and it has given me the habit of wishing to discover the Good and the Beautiful in all that meets and surrounds me."[28]

Coleridge's later works include many poems of the tragic imagination, poems basically of the inner life where truth seems most real, poems that struggle in gnarled, nightmarish, seemingly disconnected images to evoke a twilight state just short of absolute negation. The King Lear of act 4, scene 6, half-mad in his imaginings, comes to mind ("There's hell, there's darkness, there's the sulphurous pit, burning, scalding, stench, corruption"), but the "ounce of civet" is rarely found to "sweeten" his imagination, and we are left with the frightening picture of a man terrified, seemingly cut off from his inner sources of strength.

As suggested earlier, the poems of Whalley's second period, notably *Dejection: An Ode* and to a lesser extent *To William Wordsworth*, when matched with the imaginative power of the post-1807 poetry, provide a basis for the argument concerning the irony of Coleridge's cry for a lost imagination. With the seeming affirmation of Wordsworth's *Ode: Intimations of Immortality* still ringing in his ears, Coleridge wrote his *Dejection: An Ode* on 4 April 1802.[29] How different its tone, its language, its imagery, but especially its facing of similar questions from both the Wordsworth poem and his own earlier work. Using the familiar lines of the *Ballad of Sir Patrick Spence* as his point of departure and the omen of "the new Moon / With the old Moon in her arms" as an anticipation of stormy weather, the speaker pleads for "The coming-on of rain and squally blast" not simply for its physical power, but that it might minister to his deadened spirit, "Might startle this dull pain, and make it move and live" (14–20). Coleridge would have the reader see and feel his physical condition as complete. Indeed stanzas 2–3 dramatize a psychological predicament, a sense of deadness within, a sadness that transcends physical pain and that cannot be adequately conveyed in the language of common speech. It is

> A grief without a pang, void, dark, and drear,
> A stifled, drowsy, unimpassioned grief,
> Which finds no outlet, no relief,
> In word, or sigh, or tear—(21–24)

Yet—and how ironic—we see vivid images of "the western sky, / And its peculiar tint of yellow green," of "thin clouds above, in flakes and bars, / That give away their motion to the stars"; of "Yon crescent Moon, as fixed as if it grew / In its own cloudless, starless lake of blue." These are quickly followed, however, by the finality of "I see, not feel, how beautiful they are!" We find no Wordsworthian sense of the possibility of growth, of compensation, only the speaker's definitive assurance that "I may not hope from outward forms to win / The passion and the life, whose fountains are within" (25–46).

It is this deep conviction of the absolute need for an active, creative, psychological power—the imagination—that the speaker develops in the touching lines of stanzas 4–5. Only the mind's dynamic encounter with experience creates meaning. Sight and memory are inadequate; "we receive but what we give, / And in our life alone does Nature live." Meaning, felt truth, comes only from the self. The familiar Romantic image of effluence— the lamp, the fountain—comes to mind: "from the soul itself must there be sent / A sweet and potent voice of its own birth, / Of all sweet sounds the life and element!" The speaker calls the power "Joy," an inner force possessed by and given only to the "pure," a force "Which wedding Nature to us gives in dower / A new Earth and new Heaven." It creates a new reality "that charms or ear or sight" (59–75).

So much for the speaker's description of the woebegone state of his spirit, the depth of his loss, the impossibility of rebirth. Stanza 6 sharply echoes Wordsworth's opening stanza as the speaker plays on the words of the Immortality ode to dramatize the very different state of his own soul. He can, he says, recall a time when his mind could cope with misfortune, when he could hope in the midst of sadness:

> There was a time when, though my path was rough,
> This joy within me dallied with distress,
> And all misfortunes were but as the stuff
> Whence Fancy made me dreams of happiness. (76–79)

He had the gift of "hope" and could appreciate the Wordsworthian sense of the possibility of some gain in spite of eroding youthful blessings. Yet there is a finality, a firmness of tone, in his convictions about the present. "But now afflictions bow me down to earth," he says. "But oh! each visitation / Suspends what nature gave me at my birth, / My shaping spirit of Imagination." Such finality and firmness make him turn to "Abstruse research," only to have that turning result in the loss of the "natural man" and in a psychological infection that becomes "the habit of my soul" (80–93).

In the long, irregular stanza that follows, there is a flow of grotesque, terrifying imagery that graphically reveals the depth of difference in the answers of the speakers to the problems of both odes. The speaker of *Dejection* finds no "joy" in the "embers," no gathering with the children, no union with nature. His are cries of anguish as he personifies the fantasies that torment him: "Hence, viper thoughts, that coil around my mind, / Reality's dark dream!" The "joyous song" of the "young lambs," the "gladness of the May" in the Wordsworth ode give way to "the wind, / Which long has raved unnoticed." The lute, so unlike the melodious Eolian harp of Coleridge's earlier poems, sends forth "a scream / Of agony by torture lengthened out." Here is no benevolent nature; instead appropriately frightening images dominate, the product of a tormented mind no longer possessed of that great prize "Joy." The setting is "Bare crag, or mountain-tairn, or blasted tree, / Or pine-grove whither woodman never clomb, / Or lonely house, long held the witches' home." The wind is not a Wordsworthian breeze but "Mad lutanist! who in this month of showers, / Of dark-brown gardens, and of peeping flowers, / Mak'st Devils' yule, with worse than wintry song" (94–120). The story is not one of triumph over loss, but, again ironically, an imaginative adaptation of the drama of Wordsworth's Lucy Gray:

> 'Tis of a little child,
>   Upon a lonesome wild,
> Not far from home, but she hath lost her way:
> And now moans low in bitter grief and fear,
> And now screams loud, and hopes to make her mother hear.
> (121–25)

The concluding stanza has a special beauty in itself and a special significance in the way it illuminates the contrast between the two odes. Wordsworth's poem ends with a seeming confidence, firmly focused on the speaker and on his faith that age brought gifts greater than the losses, that memory had made it possible to feel thoughts "too deep for tears." Coleridge's concluding stanza begins on a similar self-centered note; he dwells on his sadness. Yet very quickly the self-centeredness gives way to an imaginative concern for the other, to a gentle good wish, a blessing for the "Lady." The lines are a prayer for an experience the speaker can no longer know—except imaginatively—but would nonetheless bestow. Fresh, vividly realized images convey his wish and prayer: "Visit her, gentle Sleep! with wings of healing"; "May all the stars hang bright above her dwelling" (126–33). His strongest prayer, however, is for inner strength, for the capacity to feel, to imagine, to know joy, to internalize the vitality of the process of nature:

Joy lift her spirit, joy attune her voice;
To her may all things live, from pole to pole,
Their life the eddying of her living soul! (134–36)

Dejection: An Ode provides a firm foundation for exploring the post-1807 poems with their pattern of physical and psychological pain, their rendering of this pain not through mere self-indulgent spurts of tormented rhetoric or maudlin religious sentiment, but through powerful images of the dark side of experience and the catharsis of hope, even when the hope is for another human being. So does the poem *To William Wordsworth*, a poem Coleridge composed, as the subtitle tells us, on the night after he had heard Wordsworth recite *The Prelude*. Again irony is striking as he addresses his "Friend" and "Teacher" and praises his poem with its recounting "Of the foundations and the building up / Of a Human Spirit" (5–6), of how:

Scarce conscious, and yet conscious of its close
I sate, my being blended in one thought
(Thought was it? or aspiration? or resolve?)
Absorbed, yet hanging still upon the sound—
And when I rose, I found myself in prayer. (108–12)

In the post-1807 poems, moments of relief are fewer; the pain is obviously deeper; the loss more decisive. Yet the poet, it seems, remains the dominant figure, ranging through the domain of his imagination for word and image to catch the state of the spirit. One notes, on the most obvious level, the simple cry of physical pain. "Sad lot, to have no Hope!" (1), he moans in a prayer for relief in *The Visionary Hope*, moving from routine abstractions to concrete feelings, sights, and sounds that dramatize his plight: "He strove in vain! the dull sighs from his chest / Against his will the stifling road revealing, / Though Nature forced" (5–7), "Sickness within and miserable feeling" (11). After a time the physical and psychological merge to create a phantasmagorical state: "Though obscure pangs made curses of his dreams, / And dreaded sleep, each night repelled in vain, / Each night was scattered by his own loud screams" (12–14). Yet pain is at least a sign of life, a basis for hope, so much so that he is tempted to "let it stay! / yet this one Hope should give / Such strength that he would bless his pains and live" (26–28). *Youth and Age*, a once-upon-a-time poem, contrasts his youthful exuberance with "This breathing house not built with hands, / This body that does me grievous wrong" (8–9), with "locks in silvery slips," with "This drooping gait, this altered size" (33–34). *The Garden of Boccaccio* records the "numbing spell" (5), "the dull continuous ache" (9). The poet in "To a Lady: With

Falconer's *Shipwreck*" identifies with the hero, William Falconer, of the poem he sends to his lady. Like Falconer, and Cowper's castaway, he is a "shipwrecked man!" (16) whose verse is inspired by "The elevating thought of suffered pains, / Which gentle hearts shall mourn" (19–20).

As pathetic and debilitating as physical pain is, it is but prelude to the state of his spirit, to isolation from the nourishment of nature, from the ever-elusive ideal that one would grasp but cannot. The best poems of these years, like all successful poems, dramatize the condition rather than narrate it, fashioning a language and an imagery that match the deeply rooted malaise of the writer, creating metaphor and symbol that participate in the reality of which they are a part.

The state of the spirit, so much a part of the great *Dejection* ode just considered, stands out most sharply in the later poems as a kind of microcosm of Coleridge's larger vision of human nature. Conventional images of darkness, shipwreck, and physical pain have already been noted. What, however, distinguishes the best of these poems is what has already been briefly suggested—the workings of the imagination on the tragic side of life, the darker nuances of the psyche, with a resulting knotted, highly complex, and frequently disconnected language and imagery. These have been associated, not quite appropriately, by some critics with the Metaphysical poetry of the seventeenth century, but perhaps more rightly they should be seen as anticipating what we might call the modern tradition, perhaps the "terrible" sonnets of Hopkins, the bleak and jarring world of Eliot's Prufrock or *The Wasteland*, the troubled fantasies of Robert Lowell. The often fragmentary quality of the poems, the lack of logical connectives between clusters of images, the condensed and often free-flowing quality of the writing—all these suggest something new and different. If symbols are, in Coleridge's aesthetic, "consubstantial with the truths of which they are conductors," they seem a fair way of describing what we are dealing with here.

What is man? What is the nature of his condition? Does he have a basis for hope given his condition? These are the recurring questions. Man is consistently imaged as inexplicable in his essence, as uncertain of his destiny at best, indeed all too often unable to decipher the code of nature provided by a once-loving God as a way of achieving the "blessed mood" of happiness. *Human Life* sketches him in richly paradoxical and frightening images; at times—interesting phenomenon—even Coleridge's abstractions and personifications seem to possess a remarkable vitality and suggestiveness. Man is a "vessel purposeless, unmeant, / Yet drone-hive strange of phantom purposes" (8–9), the drone image suggesting the male of the honeybee, stingless and making no honey, living on the labor of others, lethargic, idle. He is a "Blank accident! nothing's anomaly!" (14) whose very essence is "contradiction" (9). *Self-Knowledge*, written just two years before Coleridge's death, describes him not proudly as "What a piece of work" but grimly as "Dark fluxion, all unfix-able by thought" (7), as "Vain sister of the worm" (9), images of dehuman-ization. *Limbo* sees men caught in a strange arena between life and nonlife, shrinking from the light like "Moles / (Nature's mute monks, live mandrakes of the ground)" (6–7), frightened animals scurrying for some kind of safety.

Most terrifying is the dramatization of his spiritual life, a more com-pressed and powerful development of the nostalgic lines of *Dejection* like "I may not hope from outward forms to win / The passion and the life whose fountains are within" or "O Lady! we receive but what we give, / And in our life alone does Nature live." The power, so often seen in the figure of the fountain—"Joy's bosom-spring" (18) in *A Hymn*, the Fount of Cheer in *The Two Founts*—still remains, but it is choked, and the nature with which it must be reconciled and reunited to create life has become an Eliot-like wasteland, "A heap of broken images, where the sun beats, / And the dead tree gives no shelter, the cricket no relief, / And the dry stone no sound of water." Man is caught, indeed trapped, not in the bliss of heaven or the damnation of hell, but in "Limbo's Den," a macabre state of mental terror, "not a Place" but a realm "where Time and weary Space / Fettered from flight, with night-mare sense of fleeing, / Strive for their last crepuscular half-being" (11–14). Time and space have become meaningless scholastic categories, no longer susceptible to neat definition; poetry, however, with its image-making power, must do what philosophy cannot, must translate the untranslatable. Now one confronts

> Lank Space, and scytheless Time with branny hands
> Barren and soundless as the measuring sands,
> Not mark'd by flit of Shades,—unmeaning they
> As moonlight on the dial of the day! (*Limbo*, 15–18)

The den of Limbo is a hopeless one, a Kafkaesque existence lacking even the mild comfort of the old Christian description of Limbo. It is a condition not a place, "Wall'd round, and made a spirit-jail secure, / By the mere horror of blank Naught-at-all" (32–33). Angus Fletcher in his essay "Positive Nega-tion" sees Coleridge as like Hamlet, fearful "lest events simply may not follow. His work can be conceived as an intensely interested struggle against this fear."[30] Rejecting the abstractions of philosophy and theology, he imagines Limbo as at the very boundary line of existence where Space and Time—one "lank," the other "scytheless"—seem to have lost all their power and pre-rogatives, indeed "unmeaning they / As moonlight on the dial of the day!" (17–18). How different from human time, human life, although it too offers little consolation. Human time is a blind old man—Gloucester-like—with a face all eye, with a new silent sight gratefully accepting a special kind of illumination. Coleridge's image is powerful, sharply drawn:

> With scant white hairs, with foretop bald and high,
> He gazes still,—his eyeless face all eye;—
> As 'twere an organ full of silent sight,
> His whole face seemeth to rejoice in light!
> Lip touching lip, all moveless, bust and limb—
> He seems to gaze at that which seems to gaze on him! (25–30)

As W. J. Bate says, "But even this blind hope is denied the soul in limbo. For there, if the redemption of man is not believed, hope turns to fear."[31]

After seventeen relentlessly rhyming couplets, the poem is climaxed by a quatrain whose sense of finality and strategically positioned rhymes speak for themselves:

> A lurid thought is growthless, dull Privation,
> Yet that is but a Purgatory curse;
> Hell knows a tear far worse,
> A fear—a future state;—'tis Positive Negation! (35–38)

Fletcher's observation is again helpful as he surveys the poet's whole inner state. Coleridge, he argues, "whose heart is so full, if sometimes only of its own emptiness, its desire to be filled, seems fully aware that the between-ness of time-as-moment, pure thresholdness, barren liminality, at least in what Einstein would call a 'space-like' way, must be a nothingness."[32]

Few poems capture so well and so imaginatively the mood of Coleridge in the later years as *Time Real and Imaginary: An Allegory*. The quick rhythms and idiomatic manner of the opening lines suggest the joy and liveliness of youth when time seems an "endless race" run by "Two lovely children," "A sister and a brother!" (4–5). The sister gleefully runs onward, unaware of real time and age; in looking back, however, she spies the brother, no longer young and swift, but a blind, haggard, Bergman-like wraith who has felt the ravages of real time. The mood of the opening is abruptly reversed with the regular, almost stolid rhythm of the final couplet intensifying the pathos: "O'er rough and smooth with even step he passed, / And knows not whether he be first or last" (10–11). Coleridge in a January–March 1811 notebook entry tried to capture the sense of time that pervades the poem:

> Contrast of troubled manhood, and joyously-active youth, in the sense of Time. To the former it Time, like the Sun in a cloud

empty Sky is never seen to move, but only to *have moved*—there, there it was—& now 'tis here—now distant—now distant—yet all a blank between / To the latter it is as the full moon in a fine breezy October night—driving in amid Clouds of all shapes & hues & kindling shifting colors, like an Ostrich in its speed—& yet seems not to have moved at all—This I feel to be a just image of time real & time as felt, in two different states of Being—The Title of the Poem therefore (for Poem it ought to be) should be Time real, and Time felt (in the sense of Time) in Active Youth / or Activity and Hope & fullness of aim in any period / and in despondent object-less Manhood—Time *objective* & subjective—[33]

Ne Plus Ultra captures more powerfully in sharp, staccato lines the haunted imagination. As suggested earlier, Coleridge's allegorical figures can at times take on an unusual strength and range of suggestion, and the picture of the Demon in these lines, with its play of opposites—especially the famil-iar "Night" and "Light"—and of striking adjectives—"primal," "Condens'd," "abysmal"—takes the poem beyond the conventional into an entirely new realm of poetic effect. Note the barrage of what might be called powerfully vague images of a demonic creature aimed at creating the effect of terror:

> Sole Positive of Night!
> Antipathist of Light!
> Fate's only essence! primal scorpion rod—
> The one permitted opposite of God!—
> Condens'd blackness and abysmal storm
> Compacted to one sceptre
> Arms the grasp enorm—(1–7)

What is being dramatized, then, is a condition of imaginative and emo-tional paralysis, an entrapment by the Demon that, isolating man from the vital beauties of nature, triggers the creation of the nightmare world, a place of silent, fetid, lethargy-inducing darkness that envelops its victims and leaves them without that central Coleridgean virtue of hope. *Work without Hope*, one of the most interesting and crucial of the later poems, graphically captures the gap between the torpor of the poet and the active processes of nature:

> All nature seems at work. Slugs leave their lair—
> The bees are stirring—birds are on the wing—
> And Winter slumbering in the open air,
> Wears on his smiling face a dream of Spring!

> And I the while, the sole unbusy thing,
> Nor honey make, nor pair, nor build, nor sing. (1–6)

Every phase of nature is "at work," every creature directed toward its final cause, its proper activity; there is a wonderfully imaginative sense of an orchestrated process with self-fulfillment the goal and result. "Slugs leave their lair" to begin their annual activity; "bees are stirring," weary of their long sleep and plotting the long-range activities of later spring and summer; once again, after their annual vacation, "Birds are on the wing." These vivid, concrete images culminate in the lovely personification of Winter, still asleep, but with a magic sense of anticipation, wearing "on his smiling face a dream of Spring!" The poet seems almost categorical in describing himself as "the sole unbusy thing." He is useless. He can no longer create, find an outlet for his capacities, cannot "honey make, nor pair, nor build, nor sing." Like the antihero of *Dejection*, he can "see, not feel, how beautiful they are!" The full extent of his condition is captured in the last four lines. The first couplet juxtaposes a pathetic self-portrait, "With lips unbrightened, wreathless brow, I stroll," with a rhetorical question, "And would you learn the spells that drowse my soul?" The second, constructed around a brilliant and favorite Coleridge metaphor, answers that question: "Work without Hope draws nectar in a sieve / And Hope without an Object cannot live" (11–14). The precious nectar garnered from Work is lost in the sieve of Despair. Hope, without the vehicle of fulfillment, the power of making dreams concrete and realizable, the imagination, is a cruel hoax. The creative, life-giving fount has given way to the wasting sieve. Surely this sonnet anticipates the anguish of Hopkins's *Thou Art Indeed Just, Lord*:

> See, banks and brakes
> Now, leaved how thick! laced they are again
> With fretty chervil, look, and fresh wind shakes
> Them; birds build—but not I build; no, but strain,
> Time's eunuch, and not one work that wakes
> Mine, O thou lord of life, send my roots rain. (9–14)

A number of later poems, with varying degrees of success, focus specifically on loss of love or on the parody of love as pity or kindness. Since love is a central concern for Coleridge, the inability to love or to find reciprocation for love distresses him greatly. In a seldom-discussed *Song*, he cleverly juxtaposes two stanzas, using the second to undercut the power of the first and concluding with one of his most grotesque and painful metaphors. The opening of the *Song* celebrates love as a flashing and sharp sword, "veiled in spires of myrtle-wreath," so sharp that it "cuts its sheath" (1–2). Once the unfolding takes place, once we see "through the clefts itself has made," the sword of love is "By rust consumed, or snapt in twain; / And only hilt and stump remain" (5–8). *The Pang More Sharp Than All: An Allegory*, after describing in rather uninspired fashion the departure of the boy Love ("Hope's last and dearest child without a name!—/ Has flitted from me, like the warmthless flame," 2–3), turns inward to record how love has not so much departed from him as he has become "exiled" from love. Then in one of those extraordinary psychological images of creative interaction, one that draws on Spenser's *Faerie Queene*, Coleridge develops the motif of exile:

> For still there lives within my secret heart
> The magic image of the magic Child
> Which there he made up-grow by his strong art,
> As in that crystal orb-wise Merlin's feat,—
> The wondrous 'World of Glass,' wherein inisled
> All long'd for things their beings did repeat;—
> And there he left it, like a Sylph beguiled,
> To live and yearn and languish incomplete! (36–43)

In still another allegorical poem, *Love's Apparition and Evanishment: An Allegoric Romance*, a poem filled with echoes of *Dejection*, the tragic death of love is strangely portrayed. Using another favorite image, the "eyeless face," the poet compares himself to "a long Arab, old and blind" (1), who "listens for a human sound—in vain" (6). He describes his own "vacant mood" (8), "the sickly calm with aimless scope, / in my own heart" (15–16). The poem turns abruptly as he spies "thee, O genial Hope, / Love's elder sister" (17–18). What he sees now, however, is not the bright girl of his youth, but a Gothic horror, "Drest as a bridesmaid, but all pale and cold, / With roseless cheek, all pale and cold and dim, / Lie lifeless at my feet!" (19–21). Now Love, "a sylph in bridal trim" (22), stands beside him, but, unlike the memorable figure in George Herbert's *Love III* who finally brings warmth and hope, she has no power here. Indeed she brings despair as she "fades away / In the chill'd heart by gradual self-decay" (31–32).

In spite of pain, psychological trauma, and the onset of despair, hope flickers from time to time, hope in natural process, in human love, in poetry, in the ideal created by the power of mind/imagination. These poems, however, ultimately remove the flickers of that ideal, tracing its possibilities, its decline and fall and death, and preparing the way for a final resignation to God. Clearly one of the most beautifully realized poems in this vein is *Constancy to an Ideal Object*. It opens on a Renaissance note with a vision of the mutability of earthly things: "Since all that beat about in Nature's range, / Or veer or vanish" (1–2). The poet, inclined to hope in his ideal, quickly questions it, asking "why should'st thou remain / The only constant in a world of change, / O yearning Thought! that liv'st but in the brain?" (2–4). It is folly to "Call to the Hours, that in the distance play" (5); they will bring no "life-enkindling breath" (8). Outcasts, battered by the storms of existence, "Hope and Despair meet in the porch of Death!" (10). There can be no meeting of the "I am" and the "It is." As Boulger writes, "The ideal, fixed mode of thought, the spiritual image, must remain detached from the vibrant, mutable reality of Nature, through a paradox which is emotionally enervating for the poet."[34] Still the poet is haunted by the possibility of dreams realized, images rendered concrete, the ideal in the real. He envisions in his mind's eye "some dear embodied Good, / Some living Love" (13–14), "a home, an English home, and thee!" (18). Yet all seems vain; the ideal—of love, of hope, of peace—will vanish as two of Coleridge's recurring metaphors illustrate. The first is the familiar shipwreck image freshly conceived. The early plight of the Mariner comes to mind. Without the ideal, even the perfect home is "but a becalmèd bark, / Whose Helmsman on an ocean waste and wide / Sits mute and pale his mouldering helm beside" (22–24). The second, rooted in a much-discussed contemporary phenomenon that Coleridge had himself observed and mentioned, is that of a person following his own projected shadow and attributing mysterious powers to the effect created. The image fashioned is a ghostly embodiment of his growing despair of finding the ideal. "And art thou nothing?" he questions, confronting the image, and the answer follows quickly and disturbingly:

> Such thou art, as when
> The woodman winding westward up the glen
> At wintry dawn, where o'er the sheep-track's maze
> The viewless snow-mist weaves a glist'ning haze,
> Sees full before him, gliding without tread,
> An image with a glory round its head;
> The enamoured rustic worships its fair hues,
> Nor knows he makes the shadow, he pursues! (25–32)

As I. A. Richards says, "There is something more terrible than loneliness here. It is the Ideal itself—not the actual or the fancied embodiment—he is questioning."[35]

Some of the later poems, especially those written at the very end, develop a kind of tranquillity, a sense of a new hope, or perhaps resignation, that comes not from human resources or poetic power but from a turning to God. In *Self-Knowledge* Coleridge is angered by the familiar adage "Know thyself" and proceeds to challenge it: "Say, cans't thou make thyself?—Learn first that trade" (3). With increasing rhetorical intensity he continues, "What is there in thee, Man, that can be known?" (6). The new answer is fideistic, more a counsel of religious perfection than a line of poetry: "Ignore thyself, and strive to know thy God!" (10). The poem *Reason* seems to challenge poetic vision and the mysteriousness of life as it elevates a new power to probe and to achieve the higher knowledge:

> Whene'er the mist, that stands 'twixt God and thee
> Defecates to a pure transparency
> That intercepts no light and adds no stain—
> There Reason is, and then begins her reign! (1–4)

Coleridge's Highgate years, as Angela Dorenkamp has demonstrated, were years of great unhappiness, but years in which he came increasingly to recognize the vanity of human endeavor and the absolute need for supernatural strength, for a power beyond mind, beyond imagination. This essay has followed the poetic rendering of unhappiness in a series of remarkably powerful poems. They are poems of hope and despair but ultimately of resignation, and several of the final works are more versified prayer than inspired poetry. Most readers know the famous epitaph. Fewer know the touching *My Baptismal Birth-Day* of the same year. No longer the quester, no longer the Unitarian preacher, no longer the poet of the holiness of the "One Life," he is finally "God's child in Christ adopted,—Christ my all" (1). He now preaches confidently a new orthodoxy: "Father! in Christ we live, and Christ in thee" (5). With Donne-like militancy, with a ringing challenge to the lure of the world, he rests his case:

> Let then earth, sea, and sky
> Make war against me! On my heart I show
> Their mighty master's seal. In vain they try
> To end my life, that can but end its woe.—
> Is that a death-bed where a Christian lies!—
> Yes! but not his—'tis Death itself there dies. (9–14)

It is as if the orthodox religious thinker and man of faith and the artist meet, and poetry finally gives way. The restless Coleridge finds his rest in resignation to God.

Notes

This essay is an outgrowth of my short article "The Reptile's Lot: Theme and Image in Coleridge's Later Poetry" in *Wordsworth Circle* 8 (Autumn 1977): 349–60. I am grateful to the editor for permission to use parts of that article.

1. All references to Coleridge's poetry are to *The Complete Poetical Works of Samuel Taylor Coleridge, Including Poems and Versions of Poems Now Published for the First Time*, 2 vols., ed. with Textual and Bibliographical Notes by Ernest Hartley Coleridge (Oxford: Clarendon Press, 1912).

2. See Adair, *The Waking Dream: A Study of Coleridge's Poetry* (New York: Barnes and Noble, 1967); Bate, *Coleridge* (New York: Macmillan, 1968); Boulger, *Coleridge as Religious Thinker* (New Haven: Yale University Press, 1961); Coburn, "Reflections in a Coleridge Mirror: Some Images in His Poems," in *From Sensibility to Romanticism*, eds. Frederick W. Hilles and Harold Bloom (New York: Oxford University Press, 1965); Dorenkamp, "Hope at Highgate: The Late Poetry of S. T. Coleridge," *Barat Review* 6 (1971): 59–67; Fields, *Reality's Dark Dream: Dejection in Coleridge* (Kent, Ohio: Kent State University Press, 1967); Kessler, *Coleridge's Metaphors of Being* (Princeton: Princeton University Press, 1979); Magnuson, *Coleridge's Nightmare Poetry* (Charlottesville: University Press of Virginia, 1974); Suther, *The Dark Night of Samuel Taylor Coleridge* (New York: Columbia University Press, 1960); Watson, *Coleridge the Poet* (London: Routledge and Kegan Paul, 1966).

3. J. Robert Barth, S.J., *Coleridge and the Power of Love* (Columbia: University of Missouri Press, 1988), 105.

4. Molly Lefebure, *Samuel Taylor Coleridge: A Bondage of Opium* (London: Gollancz, 1974), 470–71.

5. Watson, *Coleridge the Poet*, 131–32.

6. Adair, *The Waking Dream*, 6.

7. Ibid., 220.

8. Ibid., 224.

9. James Boulger, *Coleridge as Religious Thinker* (New Haven: Yale University Press), 196, 198, 199.

10. Bate, *Coleridge*, 176–77.

11. Norman Fruman, *Coleridge: The Damaged Archangel* (New York: George Braziller, 1971), 332, 261.

12. I. A. Richards, "Coleridge: His Life and Work," in *Coleridge: A Collection of Critical Essays*, ed. Kathleen Coburn (Englewood Cliffs, N.J.: Prentice Hall, 1967), 23–24, 27.

13. Coburn, "Reflections in a Coleridge Mirror," 415.

14. Ibid., 433.

15. George Whalley, "'Late Autumn's Amaranth': Coleridge's Late Poems," *Transactions of the Royal Society of Canada* 2:4 (June 1964): 159.

16. Ibid., 162.

17. Ibid., 175.

18. Magnuson, *Coleridge's Nightmare Poetry*, 110.

19. Kessler, *Coleridge's Metaphors of Being*, 47.

20. Whalley, "'Late Autumn's Amaranth,'" 162.

21. Ibid., 164. Students of the dating of *Dejection: An Ode* are indebted to George Dekker's *Coleridge and the Literature of Sensibility* (New York: Barnes and Noble, 1978). Dekker argues persuasively for the poem as a later version of drafts

from as early as the late 1790s. He contends that the verse letter "is, in effect, an intermediate and in many ways deviant draft of *Dejection: An Ode*." He further argues, "Of all Coleridge's poems *Dejection* was probably the least of an *ex tempore* performance. Of all his great poems, it was at once the most dearly earned and richly inherited." See also *Coleridge's "Dejection": The Earliest Manuscripts and the Earliest Printings*, ed. Stephen Maxfield Parrish (Ithaca: Cornell University Press, 1988). Dekker connects the ode with the eighteenth-century tradition of sensibility and the genre of the nocturnal lament. See especially pp. 7–57. See also Paul Magnuson, *Coleridge and Wordsworth: A Lyrical Dialogue* (Princeton: Princeton University Press, 1988), 273–317.

22. See M. H. Abrams, "Structure and Style in the Greater Romantic Lyric," in *Romanticism and Consciousness: Essays in Criticism*, ed. Harold Bloom (New York: W. W. Norton, 1970), 201–29.

23. Richard Haven, *Patterns of Consciousness: An Essay on Coleridge* (Amherst: University of Massachusetts Press, 1969), 17.

24. *Collected Letters of Samuel Taylor Coleridge*, ed. Earl Leslie Griggs (Oxford: Clarendon Press, 1956–1971), 4:583 (2 August 1815).

25. *Lay Sermons*, ed. R. J. White (Princeton and London: Princeton University Press and Routledge and Kegan Paul, 1972), 29. This is vol. 6 in *The Collected Works of Samuel Taylor Coleridge*, ed. Kathleen Coburn.

26. Michael Friedman, *The Making of a Tory Humanist: William Wordsworth and the Idea of Community* (New York: Columbia University Press, 1979), 248–49.

27. *The Complete Works of Samuel Taylor Coleridge, with an Introductory Essay Upon His Philosophical and Theological Opinions*, ed. W. G. T. Shedd (New York: Harper and Brothers, 1856), 7:v.

28. Ibid., 7:viii.

29. The following section on the Immortality and Dejection odes is adapted from my "Teaching the Immortality Ode with Coleridge's 'Dejection: An Ode,'" in *Approaches to Teaching Wordsworth's Poetry*, ed. Spencer Hall with Jonathan Ramsey (New York: Modern Language Association of America, 1986), 92–95. Permission to adapt has been graciously granted by the Modern Language Association of America. Quotations from the Immortality ode are from *The Poetical Works of William Wordsworth*, ed. E. de Selincourt and Helen Darbishire (Oxford: Clarendon Press, 1947), 4:279–85

30. Angus Fletcher, "Positive Negation," in *New Perspectives on Wordsworth and Coleridge: Selected Papers from the English Institute*, ed. with a foreword by Geoffrey H. Hartman (New York and London: Columbia University Press, 1972), 147.

31. Bate, *Coleridge*, 177.

32. Fletcher, "Positive Negation," 140.

33. *The Notebooks of Samuel Taylor Coleridge*, ed. Kathleen Coburn (Princeton and London: Princeton University Press and Routledge and Kegan Paul, 1957–1973), 3:4048 (January 1811).

34. Boulger, *Coleridge as Religious Thinker*, 209.

35. Richards, "Coleridge's Minor Poems." A lecture delivered in honor of the Fortieth Anniversary of Professor Edmund L. Freeman at Montana State University, 8 April 1960, p. 23.

DAVID BROMWICH

A Note on the Romantic Self

To characterize the period from 1789 to 1832 as Romantic is merely to accept a convention. It is a useful convention, I think, for scholarship as well as teaching, but in accepting it one must recall that no author we now read under this heading would have recognized the description. To the extent that the authors associated themselves with a movement—Byron, at moments, did, and Coleridge and Shelley knew what he meant—they would have been surprised to see the other names and the works with which we link them. Romanticism is a term convenient for us, not them; but it can still help us to think about some motives of reflection and action that had their start two centuries ago; and given a degree of irony one need not be embarrassed by the word: the trouble with the alternative—with a detached systematic vocabulary about anything—is that its equipment for thinking is apt to come from even simpler anachronisms like class, discourse, conjuncture, or status quo. Romanticism, from Burke and Wordsworth on, had to do with thoughts of a new liberality and frankness about oneself, about the larger communities in which one was a participant, and about everything that persists beyond the reach of those communities. We may call the last thing "nature," but nature in a sense that includes mankind, since it incorporates an idea of human nature. When in Romantic writing one encounters the word nature, it almost never means to draw a

From *Raritan* 14, no. 4 (Spring 1995): 66–74. Copyright © 1995 by *Raritan*.

circle around rivers, mountains, forests, and the other constituents of the living world. These belong to the idea but are far from the whole of it. To acknowledge such elemental forms as outside the human frame of things could only mean to adopt them as symbols of the integrity of things-as-they-are. Yet a leading premise of Romanticism is that one can hardly think even of natural objects without insensibly connecting them with an idea of things as they ought to be.

The writers of the period offer fresh thoughts "about oneself." What can that mean? The beliefs we share today about the distinctness of personal identity seem so plain a given that we are apt to assume they were always so: that this kind of self-consciousness was known, quite generally, in earlier times and that it was known to carry a peculiar importance. But neither supposition is true. Nietzsche said the idea of the serf was so improbable a fruit of progress that it had remained unplucked on the tree of thought for millennia. This need not mean that in classical Greece and Rome and under the feudal system there were no individuals, not one person who once harbored the thought, "I am a unique and inseparable being; there are truths I know respecting myself and the world that nobody else knows in the same way." Doubtless there were such people. It is an important fact about them and their cultures that in every earlier time of the world they were people who had nowhere to go. There was no broader life—no life of experience and reflection—in which their intuitions of a self could be confirmed. Intellectual historians like J. H. van den Berg and Charles Taylor have variously located the beginnings of the modern idea of the self. The germ of it, we are sometimes told, was already in Luther and Montaigne; it does seem traceable to the general spirit of reformation in religion, and of secularization in letters. However, the kind of individual consciousness that we find in the Romantic poets and prose writers has a more immediate source a generation before, in the writings of Rousseau.

For French politics and social theory Rousseau's most influential works are *The Social Contract* and the *Discourse on Inequality*. For the English writers we are now considering, the great book is his *Confessions*, which opens with a remarkable sentence: "I have resolved on an enterprise which has no precedent, and which, once complete, will have no imitator. My purpose is to display to my kind a portrait in every way true to nature, and the man I shall portray will be myself." I do not think Rousseau can have meant that no one after him would write an autobiography—though his egotism certainly made him capable of such a conceit. What, then, when he spoke of an enterprise without precedent and without an imitator, did he imagine his readers would take him to be saying? Rousseau implies that he has seen and felt certain things, that there are experiences that are uniquely his; he believes that the record of those experiences will have value as an exemplary human testimony. Could the same be true of the story of any of us? The implication of *The Confessions* is: yes, potentially yes, for any of us. We cannot be sure in advance how somebody else's story may affect our imagining of our own: that is the only excuse for reading such a book and the only excuse for writing it. This may seem a simple truth about literature generally; but, even with the innovative fictions of the eighteenth century, with Diderot and Laclos as much as Richardson, we read in some measure prepared by an existing impression of character—whether the character represents a particular social role or the predicament of a whole society. On the other hand, to come to terms with Rousseau means for a self to regard another self. The effects of the discovery will not be the same in any two such encounters. This suggestion, from the opening page of the *Confessions*, will have broad consequences for criticism and interpretation in the nineteenth century. Emphatically, for Rousseau there is a truth of reading; there are wrong readings and empty readings; but it is not possible to suppose that criticism is a progress toward one right reading.

The Rousseauian thought about the individuality of any life and its unique testimony points to a psychological change in the understanding of books and writers. The fact was observed at the time—suspicion of the effects was part of the burden of the anti-Rousseau invective of Burke's *Letter to a Member of the National Assembly*—and the change was supposed to have direct political implications of a leveling sort. Any writer of whatever class, rank, or status, could now be judged individually by any reader. This is another way of saying that the interest of autobiography comes with a shift from a culture based on patronage to a culture based on public opinion. I am giving a strong version of an analysis which was itself common in the years between the French Revolution and the first Reform Bill—an analysis which took for granted that an interest in reading about the self might foreshadow the enfranchisement of many as-yet-unacknowledged persons. But the radical perception for those who first ventured it was stronger than any conceivable summary. Here is William Hazlitt in 1829, remembering what it felt like to read Rousseau in the 1790s:

> Before we can take an author entirely to our bosoms, he must be another self; and he cannot be this, if he is "not one, but all mankind's epitome." It was this which gave such an effect to Rousseau's writings, that he stamped his own character and the image of his self-love on the public mind—there it is, and there it will remain in spite of everything. Had he possessed more comprehension of thought or feeling, it would only have diverted him from his

object. But it was the excess of his egotism and his utter blindness to everything else, that found a corresponding sympathy in the conscious feelings of every human breast, and shattered to pieces the pride of rank and circumstance by the pride of internal worth or upstart pretension. . . . Till then, birth and wealth and power were all in all, though but the framework or crust that envelopes the man; and what there was in the man himself was never asked, or was scorned and forgot. And while all was dark and grovelling within, while knowledge either did not exist or was confined to a few, while material power and advantages were everything, this was naturally to be expected. But with the increase and diffusion of knowledge, this state of things must sooner or later cease; and Rousseau was the first who held the torch (lighted at the never-dying fire in his own bosom) to the hidden chambers of the mind of man—like another Prometheus, breathed into his nostrils the breath of a new and intellectual life, enraging the Gods of the earth, and made him feel what is due to himself and his fellows. . . . Shall we think only rank and pedigree divine, when we have music, poetry, and painting within us? Tut! we have read Old Mortality; and shall it be asked whether we have done so in a garret or a palace, in a carriage or on foot? Or knowing them, shall we not revere the mighty heirs of fame, and respect ourselves for knowing them?

It is a striking commentary and itself a sort of confession.

When Hazlitt speaks of Rousseau as another Prometheus, the allusion may seem a personal extravagance. But the same comparison of Rousseau with Prometheus occurs with surprising insistence elsewhere—for example, in an early notice of his writings by Mary Wollstonecraft. And in one way or another this becomes a powerful element in the Romantic idea of any original imagination. Why Prometheus? He stole the gift of fire from the gods, conveyed it to man, and by doing so made man able to rival the gods themselves. The fire, in the story Hazlitt is telling, corresponds to the new and radical standard of internal worth, the belief that a thought has some value by virtue simply of being mine. Once the gift is given, the hierarchies of the earth, the whole established order in politics and morality and religion, will be shaken to the foundations. So it appears that self-knowledge, of this unprecedented kind, is a knowledge from which there can be no turning back, any more than for paganism there could be a turning back from the humanized god of Christianity. The discovery of one self, inseparable from the discovery of "another self," is part of a long history of progress, or as Hazlitt gladly consents to call it, the March of Intellect. It is the latest step and its effects he says ought now to command our attention. His *Life of Napoleon*, written about the same time, gives a literal and historical translation of the same fable: "The French Revolution might be described as a remote but inevitable result of the invention of the art of printing." In the act of reading and judging alone are contained the seeds of a self-respect which will be broadcast as a belief in democratic equality and representation.

In this Romantic view, the discovery of the self is not a selfish discovery. By reading, by abstraction, it connects me with a community beyond the parochial demands I associate with my parents or the beliefs and prejudices I inherit from my placement in a given culture at a given time. That larger and impalpable community, which I was not given but chose, relates me conceivably to anyone, and therefore it seems to everyone. The belief in the self is thus the only faith still available that makes the sort of universalist claims we usually identify with religious commitments or with moral duties. And the makers of the French Revolution were the first to capture that intuition when they made liberty, the liberty of the individual in questions of conscience and property, the concomitant of fraternity and equality: the fraternity of people who owe something to each other as fellow citizens even before they know each other's identity; and the equality of people who do not rule out any kind of person as a possible sharer in the project of liberty. That the belief in the self had a potency to take the place of religion has been conceded by those least apt to sympathize with the belief itself. I have in mind a passage of Matthew Arnold's "Function of Criticism at the Present Time" which admits the "force, truth, and universality" of the ideas of the French Revolution and commends the same ideas for their "unique and still living power." The question that remained, for writers after Burke and Wordsworth, was how far such ideas could govern the moral conduct of a community apart from the thrall of religious authority. Today the self and its liberties are touched by the same question, though the institutions against the self now commonly shun the name of religion, and call themselves by names drawn from the quasi-religious authority of politics or culture.

The idea that the freedom of an experimenting self might belong to everyone gives the literature that followed the revolution its character of novelty and universality. This is so because, to repeat, only the self connects me with humanity at large. The point appears in the past decade or two to have become counterintuitive, and will bear some elaboration. It feels more natural, more logical, to many people now, to suppose that the self links up with local interests, and that only an actual community of persons sharing certain practices could lead us by association to the universal community of mankind. Lurking somewhere in this mental picture is a scheme of impermeable boundaries:

self tautomer local interests—tautomer universal interests

On the modern communitarian hypothesis, the self is composed of stray particulars, captivating perhaps, but with no meaning on their own; these constitutive interests pick up reality as they are shared, and the sharing happens of course in a community. The community, then, of which one is a conscious member—this entity connects one with the fate of an otherwise unfathomable humanity, itself dimly distinguishable from its contributing lesser communities.

Part of the appeal of Romantic idealism is that it reverses these now intuitive and conventional expectations. It does so by means of the imaginative identification of a self with the community of humankind. There are Enlightenment echoes in my phrasing, from Hume above all, for this power of general sympathy from an abstraction of personal experience is the single greatest inheritance Romanticism owes to the Enlightenment. In the early Wordsworth, in Shelley, and even in Keats for all his hatred of didacticism, a very different scheme is presumed:

self tautomer universal interests—tautomer local interests

When the Dissenting preacher and metaphysician Dr. Richard Price affirmed, in his sermon of 4 November 1789, that he rejoiced in the triumph of the French people over tyranny and oppression, and that he rejoiced as a "citizen of the world," he signaled the hold of this latter idea of moral association upon the minds of a generation. To celebrate "the love of our country," as Price did in the title of his sermon, implied no "conviction of the superior value of it to other countries, or any particular preference of its laws and constitution of government." One's country is the contingent home for oneself among a world of others. For me alone, in reflecting on my duties toward them alone, will the bonds of principle be absolute. Price, more than any other writer of the time, shows the long reach of Protestant liberty of conscience to a Romantic freedom of thought and action.

He was a thinking man and a genuine moralist and deserves better than to be known chiefly for Burke's attack in the *Reflections*. But Burke at any rate was consistent. He distrusted the claims of all Protestant exceptionalism, and his irony hardened into scorn when he thought he could see an argument favoring "the dust and powder of individuality." It was a central and not an incidental purpose of the *Reflections* to meet head-on the pretension of generosity in Price's cosmopolitanism. You believe, says Burke, that your liberty relates you immediately to all mankind, but a sympathy like yours is morally impossible. Before you can be a citizen of the world, you must be a member of a family, then a neighbor of others in a small community, then and only then a citizen of a nation. "To be attached to the subdivision, to love the little platoon we belong to in society, is the first principle (the germ as it were) of public affections. It is the first link in the series by which we proceed towards a love to our country and to mankind." After the abstraction of a nation, long after, comes mankind. The self in this theory can have no authority for asserting an intimate relation to humanity at large, except through the mediating layers of attachment that give a reliable texture to its experience.

We come to a puzzle here. It would seem that Romanticism in literature, so plainly associated with the dignity of the individual mind, altogether warrants the rebuke from the antirevolutionist Burke, who writes to deplore the dust and powder of individuality. And yet Burke is viewed by many historians as a predecessor of Romanticism precisely for his naturalism, the "organicism" or "localism" of his thinking about the necessary bonds of a community. Wordsworth, for one, credited him as a formative influence for just such thoughts as those. The fairest conclusion may be that Romanticism cannot mean the taking of a single side in the debate about the self. It may imply rather an engagement in the debate at a certain intensity, and a dramatic feeling for what is at stake in the choice of any side at all. Not every writer of the period recognized that something new had come into the world with the French Revolution, something on which the fate of individuals and communities might depend for a long time after. Those who wrote without some such awareness, on amusing subjects and with amusing results, we now think of as talented writers who happened to work in the years 1789–1832. But for the ones we read with the interest I have been sketching, the debate about the political and moral world could evoke so strong a personal response as to force their language into code, or elicit a response at two removes in the form of an allegory. In the Preface to *Lyrical Ballads* Wordsworth calls the poet "the rock of defense for human nature; an upholder and preserver, carrying everywhere with him relationship and love." Why is human nature in need of defense? Why now? And why this character, the poet, in this particular cause? Wordsworth's argument is really circular, as Rousseau's idea of sympathy also was, but its power is none the less sustaining for that. We look to the poet for a defense of human nature because it is from the poet that we learn the adequacies of the imagination and the inadequacies of things as they are. The person who can make us start to see this, so that we continue to see it for ourselves, is the person whom we call the poet.

JOHN BEER

Romantic Apocalypses

It was particularly appropriate that the coming of the millennium in the year 2000 should be marked by the appearance of Morton Paley's study *Apocalypse and Millennium in English Romantic Poetry*,[1] since he there concerns himself not only with the part played by those concepts in the thinking of the early English Romantic poets but with its place in Western thinking generally. Although the biblical account of the Last Things, "eschatology," as it came to be called, was always there, waiting to provide a framework for events that seemed to have a corresponding quality, Paley also notes that it did not have a finally authoritative organization among its elements. A point that he stresses in consequence, and that gives much of the shape to his study, is the degree to which the idea of the apocalypse and that of the millennium tended to go together, while still remaining separable, so that at certain times people would concentrate particularly on the one or the other. It was not very clear, for instance, whether the thousand years were to be a period preceding the Last Judgment or whether they would be a paradisal state to follow it for those who had been judged among the righteous. An interpreter could simply choose which elements to emphasize, therefore, and if in doubt place them in the order that seemed most appropriate.

Although traditionally the two ideas, those of the apocalypse and of the millennium, have gone together, the first, with its sense of doom, has recently

From *Romanticism and Millenarianism*, edited by Tim Fulford, pp. 53–69. Published by Palgrave Macmillan. Copyright © 2002 by Palgrave.

been more prominent. We saw something of this when preparations for the year 2000 coincided with premonitions of disaster, which usefully crystallized into the idea that many of the most crucial computers in the world would fail when they tried to bring up the first date of the year 2000. This, it was thought, by halting many important electronic functions, would lead to a collapse of civilization and so bring about the disasters of the apocalypse. This already illustrates the way in which the meaning of the word itself has shifted in recent times. Originally it meant simply "revelation," the name given to the English version in the New Testament, and it has always retained some of that sense. The last chapters, with their visionary picture of the heavenly city, the New Jerusalem, were particularly popular. But by way of the other events described it also came to emphasize the violence of the final events—and particularly, of course, the destructive conflict that was envisaged as marking the future end of human history.

Historically, there have been several occasions when the biblical Book of Revelation seemed particularly relevant to its readers. In the seventeenth century, when individual lay interpretations became prominent, those who came to it freshly were eager to find in its prophetic books—and especially this one—texts that could be applied to their current world. The mention of Babylon, the great Whore, suited those who were looking for ammunition against the Roman Catholic church, while the various uncomplimentary things said about the "kings of the earth," including the prophecy that they would hide in the dust, encouraged all who were of a republican frame of mind.

In one sense, then, it was predictable that the French Revolution should re-arouse such thinking. This was not the first response, however. In 1788, as a matter of fact, England had been celebrating the centenary of the English Revolution of 1688, when William of Orange was thought to have brought proper democracy to the British people and so warded off dangerous developments such as those that had provoked what was happening in France. When the Revolution first broke out it was thought at first, therefore, that France was simply following in England's footsteps into the adoption of a more democratic form of monarchy. But as the events in France unfolded, with the deposition of the king and the realization that the state being set up was atheist in nature, together with the exaltation of Reason, and when the lurking destructive potentialities became evident with the Reign of Terror, minds began to turn to the prophecies concerning the Last Days when the Devil would have power for a time. And when in the festival of Reason, a whore was crowned as its representative, the parallel with the Great Whore of Revelation seemed all too close. Surely this was a sign that civilization was passing into its apocalyptic phase.

In the 1790s events moved so quickly that the interpretative framework might have to be shifted equally quickly to adapt to them. This was particularly true in the first part of the decade. In 1793, Wordsworth's mind had been moved primarily by the fact that France and England had gone to war, thus enlisting Englishmen against figures such as the Girondins with whom he had thrown in his lot. But the matter was further complicated later that year when Robespierre, who felt that the Girondins were dragging their feet in their support of the Revolution, initiated the events leading to the Terror, in which many of Wordsworth's friends were executed. When, in the summer of 1794, news reached him that events had taken yet another turn, with Robespierre himself now dead, he found himself breaking into the rhapsodic mood described in *The Prelude*, striding along the sands by the Leven estuary where he had ridden as a boy and exulting in his belief that the ideals of the Revolution were after all going to be realized:

" . . . Thus far our trust is verified; behold!
They who with clumsy desperation brought
Rivers of blood, and preached that nothing else
Could cleanse the Augean Stable, by the might
Of their own helper have been swept away.
Their madness is declared and visible,
Elsewhere will safety now be sought, and earth
March firmly towards righteousness and peace."
Then schemes I framed more calmly, when and how
The madding Factions might be tranquillised,
And—though through hardships manifold and long—
The mighty renovation would proceed. . . .
   (*Prelude* [1805], X, 546–57)

In the previous months, with the grim, never-ending spectacle of massacre, he had found himself gazing into the heart of darkness. The revolutionary operation had seemed, indeed, like a terrible engine, consuming human beings only to demand more even as it did so (*Prelude* [1805], X, 33–46).

Whereas Wordsworth found the fall of Robespierre a straightforwardly hopeful event (even if he would then be sunk into despondency during the subsequent period), the young men whom he was shortly to meet were responding in a slightly different way. Coleridge and Southey heard the news during the summer when they were planning Pantisocracy and were equally delighted—and indeed set out to write a drama on the subject, *The Fall of Robespierre*, but had a more complex response, since in many respects they admired the Jacobin leader. They found him a resourceful, highly talented and purposeful man who had been driven to an utterly erroneous course of action—largely, Coleridge thought, through his one great failing of impatience. So there was not much of the apocalyptic in their account, more an attempt to discover how such a gifted individual might have ended up so mistaken. As a result the drama that the two poets quickly turned out was described by Coleridge, privately at least, as a "tragedy." Yet of the political significance there could be no doubt, as witnessed by their further decision in 1794 to produce a drama on the subject of Joan of Arc. Harmless enough, one might think, just another historical epic; but not in the mid-1790s, when England had just gone to war with France.

Meanwhile, as the developments on a larger stage proceeded, it was not the events of the Revolution that were now seen as apocalyptic so much as the declaration of war against France. And whereas people in England had not minded very much so long as revolutionary events were thought of in the context of the English Revolution, the new situation changed things still further. The various monarchies lining up with England to attempt defeat of the new republic could look very much like the "kings of the earth" in Revelation—who if that scenario was to be played out would end up vanquished. And in these circumstances, when there were not lacking people ready to rise up and declare themselves prophets, the most notable one being Richard Brothers, whose 1794 book, *A Revealed Knowledge of the Prophecies and Times*, affirmed, for example, that "the English government, both what is called civil and ecclesiastical, in its present form, will, by the fierce anger and determined judgment of the Lord God, be removed, annihilated, utterly destroyed,"[2] there was room for alarm.

The authorities, always fearful for the spread of sedition, and never more so than on occasions like this when the country was at war, took alarm at Brothers' sayings, which were spread by some of his associates, and had him imprisoned. There was both excitement and fear in the air, affecting the writings both of Blake and of Coleridge—which were in fact strangely similar at the time. As Jon Mee has also noted,[3] two of their writings used the birth of Christ as a point of reference. Coleridge's "Religious Musings" are written as if composed on the days before Christmas in 1794; Blake's *Europe* as a parody or pastiche of Milton's "On the Morning of Christ's Nativity":

> The deep of winter came
> What time the secret child,
> Descended thro' the orient gates of the eternal day:
> War ceas'd, & all the troops like shadows fled to their abodes.
> (Plate 3, 1–4; Erdman, p. 61)

Coleridge at the opening of "Religious Musings" figured himself as transported by his imagination to become one of the lowly shepherds who witness
the heavens explode with the vision of angels proclaiming the good news
of universal peace. He too introduces a note of cosmic vision, writing in the
first version:

> Ah not more radiant, nor loud harmonies
> Hymning more unimaginably sweet
> With choral songs around th'EETERNAL MIND,
> The constellated company of WORLDS
> Danc'd jubilant: what time the startling East
> Saw from her dark womb leap her flamy Child![4]

When the poem was re-published in the following year he omitted these
lines, thinking perhaps that they looked too pantheistic; but in 1794 they
were firmly there, envisioning the birth of the sun as a cosmic event. Blake,
meanwhile, in *Europe*, was picturing a similar birth of energy—but in more
terrible form. In his "Preludium," the Nameless Shadowy Female finds
herself about to give birth, but the son she produces is Orc, a being of unre-
stricted energy, to be experienced by her with unrelieved terror:

> I bring forth from my teeming bosom myriads of flames.
> And thou dost stamp them with a signet, then they roam abroad
> And leave me void as death:
> Ah! I am drown'd in shady woe, and visionary joy.
>   (Plate 2, 9–12; Erdman, p. 61)

Blake presents her vision ironically, since in addition to seeing energy as
terrible, she also glimpses the possibility that it might be *humanized*, which
so far from being terrible would be a mixture of the human and the divine.
She glimpses it as a divine child, in fact, not an infinite energy at all but
wrapped in swaddling clothes like the infant Jesus; not a consuming fire but
a baby needing to be fed, like the infant Zeus or the Messiah prophesied by
the prophet Isaiah, with milk and honey. And at this point she is totally non-
plussed, unable to understand at all the world in which she is living:

> And who shall bind the infinite with an eternal band?
> To compass it with swaddling bands? And who shall cherish it
> With milk and honey?
> I see it smile & I roll inward & my voice is past.
>   (Plate 2, 13–16; Erdman, p. 61)

These parallel visions of Coleridge's and Blake's give the tone of their responses to the events in France. When Blake reaches the end of *Europe*, his vision is again one of terror:

> But terrible Orc, when he beheld the morning in the east,
> Shot from the heights of Enitharmon;
> And in the vineyards of red France appear'd the light of his fury.
>   (Plate 14, 37–15, 2; Erdman, p. 65)

The book ends on the same note:

> Then Los arose his head he reard in snaky thunders clad:
> And with a cry that shook all nature to the utmost pole,
> Call'd all his sons to the strife of blood.
>   (Plate 15, 9–11; Erdman, p. 65)

The final tone is somber, relieved only by the illumination, which shows what seems to be the honest man trying to save his family in the midst of destruction.

In the cases of both Blake and Coleridge detailed chronology is particularly important, since the shift of events from year to year or even from month to month, could mean that the appropriate interpretation also changed. In the middle of the decade, for instance, the fact that Blake could follow his *America* and *Europe* with much shorter books bearing the titles of "Africa" and "Asia" suggests strongly that he had still been anticipating a worldwide movement that would take in all four continents, yet that his conviction was beginning to fade. Throughout his career, as Paley demonstrates, the theme was to recur, with the millennial suggesting, most often, less a period of time than a state of renewal. He came to believe that the Last Judgment would be realized in terms of good and bad art:

> The Last Judgment when all those are Cast away who trouble Religion with Questions concerning Good & Evil or Eating of the Tree of those Knowledges or Reasonings which hinder the Vision of God turning all into a Consuming Fire When Imagination, Art & Science & all Intellectual Gifts all the Gifts of the Holy Ghost, are [*despisd*] look'd upon as of no use & only Contention remains to Man then the Last Judgment begins & its Vision is seen by the [*Imaginative Eye*] of Every one according to the situation he holds.
>   The Last Judgment is not Fable or Allegory, but Vision. Fable or Allegory are a totally distinct & inferior kind of Poetry. Vision

or Imagination is a Representation of what Eternally Exists. Really & Unchangeably. Fable or Allegory is Formd by the daughters of Memory. Imagination is surrounded by the daughters of Inspiration who in the aggregate are call'd Jerusalem. Fable is Allegory but what Critics call The Fable, is Vision itself. ("A Vision of the Last Judgment"; Erdman, p. 554)

Coleridge, by contrast, was developing his "Religious Musings" in a much more optimistic manner. Whereas Blake leaves Europe on the point of apocalypse, with no suggestion as to what might come after, Coleridge conjures up a large and hopeful future:

> For in his own and in his Father's might
> The SAVIOUR comes! While as to solemn strains
> The THOUSAND YEARS lead up their mystic dance,
> Old OCEAN claps his hands! the DESERT shouts!
> And soft gales wafted from the haunts of Spring
> Melt the primaeval North! The mighty Dead
> Rise to new life, whoe'er from earliest time
> With conscious zeal had urged Love's wondrous plan,
> Coadjutors of God. To MILTON's trump
> The odorous groves of earth reparadis'd
> Unbosom their glad echoes: inly hushed,
> Adoring NEWTON his serener eye
> Raises to heaven: and he of mortal kind
> Wisest, he first who mark'd the ideal tribes
> Down the fine fibres from the sentient brain
> Roll subtly-surging. Pressing on his steps
> Lo! PRIESTLEY there, Patriot, and Saint, and Sage,
> Whom that my fleshly eye hath never seen
> A childish pang of impotent regret
> Hath thrill'd my heart. Him from his loved native land
> Statesmen blood-stained and priests idolatrous
> By dark lies mad'ning the blind multitude
> Drove with vain hate. Calm, pitying he retir'd,
> And mus'd expectant on these promis'd years.[5]

As we all know, there was to be no such overwhelming event in the late 1790s, or after, although there were numbers of sane people, including Priestley himself, who made such connections—which involved a course of thinking still dominated at this time by the last book of the Bible. Even at the time of its original writing that text may itself have had a political dimension, since it was possible to interpret some of the prophecies in it as covert underminings of the Roman Empire. It was a book that was being circulated among various provinces of the Empire, and so those who were responsible for its appearance there may well have been anxious for its meaning not to be too plain, a fact that may account for some of the obfuscations in it.

At all events, there were in every age elements that caught the eye of those who were looking for its fulfillment. Overarching all was the prophecy of the Last Things, including universal ruin, and of a new kingdom lasting a thousand years. But how these things were interpreted was partly a matter of individual temperament. At this time, in the 1790s, as has been suggested, such considerations were dominated by horror at the violent outcome of the French Revolution, and then by a feeling of being let down when the seemingly imminent apocalypse failed to happen.

It is this latter element that may now be focused on. Paley's study has much that is important to say about the other major Romantic poets, since apocalyptic thinking did not cease with the turn of the century. Byron, in particular, enjoyed using images drawn from the biblical apocalypse, though he was deeply skeptical about any advent of the millennium in his time; Shelley, on the other hand, constantly projected visions of a millennial age about to dawn. There had also, as Paley points out, been an interesting development at the turn of the century owing to the failure of the apocalypse to happen. It was as if all the poetic energy that had been pent up in preparation for the event needed to be used somehow, and now emerged in political commentary. So we find three poems by Coleridge in particular, "Fire, Famine and Slaughter," "The Devil's Thoughts" and "The Two Round Spaces on the Tombstone," poems that Paley groups under the term the "apocalyptic grotesque,"[6] in each of which, familiar "apocalyptic" elements appear, at the service of a sardonic imagination.

These poems are of a very different nature from the meditative poems of the period, which were to contribute particularly strongly to Coleridge's lasting reputation, but their contemporary success should not be overlooked. There was some risk involved in writing verses that were not only politically offensive but had touches of blasphemy—which was no doubt one reason why Coleridge was anxious to conceal his identity as writer. On publication "The Devil's Thoughts" sold several hundred extra sheets of the *Morning Post*, according to its editor, and copies were in demand for weeks afterwards.

The events at the turn of the century had already provided the true seedbed of a more radical response to the failed apocalypse, however, with precedents extending to the beginning of Christianity itself. We might remember at this point the career of a figure about whom much was heard earlier in the twentieth century, Albert Schweitzer. Schweitzer, as came to be well known, began his career as a theological student, working on the New Testament. As he studied the events and records of that time, it became clear to him that certain German scholars who claimed that in the early years members of the Christian church believed that the apocalypse was about to happen in their own lifetimes must be correct. Not only that, however, but he also came to believe that Jesus of Nazareth had himself shared this belief. In other words, while he continued to believe in the divine inspiration of Christianity, Schweitzer came to believe that Jesus himself had shared human frailty to the extent of being mistaken about the exact course of future events. In the face of this realization he produced a book, *The Quest of the Historical Jesus* (1910), setting out his views, and asked himself meanwhile what he *could* be sure about. He came to the conclusion that there were at least two things on which he could build his views: one was the fact of human suffering, bringing with it the need to remedy it in any way one could, and the other was the permanent value of the music of Johann Sebastian Bach. Accordingly he made himself one of the great experts on Bach's organ music for his time and also went to take over a medical mission in the Congo, where he worked for the rest of his life.

Schweitzer's views were influential in England, where the theory that the early Christians had lived in a time of imminent eschatology, expecting the Last Things to happen in their own lifetime, had hardly penetrated from Germany, so that the initial impact of his views was powerful. Gradually, however, an explanation was produced by some scholars who spoke of what they called a "realized eschatology," arguing that as the early Christians came to understand things better they came to grasp that in one sense what were regarded as the Last Things had already elapsed, leaving only the real end still to happen. Now it can be suggested that something not altogether dissimilar happened to the first Romantic writers: that in their state of confusion when the expected apocalyptic events did not after all materialize they turned back to their own experience and came to believe that the apocalypse had in one sense already happened—in their own consciousness. This process of "internalized apocalypse," as it may be termed, can I believe be traced in each of the three major poets.

After the years 1793 to 1795, the pivotal years for English apocalyptic thinking, Blake, Wordsworth and Coleridge had found themselves in a confused position. All three had been thinking apocalyptically, although only Coleridge, perhaps, had been ready to think millennially as well. But whereas earlier it had seemed quite logical to think in terms of an imminent apocalypse the balance of probabilities had now shifted so dramatically that it seemed more prudent to expect that nothing on that scale would after all happen. And of course such a shift was very difficult to record in poetry. One could not easily write an ode to a non-apocalypse; Coleridge allowed "Religious Musings" to be reprinted in 1797, and again in 1803, but then for twenty-five years omitted it from collections of his poems.

Meanwhile, however, all three poets had been passing through a crisis on the lines I suggested, which caused them to internalize their sense of apocalypse. Blake allowed the prophetic books to run out into works such as the *Book of Los* (1795), *The Song of Los* (1795), and *The Book of Urizen* (1794) where he was no longer concerned with apocalyptic events but rather with setting up his own creation myth, in order to account for the state in which humanity eventually found itself. And these in turn became part of the framework for his much longer poem, conceived on an epic scale, which was first called "Vala" and then "The Four Zoas" (1797). This did in fact enclose an apocalyptic section—indeed in one sense most of it could be regarded as an apocalypse—concluding with a last book in which, without mentioning a thousand years, Blake pictured humanity restored to a paradisal state of harmony.

"The Four Zoas" was never completed, however, and one must suspect that this had something to do with the difficulty of producing an epic poem that was viewed as happening within a single human being. The result was that when Blake set out to write a long poem that he would think good enough to produce in printed form it still had a strong apocalyptic flavor but was constructed differently. This was the long poem *Milton* (1804). Instead of building it round a central character to be called the Eternal Man, Blake wrote it around the idea of Poetic Genius, that same Genius that had been identified in an earlier poem as "the Bard." In the *Songs of Experience* only a few years before the Bard had been seen as possessing immense powers of knowledge, as the figure "Who Present, Past, & Future sees" ("Introduction," line 2; Erdman, p. 18); for the purposes of this poem he appeared first as Milton and then as himself.

This was not quite so arrogant as it may sound, since the picture of genius that emerges in the poem as it proceeds is that it is a kind of humility and self-emptying. The heroic action of the poet comes when he realizes that it is his task not to overcome Satan and try to replace him, but simply

> to teach Men to despise death & to go on
> In fearless majesty annihilating Self, laughing to scorn
> Thy laws & terrors, shaking down thy Synagogues as webs
> I come to discover before Heavn & Hell the Self righteousness
> In all its Hypocritic turpitude. . . .

    & put off
In self annihilation all that is not of God alone:
To put off Self & all I have ever & ever Amen.
    (Plate 38, 40–44, 47–49; Erdman, p. 139)

This act of the Poetic Genius corresponds also to the moment of inspiration, which in Blake's view has nothing to do with ordinary time. In these terms each period less than a pulsation of an artery is equal to six thousand years:

For in this Period the Poets Work is Done: and all the Great
Events of Time start forth & are concievd in such a Period
Within a Moment: a Pulsation of the Artery.
    (Plate 29, 1–3; Erdman, p. 127)

Just such a moment of "the Poet's Work" occurs at the end of this "Prophetic Book," when Blake brings it to a climax in a kind of Last Judgment:

And I beheld the Twenty-four Cities of Albion
Arise upon their Thrones to Judge the Nations of the Earth;
And the Immortal Four in whom the Twenty-four appear Four-
    fold
Arose around Albions body: Jesus wept & walked forth
From Felphams Vale clothed in Clouds of blood, to enter into
Albions Bosom, the bosom of death, & the Four surrounded him
In the Column of Fire in Felpham's Vale; then to their mouths
    the Four
Applied their Four Trumpets & them sounded to the Four winds.

Terror struck in the Vale I stood at that immortal sound.
My bones trembled, I fell outstretchd upon the path
A moment, & my Soul returnd into its mortal state
To Resurrection & Judgment in the Vegetable Body,
And my sweet Shadow of Delight stood trembling by my side.

Immediately the Lark mounted with a loud trill from Felpham's
    Vale,
And the Wild Thyme from Wimbletons green & impurpled
    Hills,
And Los & Enitharmon rose over the Hills of Surrey . . .
    (Plate 42, 16–31; Erdman, pp. 143–44)

Wordsworth's experience of renewal was very much less dramatic. During the same years he had been passing through a time of severe disillusionment; in a well-known passage in *The Prelude*, he describes how in contemplating the apparently insoluble problems of the time he, "sick, wearied out with contrarieties, / Yielded up moral questions in despair" (*Prelude* [1805], X, 899–900).

Interestingly, Blake's perception concerning Milton's self-emptying seems to have struck Wordsworth independently, since at about the same time he was writing the sonnet, which describes Milton as "Pure as the native heavens, majestic, free," and then continues:

> So didst thou travel on life's common way,
> In cheerful godliness; and yet thy heart
> The lowliest duties on herself did lay.
>   (WPW, III, 16)

For Wordsworth, as he came to value Milton more, it was precisely Milton's ability to reconcile the opposites of the human condition, to walk humbly as well as to write sublimely, that impressed him most. And the ability to reconcile opposites, to seize contradictions and somehow turn them into an artistic unity, came to him to seem the supreme poetic gift. This struck him with particular force when he recalled walking through the Alps as a young man and how the moment of highest revelation had come not when he reached the highest part and began to descend again, because as it turned out he had not even noticed when that happened, but in the aftermath, when he and his companion walked on down the Pass, where he found himself as "sick and wearied out with contrarieties" as he would be when he tried to think morally. Yet in spite of this, in spite of the woods that seemed to be decaying, yet never to complete the process, or the winds that were thwarting one another, or waterfalls that were frozen by distance so as to seem stationary, or clouds that seemed moving without any restraint against the background of a clear blue sky, he had a strong sense of unity and harmony. This was the moment when apocalypse became truly revelation:

> The immeasurable height
> Of woods decaying, never to be decayed,
> The stationary blasts of water-falls,
> And everywhere along the hollow rent
> Winds thwarting winds, bewildered and forlorn,
> The torrents shooting from the clear blue sky,
> The rocks that muttered close upon our ears—

Black drizzling crags that spake by the wayside
As if a voice were in them—the sick sight
And giddy prospect of the raving stream,
The unfettered clouds and region of the heavens,
Tumult and peace, the darkness and the light
Were all like workings of one mind, the features
Of the same face, blossoms upon one tree,
Characters of the great apocalypse,
The types and symbols of eternity,
Of first, and last, and midst, and without end.
   (*Prelude* [1805], VI, 556–72)

Where Blake dramatizes his own internal sense of apocalypse, Wordsworth *projects* his, into the very forms of nature. Something of the same experience of apocalypse internalized came also to Coleridge, who showed few signs of doubts and failing confidence at the time, yet was nevertheless to recall a generation later in *Biographia Literaria* how, in his small Somerset cottage, he had found himself at sea in his faith.

> I retired to a cottage in Somersetshire at the foot of Quantock, and devoted my thoughts and studies to the foundations of religion and morals. Here I found myself all afloat. Doubts rushed in; broke upon me "*from the fountains of the great deep*," and fell "*from the windows of heaven*." The fontal truths of natural religion and the books of Revelation alike contributed to the flood. . . . I began then to ask myself, what proof I had of the outward *existence* of anything? (BL, I, 220–21)

This state of his mind needs to be taken into account when we consider the background to his major poems of the time. It helps to account for the diversion of his energies into what Paley has termed the "apocalyptic grotesque," but also helps to explain much more, including the contradictions to be found in the unfinished *Christabel*, "Kubla Khan" and "The Rime of the Ancient Mariner." Like other works I have examined, the last-mentioned can be regarded as a poem of failed apocalypse, as an aspect of the condition of mind in which people—and particularly young people—were left after the French Revolution turned sour. I do not want to face this matter directly, since it is in any case very complex, but instead to look at how Coleridge dealt with it through an associated brief composition that was also poetic, yet not so much a straightforward poem as a riddle. It takes the form of an epigram of four lines that was published in the *Morning Post* for

24 January 1800. We would hardly know anything about it, in fact, were it not that he mentioned it himself in a footnote to *Biographia Literaria*, where, in describing how he had contributed the three Higginbottom sonnets in 1797, he went on to give another such anecdote, recalling how he had heard that an amateur performer wanted to meet him, but had been hesitant on the ground that he had written a severe epigram on "The Ancient Mariner" which had given Coleridge great pain. Coleridge says that he replied by saying that if the epigram was a good one he would be delighted to hear it, whereupon he recited to him the epigram that he himself had written for the *Morning Post*—which he records as follows:

To the author of the Ancient Mariner

Your poem must eternal be,
Dear sir! It cannot fail,
For 'tis incomprehensible
And without head or tail.
   (BL, I, 28n.)

It appears an innocent enough little story, introduced no doubt in order to show that Coleridge can not only take a joke against himself but even produce one if necessary. There are some strange features, however. The first is that the record is not true.[7] If one turns up the *Morning Post* for 24 January 1800, the poem is there all right, but it is not addressed to the author of "The Ancient Mariner" at all. It is entitled "To Mr Pye," who was the current Poet Laureate. Henry James Pye is, in fact, the subject of one of the most scathing entries in the *Dictionary of National Biography*, where he is described as "poetaster and poet laureate" and where his poems are described as of uniform dullness. As was the custom at the end of a century, Pye had produced a "carmen seculare"—literally, a "century poem"—and Coleridge's full title runs "To Mr Pye on his carmen seculare (a title which has by various persons who have heard it been thus translated, 'A poem *an age long*')."

The second point worth noting is that it is based on a poem by Lessing, the title of which translates as "On the eternity of certain poems."[8] But this is something of a red herring, since the idea of the poem ("must be eternal because ...") is all that Coleridge took: Lessing's poem is quite different, completing the assertion by saying that it must be eternal because there will always be poets ready to write such boring stuff.

Thirdly, however, one must ask what the point of the epigram is anyway. Why does Coleridge lay such stress on the words "eternal" and "incomprehensible," words that he actually italicizes in his original *Morning Post* version, and the phrase "without head or tail?"

I have suggested that it is not so much an epigram as a riddle, and for an answer to the riddle we need to look elsewhere in his writing. In his first major poem, "The Eolian Harp," he embarks on several brilliant intellectual speculations and then recoils from them:

> For never guiltless may I speak of him,
> The INCOMPREHENSIBLE! save when with awe
> I praise him, and with Faith that inly *feels* ... [9]

And the word was not idly chosen: within a few months he was writing to John Edwards: "has not Dr Priestly forgotten that *incomprehensibility* is as necessary an attribute of the First Cause, as Love, or Power, or Intelligence?"[10] He was still making a case for the incomprehensibility of the divine thirty years later.[11] And as for his second point we may turn to one of the most interesting letters he ever wrote, to Joseph Cottle on 7 March 1815, where he tried to intimate tactfully that he could not think that what Cottle was aiming at could very easily be conveyed, continuing,

> The common end of all *narrative*, nay of *all* Poems, is to convert a
> *series* into a *Whole*: to make those events, which in real or imagined
> History move on in a *strait* Line, assume to our Understandings a
> *circular* motion—the snake with it's Tail in it's Mouth. (CL, IV, 545)

He goes on to relate this to the knowledge possessed by the Divine Being, who sees Present, Past and Future and whose knowledge will be wholly englobed, in a way that human knowledge cannot be. And since the serpent with its tail in its mouth is a well-known image for eternity, a narrative which achieved that status would be the nearest an artist could get to not only to the divine but also to the eternal.

What I am suggesting, in other words, is that when Coleridge wrote his poem about Mr. Pye the terms he was using did not make very good sense concerning Pye except in a very general way, but they did define the qualities that a truly eternal poem would have: it would be, like the divine, incomprehensible, yet like the highest form of narrative it would resemble the snake with its tail in its mouth, and so would quite literally have neither head nor tail. Recently Coleridge himself had published just such a poem. It was hard to understand because full of contradictions. One never knows just who is in control of the universe in which the Ancient Mariner moves: is it the figures of Death and the woman "far liker Death than he" who play dice for the Mariner's fate, or is it the Spirit that bideth by himself in the land of mist of snow and who loved the bird who loved the man who shot him with his bow? And if one is looking for poetic justice why is it that, as Leslie Stephen pointed out long ago, the Mariner, who, after all, committed the crime, is the only one who survives, while his shipmates, who did nothing more than approve his action at one point, die in agonies of thirst?[12] Is the Mariner's unquestioning faith in "Mary Queen" and his own kind saint enough to account for all that happens? If one looked at the poem with such questionings in mind, it was incomprehensible. And yet it was also a narrative with its tail in its mouth. Following the Mariner's act in extremity, an act of blessing that came from outside himself, he had, in the strange logic of the poem itself, been restored to the country from which he set out and seen it as if for the first time:

> is this indeed
> The light-house top I see?
> Is this the Hill? Is this the Kirk?
> Is this mine own countrée?
>   (469–72; CPW, II, 1043)

So if I am right in seeing Coleridge's poem as a riddle, and if it is here read aright, the reason that after twenty years he remembered his poem addressed to Mr. Pye as a poem addressed to the author of "The Ancient Mariner," was because he knew at another depth of his mind that it was. As an attempt to probe the meaning of things it was incomprehensible, thwarting readers who looked for a satisfactory beginning, a middle and an end, yet also giving them a curious sense of provisional satisfaction. The best comparison, I suggest, is with one of those designs by M. C. Escher which incorporate an impossible geometry. The staircase around the building goes on and on for ever, since when one looks at it more carefully the apparent rising of each separate flight of steps is thwarted by the overall design. It is worrying when one first notices, yet the permanent effect is aesthetically pleasing, and one ceases to be concerned at its impossibility.

His considered opinion, many years later, was that it was "a poem of pure imagination"; he also said that it "might be excelled but could not be imitated" (TT, II, 359). This is another riddle. John Sterling argued (TT, II, 359n.) that it was hard to make sense of the remark, since it would be only too easy for poets to try their hands at Gothic tales of the kind; he wondered if Coleridge meant simply that it corresponded to his ideal. But I think he may have meant something else—that other poets could and perhaps would write finer imaginative poems, but that no one would ever be in quite the same position to create the kind of poem that he now saw his to be. His apocalypse, his revelation, like Wordsworth's in the Alps, was that a poem could be at one and the same time fraught with contradictions, crossing as it did all the major lines of one's discourse, and yet still be possessed of a remarkable unity—the unity, one might say, of its "chant"—so that however incomprehensible it might seem once one began asking questions of it it would remain secure in the wholeness of its appeal to the three qualities he valued most: light and energy and love. In that respect its tail would always be firmly disappearing into its mouth, giving it unity.

Coleridge had to accept—ruefully, perhaps—that his early readers showed no signs of making such connections; yet he could not escape the fact that for him its success was the result of his own internal apocalypse, the revelation of the very power of the imagination itself. And for any reader who was sufficiently seized by the attractions of the poem, the same would in some sense remain true: its positive qualities and its music would be such as to ensure that, contradictions or no, its appeal remained, in some sense, eternal.

NOTES

1. (Oxford, 1999).

2. Quoted in Jon Mee, *Dangerous Enthusiasm: William Blake and the Culture of Radicalism in the 1790s* (Oxford, 1992), p. 29.

3. Ibid., pp. 43–46.

4. Lines 9–14 in the 1796 edition: cf. CPW, I, 109, app. cr., and John Beer, *Samuel Taylor Coleridge: Poems* (London, 1993), pp. 78–79.

5. Lines 359–402 in the 1796 edition: cf. CPW, I, 122–23, app. cr., and Beer, *Coleridge: Poems*, p. 90. For the modern reader the effects of Coleridge's religious poems are somewhat confused by the fact that they have generally been included in collections (including my own) in accordance with the date of their first coherent publication. So *The Destiny of Nations* is placed after "Religious Musings," although its most interesting lines were contributed to Southey's *Joan of Arc* in 1796, while the remainder in 1797 took up the theme of Joan of Arc in Coleridge's own words; then, for the collection *Sibylline Leaves*, twenty years later, he wrote yet more lines.

6. Paley, *Apocalypse and Millennium*, pp. 140–53.

7. For bibliographical details, see CPW, II, 959 and BL, I, 28n.

8. Gotthold Ephraim Lessing, *Sammtliche Schriften*, 30 pts. in 15 vols. (Berlin, 1796), I, 11.

9. Lines 50–52 in the 1796 edition: cf. CPW, I, 102 and Beer, *Coleridge: Poems*, p. 65.

10. Letter to the Revd. John Edwards of 20 March 1796: CL, I, 193.

11. See S. T Coleridge, *Aids to Reflection*, ed. John Beer (London and Princeton, N.J., 1993) (CC), pp. 338–39 and n.

12. *Hours in a Library* (London, 1892), III, 359.

Chronology

1755	Work begun on the building of the Pantheon in Paris.
1757	Blake born in London on November 28.
1770	Wordsworth born at Cockermouth in Cumberland on April 7. Construction begins on Thomas Jefferson's Monticello.
1772	Coleridge born in the vicarage at Ottery, St. Mary, Devonshire, on October 21.
1775	American Revolution against England.
1776	American Declaration of Independence written. Thomas Paine publishes *Common Sense*; Adam Smith publishes *Wealth of Nations*. David Hume dies.
1782	Britain negotiates peace with America.
1783	Blake's *Poetical Sketches* published.
1787	United States *Constitution* written.
1788	Byron born in London on January 22.
1789	Blake publishes *Book of Thel* and *Songs of Innocence*. French Revolution.
1792	Shelley born in Horsham, Sussex on August 4. Mary Wollstonecraft publishes *A Vindication of the Rights of Women*. Louis XVI imprisoned with his family; September Massacres in Paris;

monarchy abolished in France. War of the First Coalition begins. (France declares war on Austria and Prussia.)

1793   Reign of Terror; Louis XVI guillotined; France and England declare war; Marie Antoinette executed.

1794   Blake publishes *Songs of Experience*, *Europe*, and *The Book of Urizen*. Thomas Paine publishes *Age of Reason*.

1795   Keats born in London on October 31.

1796   Coleridge publishes *Poems on Various Subjects*.

1798   Wordsworth and Coleridge publish *Lyrical Ballads*. War of the Second Coalition begins and continues through 1801.

1802   Hostilities between France and England stop.

1803   France and England declare war. Louisiana Purchase is made in the United States.

1804   Napolean made emperor. Britain at war with Spain.

1805   War of the Third Coalition against France, lasting until 1807.

1807   Wordsworth publishes *Poems in Two Volumes*.

1811   Luddite riots.

1812   Byron publishes first two cantos of *Childe Harold's Pilgrimage*. United States and England at war.

1814   Byron publishes *The Corsair* and *Lara*. France invaded by allies of the Fourth Coalition; Paris falls; Napoleon abdicates and is exiled. Peace between United States and England.

1815   Wordsworth publishes *Poems*. Napoleon returns to France, is defeated at Waterloo by allied armies, surrenders, and is exiled.

1816   Coleridge publishes *Christabel and Other Poems*. Byron publishes third canto of *Childe Harold*. Shelley publishes *Alastor*.

1817   Keats publishes *Poems*.

1818   Byron publishes *Beppo* and the fourth canto of *Childe Harold*. Keats publishes *Endymion*. Karl Marx born.

1819   Wordsworth publishes *The Waggoner*. Byron publishes cantos 1 and 2 of *Don Juan*.

1820	Shelley publishes *Prometheus Unbound*. Keats gravely ill with tuberculosis; publishes *Lamia, Isabella, The Eve of St. Agnes, and Other Poems*. George III dies. Friedrich Engels born.
1821	Keats dies on February 23. Byron publishes *Cain* and cantos 3, 4, and 5 of *Don Juan*. Shelley publishes *Adonais*. Napolean dies.
1822	Shelley drowns on July 8.
1823	Byron publishes cantos 6 to 14 of *Don Juan*. Monroe Doctrine proclaimed.
1824	Byron publishes cantos 15 to 16 of *Don Juan*; dies on April 19. Shelley's *Posthumous Poems* published.
1827	Blake dies on August 12.
1828	Coleridge's *Poetical Works* published.
1832	Édouard Manet born.
1834	Coleridge dies on July 25.
1840	Claude Monet born.
1841	Auguste Renoir born.
1843	Wordsworth becomes poet laureate of England.
1850	Wordsworth dies on April 23. Posthumously *The Prelude* is published in fourteen books.
1853	Vincent van Gogh born.
1861	Work begun on The Opéra in Paris, epitomizing the final phase of romantic architecture.

Contributors

·

HAROLD BLOOM is Sterling Professor of the Humanities at Yale University. Educated at Cornell and Yale universities, he is the author of more than 30 books, including *Shelley's Mythmaking* (1959), *Blake's Apocalypse* (1963), *Yeats* (1970), *The Anxiety of Influence* (1973), *A Map of Misreading* (1975), *Kabbalah and Criticism* (1975), *Agon: Toward a Theory of Revisionism* (1982), *The American Religion* (1992), *The Western Canon* (1994), *Omens of Millennium: The Gnosis of Angels, Dreams, and Resurrection* (1996), *Shakespeare: The Invention of the Human* (1998), *How to Read and Why* (2000), *Genius: A Mosaic of One Hundred Exemplary Creative Minds* (2002), *Hamlet: Poem Unlimited* (2003), *Where Shall Wisdom Be Found?* (2004), *Jesus and Yahweh: The Names Divine* (2005), and *Till I End My Song: A Gathering of Last Poems* (2010). In addition, he is the author of hundreds of articles, reviews, and editorial introductions. In 1999, Professor Bloom received the American Academy of Arts and Letters' Gold Medal for Criticism. He has also received the International Prize of Catalonia, the Alfonso Reyes Prize of Mexico, and the Hans Christian Andersen Bicentennial Prize of Denmark.

JEROME CHRISTENSEN is a professor at the University of California–Irvine. His publications include *Romanticism at the End of History*, as well as *Lord Byron's Strength: Romantic Writing and Commercial Society* and other works.

LESLIE BRISMAN is a professor at Yale University. He has published *Romantic Origins* and *Milton's Poetry of Choice and Its Romantic Heirs* and other works.

HELEN VENDLER is a professor at Harvard University. *Coming of Age as a Poet: Milton, Keats, Eliot, Plath* and *The Odes of John Keats* are among her publications.

PAUL DE MAN was a professor at Yale University and the author of several books, including *The Rhetoric of Romanticism*, *Blindness and Insight: Essays in the Rhetoric of Contemporary Criticism*, and *Allegories of Reading*.

JONATHAN WORDSWORTH was a professor at St. Catherine's College, Oxford. A direct descendant of William Wordsworth's brother, Jonathan Wordsworth's work focuses on Romanticism and particularly William Wordsworth. His publications include *The Borders of Vision*, the *New Penguin Book of Romantic Poetry*, and the multi-volume Cornell edition of Wordsworth.

JEAN HALL has been a professor at California State University at Fullerton. Her work includes *A Mind That Feeds upon Infinity: The Deep Self in English Romantic Poetry* and *The Transforming Image: A Study of Shelley's Major Poetry*.

JOHN L. MAHONEY is an emeritus professor at Boston College, where he also had been chair of the English department. Some of his publications are *Wordsworth: A Poetic Life* and *Wordsworth and the Critics: The Development of a Critical Reputation*. Work he has edited includes *The English Romantics: Major Poetry and Critical Theory*.

DAVID BROMWICH is a professor at Yale University. His work includes *Disowned by Memory: Wordsworth's Poetry of the 1790s* and *Romantic Critical Essays*.

JOHN BEER is emeritus professor at Cambridge and fellow of Peterhouse. His work on Romanticism includes *Coleridge the Visionary*, *Blake's Humanism*, and *Wordsworth in Time*. He also is the editor of works of Coleridge and general editor of *Coleridge's Writings*.

Bibliography

Abrams, M. H. *The Correspondent Breeze: Essays on English Romanticism*. New York: Norton, 1984.

———. *English Romantic Poets: Modern Essays in Criticism*. London: Oxford University Press, 1975.

———. *The Mirror and the Lamp*. New York: W. W. Norton, 1958.

Barfoot, C. C., ed. *Victorian Keats and Romantic Carlyle: The Fusions and Confusions of Literary Periods*. Amsterdam; Atlanta: Rodopi, 1999.

Bate, Walter Jackson. *John Keats*. New York: Oxford University Press, 1966.

Beer, John, and L. C. Knights. *Coleridge's Variety: Bicentenary Studies*. Pittsburgh: University of Pittsburgh Press, 1975.

Bewley, Marius. *The English Romantic Poets: An Anthology with Commentaries*. New York: Modern Library, 1970.

Brinkley, Robert, and Keith Hanley, ed. *Romantic Revisions*. Cambridge, England: Cambridge University Press, 1992.

Bromwich, David, ed. *Romantic Critical Essays*. Cambridge, England: Cambridge University Press, 1987.

Bush, Douglas. *Mythology and the Romantic Tradition in English Poetry*. Cambridge, Mass.: Harvard University Press, 1969.

Chandler, James, ed. *The Cambridge Companion to British Romantic Poetry*. Cambridge, England: Cambridge University Press, 2008.

Chandler, James. *Wordsworth's Second Nature: A Study of the Poetry and Politics*. Chicago: University of Chicago Press, 1984.

Christensen, Allan et al., ed. *The Challenge of Keats: Bicentenary Essays 1795–1995*. Amsterdam; Atlanta: Rodopi, 2000.

195

Christensen, Jerome. *Romanticism at the End of History*. Baltimore: Johns Hopkins University Press, 2000.

Cox, Philip. *Gender, Genre, and the Romantic Poets: An Introduction*. Manchester; New York: Manchester University Press; New York: Distributed exclusively in the USA and Canada by St. Martin's Press, 1996.

de Man, Paul. *The Rhetoric of Romanticism*. New York: Columbia University Press, 1984.

———. *Romanticism and Contemporary Criticism: The Gauss Seminars and Other Papers*. Baltimore: Johns Hopkins University Press, 1993.

Eaves, Morris, and Michael Fischer, eds. *Romanticism and Contemporary Criticism*. Ithaca: Cornell University Press, 1986.

Elam, Helen Regueiro, and Frances Ferguson, eds. *The Wordsworthian Enlightenment: Romantic Poetry and the Ecology of Reading*. Baltimore: Johns Hopkins University Press, 2005.

Erdman, David V., ed. *Blake and His Bibles*. West Cornwall, Conn.: Locust Hill, 1990.

Frye, Northrop, ed. *Romanticism Reconsidered: Selected Papers from the English Institute*. New York: Columbia University Press, 1963.

Frye, Northrop. *A Study of English Romanticism*. New York: Random House, 1968.

Fulford, Tim, and Morton D. Paley, eds. *Coleridge's Visionary Languages: Essays in Honour of J. B. Beer*. Rochester, N.Y.: Brewer, 1993.

Gassenmeier, Michael, and Norbert H. Platz, ed. *Beyond the Suburbs of the Mind: Exploring English Romanticism*. Essen: Blaue Eule, 1987.

Gill, Stephen, ed. *The Cambridge Companion to Wordsworth*. Cambridge, England: Cambridge University Press, 2003.

———. *William Wordsworth's* The Prelude: *A Casebook*. Oxford, England: Oxford University Press, 2006.

Gravil, Richard, and Lucy Newlyn and Nicholas Roe, eds. *Coleridge's Imagination: Essays in Memory of Pete Laver*. Cambridge, England: Cambridge University Press, 1985.

Hilles, Frederick W., and Harold Bloom, eds. *From Sensibility to Romanticism: Essays Presented to Frederick A. Pottle*. New York: Oxford University Press, 1965.

Johnston, Kenneth R. *Wordsworth and The Recluse*. New Haven: Yale University Press, 1984.

Johnston, Kenneth R., et al., ed. *Romantic Revolutions: Criticism and Theory*. Bloomington: Indiana University Press, 1990.

Kenning, Douglas. *Necessity, Freedom, and Transcendence in the Romantic Poets: A Failed Religion*. Lewiston, N.Y.: E. Mellen Press, 1998.

Levine, Alice, and Robert N. Keane, eds. *Rereading Byron: Essays Selected from Hofstra University's Byron Bicentennial Conference*. New York: Garland, 1993.

Lipking, Lawrence, ed. *High Romantic Argument: Essays for M. H. Abrams*. Ithaca: Cornell University Press, 1981.

Manning, Peter J. *Reading Romantics: Texts and Contexts*. New York: Oxford University Press, 1990.

McFarland, Thomas. *The Masks of Keats: The Endeavour of a Poet*. Oxford; New York: Oxford University Press, 2000.

Miller, Christopher R. *The Invention of Evening: Perception and Time in Romantic Poetry*. Cambridge, England; New York: Cambridge University Press, 2006.

Morton, Timothy, ed. *The Cambridge Companion to Shelley*. Cambridge, England: Cambridge University Press, 2006.

North, Julian. *The Domestication of Genius: Biography and the Romantic Poet*. Oxford: Oxford University Press, 2009.

Peer, Larry H., ed. *Inventing the Individual: Romanticism and the Idea of Individualism*. Provo, Utah: International Conference on Romanticism, 2002.

Reed, Arden, ed. *Romanticism and Language*. Ithaca: Cornell University Press, 1984.

Ryan, Robert M., and Ronald A. Sharp, eds. *The Persistence of Poetry: Bicentennial Essays on Keats*. Amherst: University of Massachusetts Press, 1998.

Sitterson, Joseph C. Jr. *Romantic Poems, Poets, and Narrators*. Kent, Ohio: Kent State University Press, 2000.

Stillinger, Jack. *Romantic Complexity: Keats, Coleridge, and Wordsworth*. Urbana: University of Illinois Press, 2006.

Taylor, Beverly, and Robert Bain, eds. *The Cast of Consciousness: Concepts of the Mind in British and American Romanticism*. Westport, Conn.: Greenwood, 1987.

Vendler, Helen. *Coming of Age as a Poet: Milton, Keats, Eliot, Plath*. Cambridge, Mass.: Harvard University Press, 2003.

———. *The Odes of John Keats*. Cambridge, Mass.: Harvard University Press (Belknap), 1983.

Wolfson, Susan J., ed. *The Cambridge Companion to Keats*. Cambridge, England: Cambridge University Press, 2001.

Wolfson, Susan J. *Formal Charges: The Shaping of Poetry in British Romanticism*. Stanford, Calif.: Stanford University Press, 1997.

———. 'Soundings of Things Done': *The Poetry and Poetics of Sound in the Romantic Ear and Era*. College Park: University of Maryland Press, 2008.

Wordsworth, Jonathan. *William Wordsworth: The Borders of Vision*. Oxford: Clarendon, 1982.

Acknowledgments

Jerome Christensen, "'Thoughts That Do Often Lie Too Deep for Tears': Toward a Romantic Concept of Lyrical Drama." From *The Wordsworth Circle* 12, no. 1 (Winter 1981): 52–63. Published at the Department of English, Temple University. Copyright © 1981 Marilyn Gaull.

Leslie Brisman, "Mysterious Tongue: Shelley and the Language of Christianity." From *Texas Studies in Literature and Language* 23, no. 3 (Fall 1981): 389–417. Copyright © 1981 by the University of Texas Press.

Helen Vendler, "Keats and the Use of Poetry." From *What Is a Poet? Essays from the Eleventh Alabama Symposium on English and American Literature*, edited by Hank Lazer, pp. 66–83. Copyright © 1987 by the University of Alabama Press.

Paul de Man, "Time and History in Wordsworth." From *Diacritics: A Review of Contemporary Criticism* 17, no. 4 (Winter 1987): 4–17. Copyright © 1987 The Johns Hopkins University Press.

Jonathan Wordsworth, "The Secret Strength of Things" From *The Wordsworth Circle* 18, no. 3 (Summer 1987): 99–107. Copyright © 1987 Marilyn Gaull.

Jean Hall, "The Evolution of the Surface Self: Byron's Poetic Career." From *Keats-Shelley Journal* 36 (1987): 134–57. Published by the Department of English, University of North Carolina at Chapel Hill. Copyright © 1987 Keats-Shelley Association of America.

John L. Mahoney, "'We Must Away': Tragedy and the Imagination in Coleridge's Later Poems." From *Coleridge, Keats, and the Imagination: Romanticism and Adam's Dream*, edited by J. Robert Barth and John L. Mahoney, pp. 109–34. Copyright © 1990 by the Curators of the University of Missouri.

David Bromwich, "A Note on the Romantic Self." From *Raritan* 14, no. 4 (Spring 1995): 66–74. Published by Rutgers University. Copyright © 1995 David Bromwich.

John Beer, "Romantic Apocalypses." From *Romanticism and Millenarianism*, edited by Tim Fulford, pp. 53–69. Copyright © Tim Fulford, 2002.

Index